THROWING THE MORAL DICE

just ideas

transformative ideals of justice in ethical and political thought

series editors
Drucilla Cornell
Roger Berkowitz

THROWING THE MORAL DICE

ETHICS AND THE PROBLEM OF CONTINGENCY

Thomas Claviez and Viola Marchi, Editors
Foreword by Alain Badiou

FORDHAM UNIVERSITY PRESS

NEW YORK   2022

Copyright © 2022 Fordham University Press

All rights reserved. No part of this publication may be reproduced, stored in a retrieval system, or transmitted in any form or by any means—electronic, mechanical, photocopy, recording, or any other—except for brief quotations in printed reviews, without the prior permission of the publisher.

Fordham University Press has no responsibility for the persistence or accuracy of URLs for external or third-party Internet websites referred to in this publication and does not guarantee that any content on such websites is, or will remain, accurate or appropriate.

Fordham University Press also publishes its books in a variety of electronic formats. Some content that appears in print may not be available in electronic books.

Visit us online at www.fordhampress.com.

Library of Congress Cataloging-in-Publication Data

Names: Claviez, Thomas, editor. | Marchi, Viola, editor.
Title: Throwing the moral dice : ethics and the problem of contingency / Thomas Claviez and Viola Marchi, editors ; foreword by Alain Badiou.
Description: First edition. | New York : Fordham University Press, 2022. | Series: Just ideas | Includes bibliographical references and index.
Identifiers: LCCN 2021047106 | ISBN 9780823298082 (paperback) | ISBN 9780823298075 (hardback) | ISBN 9780823298099 (epub)
Subjects: LCSH: Contingency (Philosophy) | Ethics.
Classification: LCC BD595 .T48 2022 | DDC 123—dc23/eng/20211001
LC record available at https://lccn.loc.gov/2021047106

Printed in the United States of America

24 23 22   5 4 3 2 1

First edition

Contents

Foreword: Ethics and Contingency
Alain Badiou ix

Introduction. Throwing the Moral Dice: Ethics 2.0,
Contingency, and Dialectics
Thomas Claviez and Viola Marchi 1

I   Throwing the Moral Dice: Ethics and/of Contingency

Three Notes on Contingency Today: Stress, Science—
and Consolation from the Past?
Hans Ulrich Gumbrecht 33

Cosmopolitan Ethics as an Ethics of Contingency:
Toward a Metonymic Community
Thomas Claviez 45

Dumb Luck: Jacques Derrida and the Problem of Contingency
Michael Naas 69

The Apophatic Community: Ethics, Contingency, Negation
Viola Marchi 94

II   Other Others: Ethics 2.0 and the Problem
of the "Unsynthesizable"

Commonality versus Individuality: An Ethical Dilemma?
Étienne Balibar 127

Critique, Power, and the Ethics of Affirmation
Rosi Braidotti 145

The Promise of Practical Philosophy and Institutional Innovation
Drucilla Cornell   162

Ethics of Circular Time
Slavoj Žižek   182

The Road Not Taken: Environmental Ethics, Reciprocity, and Non-Negative Nonagency
Thomas Claviez   206

"There Is No World": Living Life in Deconstruction and Theoretical Biology
Cary Wolfe   229

Works Cited   251
List of Contributors   269
Index   273

Foreword: Ethics and Contingency

Alain Badiou

The question of knowing whether ethics consists in adapting subjectivated action as best as possible to the ways of the world or, on the contrary, consists in according action with a principle itself foreign to the objective constraints of the situation is one that has always divided philosophers.

On one side, we encounter the Stoics or Spinoza, all of whom put forward appropriate knowledge of the necessary laws of the real, laws that pertain to necessity as the condition of an ethics. Ethics thereby combines a (in some sense) total knowledge of the objectivity of "that which does not depend on us" and a no less total mastery of the space left for action, namely, of "that which depends on us." It resides in the friction between two necessities, one internal, the other external.

In the case of Plato or Kant, ethics (or morality) is defined completely differently: It is on the side of an imperative, the universal value of which is intrinsic and does not depend upon any circumstances, that we must seek and find the veritable essence of moral action, which is to this extent independent of the objective necessity that it opposes to its own subjective demand. Act, Kant tells us, always "as if" the maxim of your action ought to be a universal law of the world.[1] As transphenomenal, freedom is here directly tied to thought, to the suprasensible, and imposes its paradoxical law on objective necessity.

Act "as" the world wants, or act "as if" the will of the ethical subject were worth the world? We can, I think, escape the trap of this alternative by considering some of the confusion surrounding the notion of "necessity."

Recently, in a remarkable body of work, not all of which is fully public, Quentin Meillassoux has tried to show that the laws of the world are, under the appearance of their necessity, in fact contingent.[2] Of course, these laws are the observable laws of the world in which we exist, but the being of the world, thought as such, does not impose such laws as its own. All in all, everything is necessary, except the necessity of this necessariness: The laws of the world, while immediately necessary, could be other than they are, such that their necessity is only a contingent local covering of a radical contingency.

In such a context, ethics can, as such, affirm the transtemporal validity of the Good for a determinate human life in the following sense: If this life is considered as a totality, it can never be necessary that Evil prevails over it, which would signify Evil's necessity. If, therefore, it is manifestly the case that Evil has ravaged this life, this life will be replayed again until the Good betides it, thus proving Evil's contingency. Hence a human life ravaged by Evil can rationally establish itself in the hope of its resurrection until proof is provided that it can be a "good" life, a life in accordance with justice, thus putting an end to the irrational thesis of a necessity of Evil. In sum, if my life is commensurable with justice, I thereby prove that Evil is not necessary. If injustice ravages my life, this certainly proves that the Good is not necessary. But it is rational to think that this life will be replayed until proof is given once again that Evil is not necessary either and therefore that the just life is necessarily possible.

As for me, my *dispositif* is somewhat different but aims at a related conclusion: As the experience of the world is a mixture of constraint and contingency, of chance and necessity, of being and event, the chance of a "true" life is offered to everyone.

My definition of the ethical imperative might be rendered as follows: "Become the subject of a truth, of that which every individual, including the one that you are, is capable, in general without knowing prior to an eventual encounter that he or she had indeed disposed of this capacity." Contingency here is tied to the distinction between "being" (multiplicities localized through the particular laws that form worlds) and "event" (a chance-ridden encounter with an immanent exception to the laws of the world).

This imperative has no guarantee of existential unity, since no single path of truth exists; instead, there are four. Indeed, the human individual is capable of artistic, scientific, political, or amorous truths. The eventual chances on the basis of which an individual can be incorporated into a truth process and become its militant subject differ greatly from one another: the encounter with another individual under the sign of a brush with love, the astonishment provoked by such-and-such an artwork, the luminous comprehension of a demonstration that long remained opaque, the enthusiasm raised by a mass demonstration. . . . The variants of these rubrics scatter ad infinitum the chance of an individual's transition to a subject.

I believe that I have managed to show that the subjectivation of this purely local and vanishing immanent exception, or event, is deployed, in the world touched by an event forming an exception to its laws, toward the construction of a "generic" subset, that is, a subset largely subtracted from the laws of the world to which it belongs and, notably, from this world's available knowledge.

At bottom, in any world a truth is created slowly on the basis of a contingency, whose value as exception this truth preserves in the recognizable form of a *creation*, one that is certainly internal to the world but nevertheless endowed with a universal, or transworldly, import: scientific theories, artworks, life in the love of another, communist politics. . . .

Descartes maintained that God had created eternal truths—which is a real paradox, since, as created, truths are not eternal. . . . But he was not wrong: Evental contingency means that *truths are created, by subjects, but with an eternal value, given their being immanent exceptions to the laws of the world in which they appear.*

> It can thus be demonstrated that truths are:
> —singular, insofar as they appear as well-defined multiplicities, in a particular world;
> —universal, insofar as, forming an at least partial exception to the laws of the world in which they appear, they can hold in a wholly different world;
> —absolute, or eternal, in the sense that their subjectivation, in whichever sites they are born or are reborn, subtracts individuals-become-subjects, from the strict temporal sequences of which this world is the guardian.

All these properties forcefully indicate that every ethics simultaneously requires the singularity of the world and its laws—which are the mathematized laws of the multiple as such and of its becoming object—*and* the radical contingency of an event that strikes this world, appearing only to disappear but leaving under the guard of individuals-become-subjects the possibility to create in the world that which this world had declared impossible.

NOTES

1. See, e.g., Immanuel Kant, *Groundwork of the Metaphysics of Morals*, trans., ed. Mary Gregor (Cambridge: Cambridge University Press, 1997), 15.
2. Quentin Meillassoux, *After Finitude: An Essay on the Necessity of Contingency*, trans. Ray Brassier (London: Continuum, 2008).

THROWING THE MORAL DICE

Introduction

Throwing the Moral Dice:
Ethics 2.0, Contingency, and Dialectics

Thomas Claviez and Viola Marchi

I

"Ethics 2.0—did I miss out on something? Was there another recent 'ethical turn,' comparable to the well-documented one of the '80s? And do contingency and Hegel play a prominent role there?" These might be some of the questions that the title of this collection may provoke in the well-disposed reader. And, as usual, the answer is: "Well—yes and no." What we designate here as "Ethics 2.0" is not (yet?) a "turn," in that questions of morality and ethics have not gained center stage again as one of the main foci in contemporary philosophical thought. What has happened, however, is that the oeuvres of Jacques Derrida, Jean-François Lyotard, Gilles Deleuze, Emmanuel Levinas, and Michel Foucault—which sparked the '80s turn—have been taken up and further developed, critically adapted, or refuted by scholars such as Alain Badiou, Jacques Rancière, Etienne Balibar, Jean-Luc Marion, François Laruelle, Giorgio Agamben, and Quentin Meillassoux, to mention just a few. And contingency, as Alain Badiou's foreword to this volume shows, indeed plays a huge role in at least some of these and certainly in Badiou's own approach.

An Introduction like this one, however, cannot possibly offer a serious, comprehensive account of how both Hegelian dialectics and the concept of contingency fare in such a wide scholarly debate or reflect, in any rigorous manner, on this debate itself. Allow us therefore to address just two facets that can be identified in it. One is certainly the challenge that the environmental turn has posed to traditional moral philosophy, a challenge that is reflected in numerous contributions to this volume. If anything has become clear, it is that we have to overcome the subject/object schism upon which much of our moral philosophies still rely, since it is the tenacity of this distinction that makes it almost impossible to frame the debate about our responsibilities toward, and in relationship with, our environment in ethical terms. And it is here that the philosophical interventions of Derrida and Deleuze have left their traces, as the essays of Rosi Braidotti, Drucilla Cornell, and Cary Wolfe attest to. This discussion is, however, being crisscrossed right now by one of the largest contingencies we have witnessed in our days: that of COVID-19, a contingency, moreover, that shows us in a blatant manner that our aspirations to control nature's incalculabilities have not come to fruition to the extent we might have wished—or feared. But are we then not right to try to extend our powers over a nature that shows its evil face in this manner?

This brings us to another ethical topic that has risen to some prominence through several recent publications devoted to it: that of evil, or even "radical evil." Among them—and again, just to mention a few—are Susan Neiman's *Evil in Modern Thought: An Alternative History of Philosophy* (2002), Richard J. Bernstein's *Radical Evil: A Philosophical Interrogation* (2002), Adriana Cavarero's *Horrorism* (2009), and Simona Forti's *New Demons: Rethinking Power and Evil Today* (2015). While in all of them contingency plays a more or less prominent role—as "evil" is, in most of them, defined as that which escapes sublimation through either its sheer horror or its incalculability[1]—what is quite striking is that none of them offers a philosophical discussion of this central term (in Neiman's and Bernstein's books, "contingency" doesn't even make it into the index, if this can serve as an indicator). Forti, as well as Neiman and Bernstein, are wary about the fact that a Hegelian dialectics can be used to sublate (and thus to legitimize) evil as one of the forces that drive reason's history, and thus they often define radical evil as just that: the unsublatably contingent. And for Hegel, the one enemy of his dialectical philosophy is—contingency. As he declares rather unequivocally in his Introduction *to the Lectures on the Philosophy of World History*: "The sole aim of philosophical inquiry is *to eliminate the contingent.*"[2] If, however, as Forti, Neiman, and Bernstein claim, what characterizes evil *is* its contingency, and if for Hegel contingency is the one thing that philosophy has to eradicate, then the question arises whether we are really talking about the contingency of evil or, rather, of the evil of contingency. To begin to assess the troubled relationship between dialectics and contingency (and the relevance for both to questions of ethics), maybe we should take a step back and have a closer look at one of the central instances in one of the main texts of the first ethical turn where the contingent and dialectics play an important role.

In his nominal essay "The Force of Law," Jacques Derrida for the first time addresses an issue hotly debated before its publication: whether deconstruction can provide any insights into questions of ethics. Right from the start, Derrida is at pains to warn the reader that he will not even begin to answer the question "What is to be done?" As he points out, the sheer conjunction "and" in the 1989 conference's title "Deconstruction and the Possibility of Justice" "dares to defy order, taxonomy, classificatory logic, no matter how it works: by analogy, distinction or opposition."[3] It is quite interesting to note that he mentions three different concepts by which, obviously, "order, taxonomy, classificatory logic" are usually imposed: "analogy" (that is, the logic of metaphor), "opposition" (which seems to point toward dialectics), and "distinction," which does not seem to have any clear-cut home base except, maybe, as an uneasy middle term between analogy (sameness) and opposition (absolute difference). Needless to say, there is not a single taxonomic or classificatory logic that would not be either based on or result in distinctions. However, according to Derrida, the "and" in the conference title even goes beyond that. In fact, this "and" defying all classificatory logic comprises, if anything, the question of justice itself; it is but a prolegomenon or a synecdoche for justice. Justice, from a deconstructive "point of view" (if such a thing exists), is itself the "and" between two poles:

> How are we to reconcile the act of justice that must always concern singularity, individuals, irreplaceable groups and lives, the other or myself *as* other, in a unique situation, with rule, norm, value or the imperative of justice which necessarily have a general form, even if this generality prescribes a singular application in each case? If I were content to apply a just rule, without a spirit of justice and without in some way

inventing the rule and the example for each case, I might be protected by law (*droit*), my action corresponding to objective law, but I would not be just.[4]

Just as the "and," however, justice is not—must not be—of the order of the calculable to be worthy of its name:

> In short, for a decision to be just and responsible, it must, in its proper moment if there is one, be both regulated and without regulation: it must conserve the law and also destroy it or suspend it enough to have to reinvent it in each case, rejustify it, at least reinvent it in the reaffirmation and the new and free confirmation of its principle. Each case is other, each decision is different and requires an absolutely unique interpretation, which no existing, coded rule can or ought to guarantee absolutely.[5]

This thought, that an act of judgment has to take into account both the rule of law and the singularity of the case at hand, is in itself nothing new: Already Aristotle defines the wise judge, the *phronimos*, as someone who cannot base his decisions on principles of scientific exactness, as these "are impossible in reasoning upon particular ethical cases. They do not fall under any art or any law, but the agents themselves are always bound to pay regard to the circumstances of the moment as much as in medicine and navigation."[6] For Aristotle, however, this dilemma is covered by a dialectics that is able to "navigate" between the "particular ethical case" and the "arts" and "laws" that neither a captain nor a doctor can simply disregard but that they must not slavishly follow, either. The singular case, then, constitutes something like a contingency that must be negotiated with established rules and norms.

This, however, is emphatically not Derrida's view. What he points out is that there is another form of contingency at work here: that of the decision itself.

> The undecidable, a theme often associated with deconstruction, is not merely the oscillation between two significations, or two contradictory and very determinate rules, each equally imperative (for example respect for equity and universal right but also for the always heterogeneous and unique singularity of the unsubsumable example). The undecidable is not merely the oscillation or the tension between two decisions; it is the experience of that which, though heterogeneous, foreign to the order of

the calculable and the rule, is still obliged—it is of obligation that we must speak—to give itself up to the impossible decision, while taking into account laws and rules. . . . That is why the ordeal of the undecidable that I just said must be gone through by any decision worthy of the name is never past or passed, *it is not a surmounted or sublated (aufgehoben) moment in the decision.*[7]

If the singular case remains an "unsubsumable example," it is not its "unique singularity" that defies dialectics: It is the moment of *decision itself* that cannot be "sublated." That is, dialectics—although it would seem to be prepared to negotiate the universal and the singular, according to Hegel—not only does not seem to work here, but, according to Derrida, it has to be suspended since "a just decision . . . *must rend time and defy dialectics . . .* acting in the night of non-knowledge and non-rule."[8]

We are, obviously, in the face of two "contingencies," which are both connected but still different: The first one is the contingency of the single historical moment, as it is juxtaposed to the universal laws and rules, a singularity that, though "unsubsumable," is still not "unsublatable." Contrary to Aristotle's *phronimos*—whose wisdom allows him or her to negotiate between the particularity of the case and the generality of the laws—in Derrida this wisdom turns into "madness," as a second contingency (that of the decision) enters, which is explicitly "unsublatable." Now, when we said that the two are both connected but different, this refers to the fact that, if it weren't for the one having to make a decision, the unsubsumable contingency of the first event would not even matter, let alone be taken into account: It is the fact that a judge *has* to make a decision (without which, as Derrida rightly points out, there is no justice) that the second contingency even comes up. What this implies, however, is that contingency is split against itself as that which is both sublatable *and* unsublatable. But even in stating that much, we are in the danger of falling back into dialectics itself, as we feed into, reinvoke, and thus reinstall and affirm its very logic.

What is quite interesting in Derrida's essay is that he invokes, a propos this logic of dialectics, another tropological figure at the end of his essay when he writes: "And the example or index could be carried by metonymy back toward the conceptual generality of the essence."[9] When Derrida uses the concept of metonymy here, he is—as many others—declining metonymy into synecdoche: It is only via the *pars pro toto* of synecdoche that the "example or index" can be "carried back toward the conceptual generality of the essence." As we have argued elsewhere,[10] however, synecdoche (to which metonymy, as in Derrida's case, is reduced) is conceptually much closer to metaphor than to metonymy, since its spatial logic is based upon a third—space itself—that the tenor shares with the vehicle. In fact, what synecdoche is able to do is to reduce the entire conceptual difference between the singular and the general to naught, as the difference between *pars* and *toto* virtually disappears in what is in fact a metaphorical structure—*pars* est *toto*—in which the metaphorical third *becomes space* itself.

Now what does all of this have to do with ethics? Well, if the singular case and the "generality of the essence" are easily sublated by means of a synecdochal logic, then nothing of either contingency remains. Which brings us to a problem of ethics as regards dialectics: What is the status of *difference* within dialectics? And it brings us back again to where we started out from: Derrida's ascription of "analogy, distinction or opposition" to modes of imposing order that, in his view, justice not only defies but needs to defy to deserve its name. We have already pointed out the strange status that "distinction" has in this list. If it indeed fills the gap between analogy and opposition, as we have argued, then we would have to address, in particular, its relation to the latter. If "opposition" demarcates "absolute difference," then "distinction" would seem to imply a sort of "relative" difference. But then the question arises as to what specifically the difference between absolute difference and relative difference boils down to. "Relative difference" would seem to imply that there still is a common third on the basis of which the relativity of the difference could be gauged; thus, what is presumed is a third that makes such a comparison possible. However, to thus distinguish between "relative" and "absolute" difference becomes difficult, as in Hegel's dialectics opposites—and there are only "absolute" differences in dialectics (and that's for a reason)[11]—are finally sublatable into a third as well, a third, moreover, that would have been there right from the beginning, in the very unity that self-sublates itself. That is, there is no difference—neither "relative" nor "absolute"—that would not fall prey to a logic of the third that empties it, in subjecting it to its laws.[12] Ironically, we might have to look for a "third" form of difference that would escape the "third" of dialectics . . .

It would seem that the almost cosmological grasp of dialectics leaves no room for genuine contingency not only to occur but to be seriously taken into account without falling prey to these laws. The "We" that Hegel evokes is always already a dialectically sublated "We," a "We," moreover, that, as the *Phenomenology of Spirit* makes clear, has to be created through a logic of

(a) war and (b) a dialectics of master and slave. What is quite interesting to note is that what dialectics shares with war is that both turn "relative" into "absolute" difference; moreover, it can conceive recognition between people only in the framework of this master/slave dialectic. And, if we are honest to ourselves: How far does the master/slave dialectic reflect reality? How often do we see slaves heroically achieving recognition through their work, while the masters, chewing their fingernails, howl at the moon for not getting the recognition they feel they deserve?

Thus Hegel perpetuates a paradox at the heart of ethics that is to be found in all three of the "classic" moral philosophies: those of Aristotle, Kant, and the utilitarian variety. This paradox consists in the fact that, whereas ethical problems arise only if there is contingency and otherness, all three moral philosophies mentioned are based upon a prior assumption of a normative and regulatory sameness: in Aristotle's case, the assumption of a telos inherent in a human being (though not all beings);[13] in Kant, the principle of reason; for utilitarians, what is best for the majority. And in Hegel, as we have seen, the law of dialectics. Any otherness or contingency located outside these norms accordingly poses a challenge to these respective norms. The one philosophy that does not only take into account but actually bases its premises on the radical contingency of Otherness is the one offered by Emmanuel Levinas's "ethics as first philosophy," which has also strongly influenced the work of Derrida.

One of the most striking instances in which this clash becomes visible for the Kantian variety is in Kant's exchange with the French philosopher Benjamin Constant. The latter challenges Kant's insistence that in no case would one be allowed to tell a lie by means of an "exemplary" story, indeed, an exemplary contingency: A friend of mine, who is pursued by a killer, seeks protection in my home. Having granted him that, I leave my house, only to meet the killer, who asks me about the whereabouts of said friend. Do I—and such is the title of Kant's response—have a "supposed right to lie because of philanthropic concerns"? Constant argues that I do, since "no one has the right to a truth that hurts others."[14] Not surprisingly, Kant sticks to his guns, arguing that even in the case of such a contingency, the only "contingency plan" available for me is to tell the truth. In Kant's view,

> "to have a right to the truth" is meaningless. One must say, rather, that man has a right to his own truthfulness (*veracitas*), i.e., to subjective truth in his own person. For to have objectively a right to truth would

be the same as to say that it is a matter of one's will (as in cases of *mine* and *thine* generally) whether a given statement is to be true or false; this would produce an unusual logic.[15]

What Kant here euphemistically describes as "unusual logic" is, indeed, just that, one that Derrida calls the "madness" at the heart of any such decision. What is striking, however, is that, in what follows, Kant's own argument pursues another, rather "unusual logic." Obviously not prepared to admit openly what will result when I do tell the truth, Kant offers us a whole array of alternative scenarios—each one more improbable and contingent than the next:

> For example, if by telling a lie you have in fact hindered someone who was even now planning a murder, then you are legally responsible for all the consequences that might result therefrom. But if you have adhered strictly to the truth, then public justice cannot lay hand on you, whatever the unforeseen consequence might be. It is indeed possible that after you have honestly answered Yes to the murderer's question as to whether the intended victim is in the house, the latter went out unobserved and thus eluded the murderer, so that the deed would not have come about. However, if you told a lie and said that the intended victim was not in the house, and he has actually (though unbeknownst to you) gone out, with the result that by so doing he has been met by the murderer and thus the deed has been perpetrated, then in this case you may be justly accused as having caused his death. For if you had told the truth as best you knew it, then the murderer might perhaps have been caught by neighbors who came running while he was searching the house for his intended victim, and thus the deed may have been prevented. Therefore, whoever tells a lie, regardless of how good his intentions might be, must answer for the consequences resulting therefrom even before a civil tribunal and must pay the penalty for them, regardless of how unforeseen those consequences may be.[16]

Once, that is, the Pandora's box of contingency is opened, there seems to be no reining in of its subversive potential; other contingencies—and, as mentioned, even more improbable ones—have to be mustered in order to defend and reinstall the rule of order and truth.[17] From a Kantian point of view, contingency, even if it is acknowledged or raises "philanthropic concerns," must by all means be held at bay—or, as Hegel puts it, "eliminated." But can it?

The questions that then pose themselves—and to which the contributors to this volume were asked to respond in their individual fashion—were the following: What is the status of contingency in or for ethics? And provided that the problems diagnosed above are correct, where do we go from here? Do we have to conceive of alternative ethics that address these and other questions in a different, and potentially more fruitful, manner? The answers to these questions provided by the contributors to this collection seem—on the occasion of Hegel's 250th birthday in 2020—to have inadvertently turned into something like an inventory as to how far his oeuvre might take us in the twenty-first century.

II

The challenge of any introduction, as anyone who has ever written one will readily admit, is to turn what is, in most cases, a metonymic relation—the contiguity in space (provided here by a book cover) of many different viewpoints—into a metaphoric one that creates the impression that all these single elements are somehow connected by a third.[18] Ironically, this third is, in our case, made up of (1) the concept of contingency, for which metonymy provides the trope, and (2) ethics, which is usually conceived as a metaphorical means to provide us orientation in order to overcome contingency, as we have learned from Aristotle and Kant.[19] In a very peculiar way, thus, this Introduction to a volume dedicated to the topic of ethics, contingency, and dialectics faces the very problems it addresses. What we will do, for purposes both "contingent upon" the pragmatics of publishing but also indebted to a possible "ethics" of contingency, is to provide the reader with a narrative that, on the one hand, will attempt to create the impression of a sequential order but that, on the other hand, will hopefully allow for the different contributions to stand in their unsublatable particularity.

Our volume opens with Alain Badiou's foreword, "Ethics and Contingency." There he addresses contingency's relationship not only to ethics but to its (necessary?) counterpart—necessity. Referring back to the influential work of his pupil Quentin Meillassoux,[20] he states: "Everything is necessary, except the necessity of this necessariness: The laws of the world, while immediately necessary, could be other than they are, such that their necessity is only a contingent local covering of a radical contingency." That is, the laws—although designed to overcome contingency—are themselves but the product of a "radical contingency."[21] From this, Badiou concludes that "as the experience of the world is a mixture of constraint and contingency, of chance and necessity, of being and event, the chance of a 'true' life is offered to everyone"—"true life" meaning for him an ethical life that is "faithful" to the event.

What is so striking is that there seems to be a paradox at the heart of his ethics: On the one hand, there is the *cause* of an ethical life—the event—that features all the qualities of the contingent as incalculable, law defying, "un-necessary," or, as Badiou defines it, "a chance-ridden encounter with an immanent exception to the laws of the world." On the other hand, there is the ethical life itself, conceived of as a "faithfulness" that, while inaugurated by a chance encounter with the contingency of events,[22] is driven by almost pure necessity and characterized by the demand to "keep going!"[23] However, Badiou's paradoxical description of truth's evental contingency as "singular," "universal," and "absolute" may lose something of its paradoxicality. Or, rather, it may help us understand that his ethics are a "faithful" reflection of the paradoxical nature of his own concept of truth. As Badiou concludes:

> Ethics simultaneously requires the singularity of the world and its laws—which are the mathematized laws of the multiple as such and of its becoming object—*and* the radical contingency of an event that strikes this world, appearing only to disappear but leaving under the guard of individuals-become-subjects the possibility to create in the world that which this world had declared impossible.[24]

It might be worth noting here that—to resort to a Hegelian vocabulary once again—the alleged "impossible" that Badiou refers to is what will, retrospectively, become a contingency that the laws, be they mathematical or juridical, will strenuously attempt to turn into a necessity.[25]

In a manner not unlike Badiou, Hans Ulrich Gumbrecht also starts his contribution, "Three Notes on Contingency Today: Stress, Science—and Consolation from the Past?," from the assumption that contingency plays a decisive role in our everyday life. He specifically points out the implicit connection of contingency to freedom and the—again paradoxical—role that it plays in how we designate our private realm. On the one hand, we celebrate the growing contingency (qua non-necessity) that characterizes our experience of the everyday as what allows for the expansion of our individual freedoms and independence from state institutions. On the other, however, the virtually infinite choices and possibilities that new technologies make available to us constitute the very source of increasingly unmanageable feelings of insecurity and stress. As a result, as Gumbrecht points out, "our everyday as a field of contingency is fast approaching the form of a universe of contingency." This, in turn, gives rise to an assortment of fundamentalisms that shine like beacons of security in said "universe of contingency."

Strangely enough, however, another well-known contingency-overcoming strategy—science—Gumbrecht stipulates, lost some of its allure in the nineteenth century. The trajectory of this loss is what he then traces in the remaining part of the essay, in which he outlines the emergence and decline of what he calls the "historical worldview," one characterized by an "obsession with contingency." This development manifests itself as a "transition from a mirror-like, one-to-one pattern of world representation to a narrative principle of world representation, as we can trace it in the early nineteenth century." This new narrative principle, writes Gumbrecht, has the "elementary capacity of integrating multiple views regarding one and the same object of reference and of arranging them as a sequence"—a diagnosis very much in line with Mikhail Bakhtin's theory of the novel as "polyphonic."[26] Gumbrecht then illustrates this phenomenon in his reading of Denis Diderot's novel *Jacques le fataliste et son maître*, which, according to him, illustrates that even a materialist like Diderot was aware of the fact that all claims to necessity can only and exclusively be made a posteriori and not, to refer back to Badiou, from the *in situ* of the "evental" situation itself.

Contingency and its "narrative principle" are also at the center of Thomas Claviez's contribution, "Cosmopolitan Ethics as an Ethics of Contingency: Toward a Metonymic Community." The essay addresses the highly disputed and almost paradoxical idea of a "cosmopolitan community." The paradoxical status of this formulation derives from the fact that, while community has always necessitated an "outside" in order to establish its external boundaries and internal homogeneity, the main result of thinking this concept in a cosmopolitanism vein would be to effectively dissolve the very divide between inside and outside that makes community possible. But what is it exactly that constitutes this outside? After a brief sketch of a long conceptual trajectory, Claviez concludes that from Aristotle's *Politics*, to Ferdinand Tönnies's romantically inflected *Gemeinschaft*, to Zygmunt Bauman's more recent account of community, "instances of contingency and concepts of otherness are immediately collapsed into each other and thus form . . . an imaginary outside." In other words, the traditional strategies of community construction—such as the institution of a boundary between same and other—are in fact subordinated to and directly dependent upon community's main goal: overcoming contingency.

The crucial function of community as contingency-overcoming device becomes even more apparent in the philosophies of Hobbes, Kant, and Heidegger. Not only is the very inception of modern political thought characterized by the attempt at dealing with the (dangerous) contingency that would constitute humanity's natural state; what is more, the only way of limiting the exposure to the immanent risk it generates would be to submit oneself to the transcendent "hypercontingency" embodied by the Leviathan. The vicious circle also marks Kant's normative approach to cosmopolitanism and Heidegger's sketch of community in *Being and Time*. As Claviez's analysis reveals, the rhetorical exercise that allows Heidegger to govern the contingency of Being-with the "Man" by turning it into a "destiny" is an inherently metaphorical one. It is against the community of destiny's metaphorical regime and in the face of the very pragmatic demands of our globalized world that Claviez reclaims the notion of contingency and its cognate trope of metonymy to contend that, in order to think cosmopolitanism, we would need to approach it "along the lines of a community conceived as metonymic."

Drawing on Roman Jakobson's famous discussion of the difference between metaphor and metonymy, and through a reading of Amitav Ghosh's Ibis trilogy as a contingent narrative of a metonymic community, Claviez suggests that to acknowledge contingency does not mean, necessarily, to paint it in Romantic colors; nor does it mean to do everything to overcome it, either. It means to recognize it for what it is: Chance/change and/as crisis/creation.

In the light of what has been said, the notion that Michael Naas takes up in his essay, "Dumb Luck: Derrida and the Problem of Contingency," acquires a new valence: If our assumption that contingency can (and ever so often does) go both ways—chance and change, crisis and creation, as Claviez suggests—then to designate the possibility that it actually acquires a positive aspect leads us to call it "dumb luck," which, as Naas defines it, describes "a good or fortunate occurrence that arrives completely by chance, without any planning or preparation, in a purely gratuitous, unmerited, or undeserved way." To classify such an occurrence as "dumb" implies a whole narrative—and one that transports its own ethics, namely, an ethics of desert: It means that (1) no intelligence was involved in being thus lucky and that (2) because of this it is somehow "unmerited," which, in turn, implies that (3) only intelligent people deserve such luck, because (4) intelligent people do not have to rely on luck (a.k.a. contingency), since (5) intelligence is the contrary to contingency because it is designed to overcome it.

However, as Naas reminds us, "a bit of dumb luck is lodged within the expression *dumb luck* itself, since 'dumb' also means, of course, to be lacking not in intelligence but in the ability to speak, to be without a voice, that is, to be mute." Naas follows this trace through Herodotus's *Persian Wars* and Aristotle's *Nicomachean Ethics*, arguing that the "dumbness" of contingency ought to be read in both ways: as not only outside of what can intelligibly be *expected before its occurrence* but also outside of what can intelligibly *be said about it post factum*.[27] Which leads Naas to conclude that "dumb luck, chance, is perhaps the very logic of the living."

In what follows, Naas reads Derrida's 1975/1976 seminar *Life Death*, focusing on Derrida's take on François Jacob's *The Logic of the Living* and, specifically, on the role that the concept of "program" plays in Jacob's analyses as a notion that, with its connotations of a telos and a destiny, seems to rigidly exclude any contingency from the evolutionary process. Naas concludes by returning to *Of Grammatology*, where Derrida, as in the final paragraph of "Structure, Sign, and Play," alludes to the "monstrosity" of the as-yet unknown, a monstrosity that, in retrospect, might unveil itself in its benign features as dumb luck—at least for some undeserving individuals. If this, on the one hand, might explain its potential monstrosity, on the other hand it also raises the question of why we feel forced to designate contingency in terms of monstrosity in the first place. This question will be taken up, in a similar manner, by Cary Wolfe's contribution later in this collection.

The potential "monstrosity" that contingency might harbor, however, is by no means restricted to the "formless"—and thus "mute"—infancy of a future not only "to come" but to be "born(e)" by us. It is and has been also part and parcel of our present and our past, the latter enjoying the advantage of having offered us either the time to rationalize contingency as, after all, necessary or the perfect justification for excluding it from our considerations by labeling it as "irrational," "dumb," or somehow "other." The latter is, basically, the job description of another highly disputed concept, that of community, already interrogated by Claviez and that returns here at the center of Viola Marchi's contribution.

In her essay, "The Apophatic Community: Ethics, Contingency, Negation," Marchi starts out from what Derrida, again, has called a "seismic event"[28]—a term that seems to carry all the connotations and implications of a contingent event à la Badiou: the appearance of Jean-Luc Nancy's essay "The Inoperative Community" in 1983 and of Maurice Blanchot's response, immediately afterward, with the title *The Unavowable Community*. As Marchi remarks, we are again in the face of a necessity that is being born(e) out of a contingency. Or, as she argues: We need a new poetics—which, in a way that needs further clarification, seems able to offer such services—in order to "deliver ourselves over" to "the necessity" that this contingent event has created. The "paradoxical force" that Derrida attributes to these texts is, philosophically speaking, nothing new; it has become known, if not with Plato, then with Hegel, as the force that drives dialectics. However, as Marchi goes on to show, if we are to think community in the new way that this seismic event points to, we have to leave dialectics behind.[29]

By means of an "apophatic," or "negative theological," reading of Nancy and Blanchot around the work of Georges Bataille, Marchi establishes a concept of negation that defies the sublative force of dialectics. Applied to the concept of community, this allows her to carve out her main thesis: that we need to develop a notion of "nonpositive affirmation," which escapes the cosmological force of dialectics, in order to defy the unifying force—the Hegelian "We"—that still underlies many conceptions of community. What is at stake here—which refers us back to what was said in the first part of the Introduction—is that, in order to escape the sweeping force of dialectics, we are forced to think of a "third kind of difference": one that escapes the third that the relative difference of metaphorical difference presupposes and that also circumvents the all-devouring, cosmological force of dialectics, based upon a prior unity. What an ethics of nonpositive affirmation that evades the traps of dialectics would then oblige us to is, as Marchi insists, "the difficult task of finally finding a way to disjoin the seemingly indissociable connection that ties community to the 'proper,' at a moment in which every invocation of community functions as a call to the righteous defense of the proper," the proper being another instance that strangely seems to escape its deconstruction—dialectical or else.[30]

III

The contributors to the second part of the present collection were asked to present their ideas about alternative ways of thinking ethics in the twenty-first century—specifically in light of the dead ends that some of the more established ways of doing so, as critically addressed in the previous section, have done. In his essay with the title "Commonality versus Individuality: An Ethical Dilemma?" Étienne Balibar, as Marchi before him, addresses the concept of community, arguing that we need to assess "the value of the individual from *within* the idea of the community, in relation to its existence." To do so, we have to start thinking about these matters "in *relational terms*" and critically assess some of the dialectical underpinnings of what he calls the "grand narrative" of sociological community construction.[31] This grand narrative of sociology, which we are familiar with also under the name of Enlightenment, establishes, through processes of abstraction, a subject in isolation, which, in turn, leads to both alienation and liberation. Tracing these abstractions—and their incapability to account for the concrete subject—Balibar argues that to achieve a balanced "Equaliberity,"[32] "constitutional regimes substitute the 'pure' political principle with social mediations that variously combine regimes of property and regimes of community, the distribution of ownership and the conditions of membership." However, in so doing, these regimes of property tacitly introduce and implement a normativity of normality and deviancy.

Balibar then pursues the question whether, and in how far, either Marx or Foucault (who, he claims, is more strongly indebted to Nietzsche than to Marx) can provide a convincing answer to this dilemma. Whereas he diagnoses in Marx the introduction of a certain form of "transindividuality" that while going against "abstract universalism" still retains traces of universalism, in Foucault's trajectory Balibar distinguishes two distinct phases. In the first, Foucault's Nietzschean heritage (via Bataille and Blanchot) leads to the conception of a subject that, if torn in itself, becomes decidedly ahistorical—and thus unHegelian: "masters without slaves," as Balibar insists. A later Foucault, however, turns this "sovereign" and "dangerous" individual into a relational self, one that is "*becoming* more autonomous rather than *being* transcendentally free," thus suggesting that "Marx and Foucault are both, although on very different premises, *relational thinkers*." Such relational thinking, as becomes clear, would have to remain outside the parameters of dialectics, since, as Balibar concludes, what we need is "a problematic of 'relations' and relationality that overcomes the dilemmas of organic fusion (or teleological unity) and dialectical mediation."

While Balibar tries to overcome dialectics from within the exclusionary/inclusionary seductions of both capitalism and the Hegelian tradition of Marx, Rosi Braidotti, in her essay, "Critique, Power, and the Ethics of Affirmation," argues for an ethics that foregrounds "the praxis of extracting knowledge from pain, the better to transform its negative effects." In such an ethical framework, based on "political passions, affirmative affects, and a rigorous vision of the role of the imagination," the normative opposition between good and evil is

> replaced by that between affirmation and negation, or positive and negative affects. . . . This ethics consists not in denying negativity but in reworking it outside the dialectical oppositions, because negative passions diminish our relational competence and deny our vital interdependence on others.

This project, at first glance, seems to share some points with Badiou's, which also puts affectivity (love) and imagination (arts) at the center of a practical ethics (politics). However, if Braidotti's contribution aligns itself with a certain "ethics of the event," her immediate philosophical antecedent is to be found in Deleuze rather than Badiou,[33] and in her essay Braidotti provides an overview of the trajectory of her own impressive oeuvre in this direction. At the center of her thought—as of that of Deleuze and Guattari—is the idea of the virtual as "a reservoir of yet unrealized possibilities that cannot be brought about by dialectical opposition to the present (that is, actual) conditions." These unrealized possibilities are, needless to say, the contingencies and potentialities that have not as yet reached the status of necessities or actualities; nor, as Braidotti insists, will they reach such a status through a dialectical process of sublation, which, as has become clear in the meantime, will always carry the traces of the unity that it started out from. The creativity initiating a nondialectical notion of becoming, according to Braidotti, finds its expression foremost in a poetics that would be able to help us not only imagine—but also to practically constitute—a "We." A "We," however, that is emphatically non-Hegelian and that is "conceived following a 'logic' of the assemblage"[34] thought in a "trans-species manner."[35]

In line with an ethics of the event, Braidotti insists that what urges us to engage ethically with an event "resides not in its intrinsic value according to given standards of moral or political evaluation but rather in the extent to which it contributes to conditions of becoming." The ultimate goal of such an approach to ethics is to pave the way for an active process of "*counteractualization*" of the (by no means necessary) state of affairs—a central concern also for Drucilla Cornell's essay to follow—or, in the words of Deleuze, "to affirm and ramify chance, instead of dividing it *in order to* dominate it, *in order to* wager, *in order to* win."[36]

What becomes obvious more and more in the contributions so far is that what we are dealing with is a decisive clash: a clash between a discriminating logic based upon exclusion—to which notions of community and otherness are still subjected—and a potentially "indiscriminate" ethics of inclusion, with a dialectics that, growing out of the former, uneasily rubs against the latter, its cosmology of comprehensiveness notwithstanding. When framed within a teleology of sublation, the incalculable contingency of the event—and its capacity to engender innovation and newness—loses its sting by being inexorably linked to a former unity it presumably grows out of and inescapably will sublate back into.

This dilemma is also the starting point of Drucilla Cornell's contribution, which, in its very title, "The Promise of Practical Philosophy and Institutional Innovation," already conjures up what, for some, would be a *contradictio in adjecto*: Can we actually think innovation in any way connected to something that, in its name, evokes that which is established?[37] And, as she resorts to Marx's famous dictum from his *Theses on Feuerbach*—"the purpose of philosophy is to transform the world, and not just to understand it"[38]—how does the normative claim that philosophy ought to change the world clash with the descriptive task to understand it? The inconspicuous junctim "not just" plays an important role in a sentence that dramatizes what has become known in philosophy as the "naturalist fallacy": the alleged impossibility to deduce a normative claim, designed to change the status quo, from a description of said status quo.

As Cornell states with regard to Derrida, this dilemma between the normative and the descriptive has to be "negotiated." If, as Derrida explains, an affirmation remains empty without someone taking a position as regards this affirmation, then this phenomenon is rather similar to the fact that justice is rendered only if a decision is taken.[39] However, if both ethical actions and decisions are "mad,"[40] it is also because the truth—that is, the complete information—about the situation we are called to act and decide upon is never available to us. And when we frame the issue in these terms, another strange paradox (or, rather, chiasm) emerges: In this scenario, the very fact that comprehensive access to the truth can never be ascertained turns our "mad" insistence that we need to transgress the status quo of knowledge into something perfectly reasonable. If anything, the trajectory that Cornell draws of the living development of her ethical thought exemplifies just that: that the "ought" inherent in thinking ethics will always have to go beyond the lay of the land and the rules attached to it and that transgression is—indeed *has to be*—part of any ethical thinking.

Interestingly, at a pivotal point in the essay, dialectics again takes center stage as Cornell quotes Derrida and his claim that "the dialectic is not the dialectic: the dialectic is the dialectic of the nondialectic and the dialectic."[41] The most noticeable aspect of this quote is certainly the claustrophobic atmosphere these lines evoke, with the omnivorous quality of a dialectics that even swallows the nondialectic whole.[42] For Cornell, what Derrida is pointing to here is the "undecidable," which—if it can be thought at all—has to be thought as that which has not yet entered the (cosmo)logics of dialectics. According to Cornell, this undecidable, as the realm of imagination and affects, is what can actually provide the space for a distinctly aesthetic approach to ethics, one able to produce "visions of justice," and for a feminism-inflected ethics in which "the feminine *can always be actualized otherwise.*"

It does not come as a surprise that Cornell then turns to an ethics of practice that stems from outside the frightening, because allegedly inescapable, cage of Greco-Judaic Western metaphysics. It is the philosophy of uBuntu that she turns her attention to in the last part of her essay. The seminal difference between uBuntu and the ethics of Western metaphysics is that—comparable to Levinas's ethics but clearly distinct from it—difference does not entail a problem to be overcome but an asset, in that said difference "means that each one of us is different from the others but also that part of this difference is a responsibility toward the creation and sustenance of a human and ethical community." This would seem to imply that the first difference—the one that could potentially raise ethical problems—is complemented, offset, and to a degree overridden by a responsibility toward a "higher good" (and one cannot but fail to notice a certain utilitarian element in this). A higher good, however—and here the superficial parallels to utilitarianism end—that is *dependent upon the very difference between those who feel this responsibility*. More than a mere challenge to Eurocentrism and its self-proclaimed philosophical primacy, for Cornell uBuntu represents "a better way of thinking about transindividuality and why the ethical relationship can never be separated from the collective struggles that empower us and maximize the force and life of beings."

After what appears like an array of scholars devoted either to taking Hegel down from his pedestal or at least to reading him in a critical light had the opportunity to voice their concerns, it is interesting to read what a staunch Hegelian—or, rather, a Hegelian strongly inflected by Lacanianism—offers as regards his take on ethics. In his essay "Ethics of Circular Time," Slavoj Žižek addresses what has also been a topic in Gumbrecht's and Braidotti's contributions: the impact of digitalization upon our contemporaneous thinking.

Starting out from the seven cardinal sins, Žižek identifies one of them as apparently escaping the logic of thinking in opposites of Self and Other: This sin is Sloth, since, as he claims, it is the one that calls for historicization: "Before modernity, it was melancholy (resisting to pursue properly the Good); with capitalism, it was reinterpreted as simple laziness (resisting the work ethics); today, in our 'post-' society, it is depression (resisting to enjoy life, to be happy in consumption)." All three varieties, as Žižek points out, are in breach of one of Lacan's central ethical criteria, as they go against the injunction "*de ne pas ceder sur ton desire*"—not to "compromise your desire."[43] But they also seem to defy a contemporary culture saturated by seemingly endless opportunities to guarantee just that: that your desires *can* be fulfilled—any time, any place, any way. However, what looks like a phantasmagoria of Lacanian ethics proves, upon further inspection, to be something quite different, the reason being that the logic behind this state of affairs relies on the circular premise that while "there is no pleasure without guilt," "in a more radical sense, guilt provides the surplus-pleasure that transforms a simple pleasure into intense *jouissance*."

Žižek then goes on to illustrate this circular logic and its ramifications, in the slightly eclectic way that we have come to expect from him, using a number of films—Kevin Costner's *Postman* (1997) and Terry Gilliam's *Brazil* (1985)—and the magazines *Business Insider* and *Mad*, to ask whether the digital big Other is not, after all, "just a new case of the symbolic big Other." To this question, Lacan's (and Žižek's) answer is "a resolute no: What is threatened in the digitalization of our daily lives is not our free subjectivity but the big Other itself, the agency of the symbolic order, in its 'normal' functioning."

The "cure," so to speak, comes, in typically dialectical fashion, from within, since "it is this separation in the heart of the big Other itself that sustains the space for subjectivity." Žižek's conclusion is that digitalization does not decenter the subject; it decenters decentering itself. Thus, it is the question of (ethical) subjectivity itself that is wrongly put. As he claims, the "very alternative between autonomous/authentic human subjectivity and a posthuman(ist) machinic flux of desire (celebrated, among others, by Guattari) is false, as it obfuscates the true shift, the shift in the status of the big Other."

The second part of his essay is devoted to the concept of circular time as the specific time structure that virtual space allows us to inhabit.[44] Carving out the paradoxes that such a circular time engenders, again through provocative readings of various movies—among them Charly McDowells's *The Discovery* (2017) and Denis Villeneuve's *Arrival* (2016)—Žižek rather surprisingly (and in a manner starkly different from an ethics of the event or an affirmative ethics of practice) concludes that the paradoxes of circular time these movies dramatize go to show that "willing the inevitable (choosing the future we know will happen) is not just an empty gesture that changes nothing. . . . If we don't do it, if we don't choose the inevitable, the entire frame which made it inevitable falls apart, and a kind of ontological catastrophe occurs."

"Choosing the inevitable," in our view, does not exactly sound like an exciting political program—revolutionary or else. It raises, however, once again the question about the status of agency within a structure of dialectics—even one as advanced as Žižek's Lacanian variety.

This question of agency is taken up again in Thomas Claviez's second contribution to this collection, "The Road Not Taken: Ethics, Environment, and Non-Negative Nonagency," which takes its cue from the observation that agency seems to be one of the few concepts that hasn't fallen under the purview of dialectics proper, in that its opposite—passivity—has not as yet (with the exception of Emmanuel Levinas) comprehensively been addressed, and specifically not in the realm of ethics.

The preliminary question that needs to be raised in this regard—and whose answer is far from trivial—is: What is this opposite of agency, exactly? What seems to be lacking in our moral philosophies is a basic vocabulary that would be able to avoid the pathological undertones that terms like "suffering," "patient," or "passivity" inevitably carry. The one notable exception to this tendency, mentioned earlier, is to be found in Levinas, who, by placing the notions of passivity and irreciprocity at the foundation of his theoretical edifice, is possibly the only ethical thinker that has attempted to reflect *explicitly* on passivity before and beyond the agent/patient divide. However, as already hinted at in this Introduction, if not exactly pathological, the passivity Levinas talks about still retains at least the distinctive features of the traumatic event. The reason for this isolated example of an ethical discourse arguing for the primary role of passivity is, according to Claviez, clear enough if one considers that, at least from a Western perspective, to conceive of moral (let alone legal) subjecthood without resorting to agency seems to amount to a logical impossibility.

However, as Claviez notes, if Levinas's explicit focus on passivity represents a unique exception, the same attempt to address the opposition between agency and its opposite can also be located at the core of "almost all recent contributions to ecocriticism, especially of the posthuman variety." In contrast to Levinas, the main aim here is not to rethink passivity but to grant agency and thus ethical status "to that part which, up to now, has been considered on the losing side of the subject/object divide: the object," or, more generally, "to parts of our environment that, up to now, have been excluded from our moral considerations because they haven't been granted agency." The most pertinent example in this regard is certainly Bruno Latour's Actor-Network Theory, with which Claviez engages in the last part of the essay, underlining the unsolvable contradictions that the attempt at thinking that "impossible thing" that is a *moral object* gives rise to, especially given the Kantian moral lexicon that Latour, quite surprisingly, ultimately resorts to. It is precisely Kant's moral philosophy and his famous "Golden Rule'" that allows Claviez to unveil the "perverse logic" that sustains every ethical discourse based on (rational) agency as the foundation of moral subjecthood.

If, as Kant's formulation (and implicit caveat) goes, we should treat others "*also* as an end and *not only* as means," and if what defines me as a moral subject is the capacity to act rationally (with its corollaries of responsibility and accountability), what happens when I find myself on the receiving end of action? Does that imply that, "as someone 'being acted upon,'" I will, "by temporarily becoming a means, lose my status as a moral subject?" Or, even more dangerously: Do "I, morally speaking, achieve my subjectivity only at the cost of others who suffer my actions and thus lose their moral subjecthood" in turn?

To travel "the road not taken" Claviez indicates—surely a difficult one, burdened with exorbitant political and juridical implications, but one that might allow for a different ethics, finally able to truly include environmental issues—is "to try to disentangle moral subjecthood and agency, or, to be more precise, to come up with a non-negative concept of the contrary to agency that still would allow a patient to retain his/her/its status as a moral subject."

In his contribution, "'There Is No World': Living Life in Deconstruction and Theoretical Biology," Cary Wolfe also addresses, as do Naas, Braidotti, and Claviez, issues related to the intersection between ethics and the environment. Taking his cue from Wallace Stevens's 1942 poem "The Noble Rider and the Sound of Words" and from a comment that appeared in the same year, claiming that the poet's task is "to help people to live their lives,"[45] Wolfe raises the question as to what this rather demanding responsibility entails and takes it toward the question of ecology. His intent is to take issue with a tendency within recent debates on ecology to dismiss the relevance of deconstruction for addressing pressing questions that the rise of the Anthropocene confronts us with. To do so, Wolfe suggests "bringing deconstruction into conversation with work in both biological and social systems theory," as he has done in numerous previous works.[46]

He starts out with an analysis of the second volume of Derrida's *The Beast and the Sovereign* (2011) and, more specifically, of Derrida's Heidegger-inflected reading of the Swedish-German philatelist Jakob von Uexküll's work *Umwelten*. According to Wolfe, Derrida's statement "there is no world, there are only islands"[47] deserves scrutiny, specifically in light of what he later has to say about Paul Celan's poetry and the famous quotation "the world is gone, I must carry you."[48] Wolfe points out that the finitude that both Derrida and Celan evoke is what binds human and non-human together and that this sharing "is precisely where ethics and ecological responsibility begin." He then goes on to carve out the implications of the notion of the "program" of the genetic code—and the connotations this evokes (not unlike dialectics) in terms of calculability, inevitability, and inescapability—that Christopher Johnson has traced in his 1993 book *System and Writing in the Philosophy of Jacques Derrida*. Including further work by Conrad Waddington, Denis Noble, and Stuart Kauffman, Wolfe argues that, as early as *Of Grammatology*, Derrida offers us "a theory of something like the relationship of the genetic (or systemic, formally code bound) and the epigenetic factors (the environmental or contextual setting in which the code is deployed)." That is, there do exist incalculable and random processes that escape the determinations of the genetic code, which leads Kauffman to presume that "evolution literally creates its own future adjacent-possible opportunities for further evolution without selection in any way 'achieving' this."[49]

In light of Derrida's quotation above—and in stark contrast to Žižek—Wolfe concludes that "if there is to be a 'world,' a 'shared world,' in other words, *we* must make it, without any taking for granted of who or what this 'we' might be. The ethical point . . . is that the world is not given; it is *made*, and it therefore matters how we make it." And, closing the (hopefully not vicious) circle by returning to the concept of contingency and its importance for any kind of creation, Wolfe adds—and we could not possibly imagine a more fitting closing statement for the Introduction to this collection:

> The point is not so much epistemological as it is pragmatic and ethical, and it is driven by—made unavoidable by—a contingency that is radical precisely because it is not the privileged domain of the human alone. In fact, it is what makes the domain of life and the living . . . "creative."[50]

NOTES

1. Susan Neiman, *Evil in Modern Thought: An Alternative History of Philosophy* (Princeton, NJ: Princeton University Press, 2002), 20, 42–45, 93, 260; Richard J. Bernstein, *The New Constellation* (New York: Polity, 1991), 5, 60–72, 175–79; Adriana Cavarero, *Horrorism: Naming Contemporary Violence* (New York: Columbia University Press, 2011); Simona Forti, *New Demons: Rethinking Power and Evil Today*, trans. Zakiya Hanafi (Stanford, CA: Stanford University Press, 2015), 45–51, 122–35, 298–302.

2. Georg Wilhelm Friedrich Hegel, *Lectures on the Philosophy of World History*, trans. H. B. Nisbet (Cambridge: Cambridge University Press, 1975), 28.

3. Jacques Derrida, "Force of Law: The 'Mystical Foundation of Authority,'" in *Deconstruction and the Possibility of Justice*, ed. Drucilla Cornell, Michel Rosenfeld, and David Gray Carlson (New York: Routledge, 1992), 3.

4. Derrida, "Force of Law," 17.

5. Derrida, "Force of Law," 23.

6. Aristotle, *Nicomachean Ethics*, trans. Harris Rackham (Cambridge, MA: Harvard University Press, 1982), 1104a 5–12.

7. Derrida, "Force of Law," 24; emphasis ours.

8. Derrida, "Force of Law," 26; emphasis ours.

9. Derrida, "Force of Law," 37.

10. Thomas Claviez, "Traces of a Metonymic Society in American Literary History," in *American Studies Today: New Research Agendas*, ed. Winfried Fluck et al. (Heidelberg: Winter, 2014), 299–322.

11. As Thomas Claviez argues in his essay "Neorealism, Contingency, and the Linguistic Turn," *Humanities* 8, no. 4 (2019): 176–92, there is a strong affinity between the (tropo)logic of metaphor and dialectics. As regards "absolute difference," Hegel is pretty clear that identity and difference can be collapsed into a dialectical unity: "This difference is difference *in and for itself, absolute difference, the difference of essence*. It is difference in and for itself, not difference resulting from anything external, but *self-related*, therefore *simple* difference. It is essential to grasp absolute difference as *simple*. In the absolute difference of *A and not-A* from each other, it is the *simple not* which, as such, constitutes it. Difference itself is the simple Notion. Two things are *different, it* is said, *in that* they, etc. 'In *that*' is, in one and the same respect, in the same ground of determination. It is the *difference of reflection*, not the *otherness of determinate being*. One determinate being and another determinate being are posited as falling apart, each of them, as determined against the other, has an *immediate being* for itself. The *other of essence*, on the contrary, is the other in and for itself, not the other as other of an other, existing outside it but simple determinateness in itself. In the sphere of determinate being, too, otherness and determinateness proved to be of this nature, to be simple determinateness, identical opposition; but this identity revealed itself only as the *transition* of one determinateness into the other. Here, in the sphere of reflection, difference appears as reflected difference, which is thus posited as it is in itself." Georg Wilhelm Friedrich Hegel, *The Science of Logic*, trans. and ed. George di Giovanni (Cambridge: Cambridge University Press, 2010), §886.

12. That is why Levinas's "ethics as first philosophy," which Derrida so often refers to, makes a categorical distinction between the face-to-face of the ethical encounter and the entrance of the third that—comparable to the two contingencies outlined earlier, which are both causally connected but seem to contradict each other—"betrays" the initial encounter, in the double sense of the term, as it is both a trace and a negation of the latter.

13. Thomas Claviez, *Aesthetics and Ethics: Otherness and Moral Imagination from Aristotle to Levinas and from "Uncle Tom's Cabin" to "House Made of Dawn"* (Heidelberg: Winter, 2008), 53–77. This presumed telos will reappear as a driving force in Hegel's dialectics and in Heidegger's philosophy as "authentic potentiality of being."

14. Immanuel Kant, *Grounding for the Metaphysics of Morals with "On a Supposed Right to Lie because of Philanthropic Concerns,"* trans. James W. Ellington (Indianapolis, IN: Hackett, 1981), 64.

15. Kant, *Grounding for the Metaphysics of Morals*, 64.

16. Kant, *Grounding for the Metaphysics of Morals*, 65.

17. For a more comprehensive analysis of this exchange between Constant and Kant and what it means for a literary ethics, see Claviez, *Aesthetics and Ethics*, 22–29. And it is important to point out that what contingencies ever so often have served to implement is—and again, COVID-19 might serve as a proof for this—another one: that of the "state of exception."

18. On the connection between metaphor and metonymy to contingency, see Claviez, "Traces of a Metonymic Society"; "Neorealism, Contingency, and the Linguistic Turn"; and his first contribution to the present volume.

19. In Aristotle's case, this "third" is provided by what he calls the telos of any human being; in Kant's case, it is the fact that we are all rational beings.

20. Quentin Meillassoux, *After Finitude: An Essay on the Necessity of Contingency*, trans. Ray Brassier (London: Continuum, 2008); Quentin Meillassoux, *The Number and the Siren*, trans. Robin Mackay (New York: Sequence, 2012).

21. It might be important to note that the term "contingency" does not play a prominent role in Badiou's *Ethics*; in fact, the only time Badiou brings it up is in the context of his critique of what he considers to be a dangerous relativism that inhabits any ethics of difference: "It is only through a genuine perversion, for which we pay a terrible historical price, that we have sought to elaborate an 'ethics' on the basis of cultural relativism. For this is to pretend that a *merely contingent* state of things can found a law." Alain Badiou, *Ethics: An Essay on the Understanding of Evil*, trans. Peter Hallward (London: Verso, 2012), 28; emphasis ours. This use of contingency certainly differs from the way he uses it here.

22. As readers familiar with his work are aware of, and as he also states in his foreword, such a truth is being offered not only in one but in four different, specific truth realms: art, science, politics, and love. And in his *Ethics*, he notably describes the "encounters" with the contingency of events that these realms offer in exclusively positive terms: "We can name them: in love, there is *happiness*; in science, there is *joy*; . . . in politics, there is *enthusiasm*; and in art, there is *pleasure*." Badiou, *Ethics*, 52, emphasis ours. We think that this is important to point out, since to describe the encounter with contingency in such decidedly positive terms is what distinguishes him from the rather "traumatic" encounter with otherness that characterizes, e.g., Emmanuel Levinas's "ethics as first philosophy." Emmanuel Levinas, *Otherwise Than Being or Beyond Essence* (The Hague: Nijhoff, 1981); Emmanuel Levinas, *Totality and Infinity* (Pittsburgh, PA: Duquesne University Press, 1969). See also Badiou's critique of Levinas in his *Ethics*, 21–23.

23. Badiou, *Ethics*, 52. This link between the event and the ethics of following a truth process seems to partake in the paradoxical structure of betrayal that characterizes the "trace," a term both Derrida and Badiou use. The trace both betrays the former existence of something but indicates, at the same time, its absence. Not unlike the relationship between "saying" and "said" or ethics and justice in

Levinas—or, for that matter, between "event" and "structure"—my faithfulness to the event is characterized, according to Badiou, by qualities (steadfastness, purpose) that are diametrically opposed to the contingent qualities of the event itself. Thus, it is not unlike the paradox that inhabits the demand "Be spontaneous!" But then, as Christopher Norris points out, "turning paradox into concept" is what Badiou's philosophy is all about. Christopher Norris, "Alain Badiou: Truth, Ethics, and the Formal Imperative," *Revista Portuguesa de Filosofia* 65 (2009): 1108.

24. In order to avoid any misunderstandings, it might be worth pointing out that the "multiple" that Badiou refers to here is one that, to use Norris's words, is a secondary "consistent multiplicity" that "always results from a restrictive operation of the count-as-one, in its various modes and object-domains whose effect is to repress, dragoon or dissimilate the 'inconsistent multiplicity' which, as a matter (at least since Cantor) of formally demonstrable truth always precedes it." Norris, "Alain Badiou," 1128. See also Alain Badiou, "Ontology Is Mathematics," in *Theoretical Writings*, ed. and trans. Ray Brassier and Alberto Toscano (London: Continuum, 2004), 3–93; Alain Badiou, *Number and Numbers*, trans. Robin MacKay (London: Polity, 2008).

25. It is quite interesting to note that, while he clearly identifies Hegel as one of the culprits to philosophically pursue Romanticism, he admits to following a dialectical method, as he repeatedly does in his interview with Bruno Bosteels. Bruno Bosteels, "Can Change Be Thought? A Dialogue with Alain Badiou," in *Alain Badiou: Philosophy and its Conditions*, ed. Gabriel Riera (Albany: SUNY Press, 2005), 237–61. For a comprehensive assessment of his (changing) relationship with Hegel, see Jim Vernon and Antonio Calcagno, eds., *Badiou and Hegel: Infinity, Dialectics, Subjectivity* (New York: Lexington, 2015).

26. See Tzvetan Todorov, *Mikhail Bakhtin: The Dialogical Principle* (Minneapolis: University of Minnesota Press, 1984). The "sequential" arrangement that Gumbrecht notes here comes close to Claviez's argument in this volume of a close connection between the metonymic character of narrative and the nature of contingency.

27. It cannot come as a surprise that the possibility of "undeserved luck" doesn't sit too well with an Aristotelian ethics based upon desert. The "sublime" aspect of the "truth process" (as unnamable and thus incommunicable) is also emphasized by Badiou, who in his *Ethics* states that "what arises from a truth-process . . . cannot be communicated" (51). This, however, opens the question of the distinction between the contingency of the event proper and the "truth process" that arises from it. In any case, Peter Hallward's claim—in his defense against Simon Critchley's objection that Badiou's ethics partakes in the very religious discourse that he so criticizes in others—that "in Badiou's own philosophy, there is simply no place for an 'inaccessible' transcendence in any sense of the word" at least raises the question. While the event might not be transcendent, it certainly is characterized by an amount of

inaccessibility that approaches the sublime. Peter Hallward, "Ethics without Others: A Reply to Critchley on Badiou's Ethics," *Radical Philosophy* 102 (2000): 28. Simon Critchley, "Demanding Approval: On the Ethics of Alain Badiou," *Radical Philosophy* 100 (2000): 16–27.

28. Jacques Derrida, *The Politics of Friendship*, trans. George Collins (London: Verso, 2005), 47n15.

29. Marchi explicitly states: "My central claim is that, in both thinkers, the apophatic strategy signals the attempt at thinking community nondialectically and, more specifically, outside of a dialectic of the 'proper.'"

30. On this, see Viola Marchi, "'The Alienation of the Common': A Look into the 'Authentic Origin' of Community," in *Critique of Authenticity*, ed. Thomas Claviez, Kornelia Imesch, and Britta Sweers (Wilmington, DE: Vernon, 2019), 73–100.

31. The concept of "relationality" will be taken up numerous times in the essays that follow.

32. See Étienne Balibar, *Equaliberty: Political Essays*, trans. James Ingram (Durham, NC: Duke University Press, 2014).

33. It is Badiou himself who, in his essay "The Event in Deleuze," *Parrhesia* 2 (2007): 37–44, carefully lays out the central differences that separate his approach to the event from that of Deleuze. For instance, while for Badiou the event constitutes a radical immanent break, a supplement that cannot be accounted for by established norms, languages, and knowledges, for Deleuze the event is coextensive with becoming, operating on it in terms of "intensities." Against what Badiou interprets as Deleuze's philosophy of the One and of the "univocity of being"—a reading already articulated in depth in his *Deleuze: The Clamor of Being*, trans. L. Burchill (Minneapolis: University of Minnesota Press, 2000)—Badiou advances an idea of the event as the "decomposition of worlds by multiple eventual sites," in order to safeguard the "without-One of the event, its contingent dissemination" (40).

34. Gilles Deleuze and Felix Guattari, *A Thousand Plateaus: Capitalism and Schizophrenia* (Minneapolis: University of Minnesota Press, 1987). For a closer analysis of the concept, see Manuel DeLanda, *A New Philosophy of Society: Assemblage Theory and Social Complexity* (London: Bloomsbury Academic, 2006). The most concise definition of what constitutes an assemblage is provided by Deleuze in an interview with Claire Parnet, published in 2007 in *Dialogues II* (New York: Columbia University Press, 2007): "What is an assemblage? It is a multiplicity which is made up of many heterogeneous terms and which establishes liaisons, relations between them, across ages, sexes and reigns—different natures. Thus, the assemblage's only unity is that of a co-functioning: it is a symbiosis, a 'sympathy.' It is never filiations which are important, but alliances, alloys; these are not successions, lines of descent, but contagions, epidemics, the wind" (69).

35. This strongly resonates with a Derridean ethics of hospitality, one that obliges

us to "say yes to who or what turns up, before any determination, before any anticipation, before any identification, whether or not it has to do with a foreigner, an immigrant, an invited guest, or an unexpected visitor, whether or not the new arrival is the citizen of another country, a human, an animal, or divine creature, a living or a dead thing, male or female." Jacques Derrida, *Of Hospitality: Anne Dufourmantelle Invites Jacques Derrida to Respond* (Stanford, CA: Stanford University Press, 2000), 77.

36. Gilles Deleuze, *The Logic of Sense*, trans. M. Lester and C. J. Stivale (London: Bloomsbury, 2004), 71.

37. To "institute" goes back, according to the *Online Etymology Dictionary*, to the Latin verb *statuere*, which means to "establish, to cause to stand."

38. Karl Marx and Friedrich Engels, *The German Ideology* (New York: International Publishers, 1972), 121–24.

39. Jacques Derrida, *Negotiations: Interventions and Interviews, 1971–2001* (Stanford, CA: Stanford University Press, 2002), 25–26.

40. "The moment of *decision as such*, what must be just, *must* always remain a finite moment of urgency and precipitation; it must not be the consequence or the effect of . . . theoretical or historical knowledge, of . . . reflection or . . . deliberation, since the decision always marks the interruption of the juridico-, ethico-, or politico-cognitive deliberation that precedes it, that *must* precede it. The instant of a decision is a madness, says Kierkegaard." Derrida, "Force of Law," 26.

41. Derrida, *Negotiations*, 26.

42. The tone of this passage stands in remarkable contrast to the urgency that characterizes his preface to Catherine Malabou's *The Future of Hegel*, trans. Lisabeth During (London: Routledge, 2005), in which Derrida admonishes the reader to read her book, as he clearly considers it a milestone in Hegel scholarship.

43. Jacques Lacan, *The Seminar of Jacques Lacan Book VII: The Ethics of Psychoanalysis 1959–1960*, ed. Jacques-Alain Miller, trans. Dennis Porter (London: Routledge, 2008), 303, 243, 313. It is worth mentioning, in the light of what follows, that Jason Glynos, "Thinking the Ethics of the Political in the Context of a Postfoundational World: From an Ethics of Desire to an Ethics of the Drive," *Theory and Event* 4, no. 1 (2000): 1–16, takes this ethics to mean "stay true to the senselessness of the master signifier" (4).

44. It is interesting to note, in this regard, that a "circular" concept of time is usually connected to the cosmology of myth.

45. Wallace Stevens, *The Necessary Angel: Essays on Reality and the Imagination* (New York: Random House, 1942), 29.

46. As regards specifically the intersection between systems theory and deconstruction, see William Rasch and Cary Wolfe, eds., *Observing Complexity: Systems Theory and Postmodernity* (Minneapolis: University of Minnesota Press, 2000);

Cary Wolfe, *What Is Posthumanism?* (Minneapolis: University of Minnesota Press, 2010).

47. Jacques Derrida, *The Beast and the Sovereign, Volume II*, trans. Geoffrey Bennington, ed. Michel Lisse, Marie-Louise Mallet, and Ginette Michaud (Chicago: University of Chicago Press, 2011), 9. In a way worth pursuing further, Derrida's mentioning of islands echoes Deleuze and Guattari's concept of "archipelago" as an instance of assemblage, although the assemblage's characterization as bits and pieces achieving relation to others is what Derrida's islands, at least according to Wolfe's quotation, are emphatically not designed to do.

48. Derrida, *The Beast and the Sovereign, Volume II*, 9.

49. Stuart Kauffman, *Humanity in a Creative Universe* (Oxford: Oxford University Press, 2015), 73. See also Christopher Johnson, *System and Writing in the Philosophy of Jacques Derrida* (Cambridge: Cambridge University Press, 1993).

50. If this Heideggerian quip be allowed us—that the mechanism inside a watch that is designed to capture the passing of time is called *Unruhe*, which could be translated into English as "restlessness" or "disquietude."

Throwing the Moral Dice
            Ethics and/of Contingency

Three Notes on Contingency Today
Stress, Science—and Consolation from the Past?

Hans Ulrich Gumbrecht

I

In the context of philosophical arguments and discussions, rather than in everyday conversations, the word "contingency"[1] refers to the status of future events or circumstances that may happen but do not have to. It thus necessarily evokes a viewpoint that links present to future and marks, in the future, the status of a horizon between necessity and impossibility. This explains why sociologists frequently use the phrase "double contingency" to describe the initial situation of persons participating in an interaction. The participants will always have some expectations about each other's behavior that cannot be certain (in the sense of being "necessary" expectations), whereas some other behaviors that they are able to imagine can be excluded from their expectations as "impossible." If we say in such contexts that events, circumstances, or behaviors are "random," then we refer to our inability, at least indirectly, to explain why they came to happen—but we sometimes also want to say, as an implicitly ontological claim, that the reasons why they became real do not exist.

In recent times, this very conception of a horizon of "contingency" has shaped an increasingly dominant individual view of our everyday life. We normally do experience and often refer to the everyday where our actions and our behaviors are taking place as a "field of contingency," that is, as a horizon provoking choice between necessity and impossibility. Perhaps more than ever before, this "in between" dimension of contingency has been enshrined and obsessively protected against all outside interferences as the place of our individual freedom. In other words, it has become the latest version of our sphere of privacy, where, on the one hand, we do not want to think too much of what is "impossible" for us and where, on the other hand, we do not want to be reminded too much of what is "necessary," in the sense of being subject to fate and even destiny. Within our "own" field of contingency as a space of private freedom, we want to constantly choose, decide, and perhaps revise what we chose, and we thus strongly resent any type of surveillance or documentation of our choices (hence the loud protest against all attempts to anonymously store traces of our behavior and then trade them as market-relevant data). The claim of independence from all kinds of institutions, above all from state institutions and their demands, may indeed be more intense than ever before, while our expectations about individual needs being covered by the same institutions are constantly growing.

As a collateral effect of the tendency to shelter our private life, as a field of contingency, against all hints of "necessity" (that is, duty or fate) or "impossibility" (that is, limiting our choices), we have inadvertently entered a coalition with contemporary (mainly electronic/data processing) technology, whose achievements and conquests are progressively transforming the poles of necessity and impossibility into an ever broader horizon of contingency. More metaphorically speaking: As the poles of impossibility and necessity are melting under the impact of electronic technology, our everyday as a field of contingency is fast approaching the form of a universe of contingency.

A few illustrations, starting with the necessity pole: The sex into which (the genitals with which) we were born has always been considered fate or destiny, with devastating existential and social consequences, well known to all of us, for humans who were born into a sex with which they could not psychically identify. Transsexual surgery now holds the promise for a progressive substitution of fate by choice. On the impossibility side of our everyday as a field of contingency, and presupposing that predicate is used for (above all) monotheistic Gods, the latter have always been examples of the human talent to imagine forms of existence that do not seem attainable for us; on the impossibility side of our everyday, it is obvious how the development and expansion of the internet have given the traditionally divine conditions of individual omnipresence and individual omniscience a new status as dimensions of human life available on a global level. In addition, the divine condition and the human dream of eternal (physical) life have become an increasingly realistic target for medical research in recent years.

Of course, we should celebrate such ongoing transformations of necessity and impossibility into objects of choice, that is, the transformation of our field of contingency into a universe of contingency, as a substantial increase of human freedom. At the same time, however, we cannot overlook how this growth of freedom and choice produces an unprecedented level of individual stress and insecurity. Even the planning of our weekends, within a perceived infinity of leisure choices offered by the web and always ready for "immediate reservation," has become a daunting task—in a never-ending seven-day rhythm. The daily communication within our families and at our workplaces is now part of a potentially global hypercommunication taking place in front of laptops and with iPhones in our hands. Nothing indeed can appear necessary today (even in the sense of "casual" or "natural"), while hardly anything seems to be absolutely impossible, either.

The unavoidable stress caused by living in a universe of contingency facilitated by contemporary technology, a level of stress for which neither our minds nor our bodies have ever been prepared, may well explain the two most frequently mentioned pathologies within contemporary everyday culture: the (in)famous burnout syndrome (despite decreasing amounts of obligatory working time) and the widespread longing for simple values, for figures to believe in, and for orientations "to hold on to." They all seem to be a matrix and a fertile ground for what present political commentators identify and criticize as a new wave of "fundamentalism." Whoever inhabits this still obsessively protected private sphere of incessant choice under the condition of growing internal complexity now faces the temptation of longing for a public sphere of simple and highly transparent structures. This does not only provoke political messages with a connotation of being "clear" and "elementary" but, more interestingly, some new and at the same time archaic-looking forms of sociability.

The most appealing forms of sociability today no longer exclusively rely on shared interests (like political parties and labor unions used to do) and provide solidarity and mutual support. What makes them different from traditional forms and at the same time fascinating for many of us is the joint desire of bringing the human body back into interaction and community. I am thinking of open-air concerts and religious events with broad participation (like solemn high masses read by the pope on his travels all over the world, where, quite often, the majority of people gathered know little or nothing about the Eucharist as core of the ongoing ritual); of the spectators at sports events, the groups coming together for public viewing (who are far from being unanimously interested in the competition to be seen); and of mass-participation long-distance running events. As modern sociology has always worked under the (mostly silent) premise of the human body belonging to the outside of human sociability, we lack well-defined concepts for the analysis of such phenomena. Therefore, I like to go back to one of the earliest concepts that Christian theology has used to describe its community of believers, that is, the concept of "Christ's mystical body."

When I am part of a—secular—"mystical body" in a stadium, at an open-air event, or even in one of its political manifestations, I can feel free of (the freedom and the stress of) constantly making choices in a universe of contingency. Rather, I become physically linked to an intensity and a flow that are not exclusively mine. It is this perspective, I believe, that can explain how "resonance" has replaced deliberation and consensus as a central medium of politics during the past years. For what we call "resonance" is the existentially assuring sentiment of growing into one secular mystical body under the impact of an (often) charismatic speaker and her or his (often confused and sometimes dangerous) message. Resonance in this sense, as we gather from many scenarios within the global political situation today, can be ugly and precarious, high-risk and threatening. But we should not only demonize this phenomenon or engage in a ritual self-flagellation for having allowed it to grow, typical responses of intellectuals, who always tend to overestimate their influence and responsibility. Resonance and mystical bodies, after all, may also help us rediscover some essential—and comforting—aspects of human existence that we have lost as our everyday turns into a universe of contingency.

II

Life within mystical bodies is, of course, not the only imaginable redemption from the stress caused by what we so seem to cherish, that is, our private sphere and everyday world as a universe of contingency. During the late nineteenth and the first half of the twentieth century, for example, the public admiration and trust in natural science and in the "laws" that it claimed to uncover fulfilled the function of a horizon for human existence that gave "absolute" certainty about what had to be considered impossible and necessary (or unavoidable). It is no coincidence that the names and the faces of some early Nobel laureates in the sciences, the Einsteins, Schrödingers, and Heisenbergs, have reached a quasi-transcendental (more than just iconic) status, even among those of their contemporaries who only have a vague level of understanding about their research.

Something profound (or at least something culturally decisive) must have changed since then. Today, my students and I will only remember for a few days after the annual announcements the names of even those Nobel laureates who work at our own university. One could argue, for instance with Martin Heidegger and based on his essay "The Age of the World Picture," that science has altogether failed to develop an existentially relevant influence on our relationship to the material environment because, instead of finding perspectives of convergence between our own physical being and nature, it has further separated us from nature by hiding the material world behind a curtain of mathematical equations.[2] This might also explain why engineering, as a less intellectually aristocratic but more hands-on approach to nature, has long left science behind in terms of its everyday perception and impact in the public sphere.

Yet science has also become more powerful today in fulfilling those functions that were formerly decisive for its role as a source of existential assurance. Largely owing, again, to the data processing capacities of the most recent generations of computers, science is now able to transform, in many different contexts, what used to be considered randomness into almost certainty and almost necessity. Think of short-, mid-, and long-term weather forecasts today; think of prognostics regarding global climate change; think of our ability to anticipate macroeconomic fluctuations. Not to speak of the impressively developed competence that can explain, retrospectively and in detail, the origin and the development of events of nature that we are not yet able to predict: for example, earthquakes and tsunamis.

But why does science, in spite of such a truly amazing increase of knowledge, no longer manage to fulfill its former function as a compensation and a balance for the destabilizing existential impact of our everyday turned into a universe of contingency, as it had so impressively done during the decades after 1900? There are multiple answers. In the first place and quite obviously, the great scientists of our present hardly ever conceive of themselves as public intellectuals, as most protagonists of the Einstein generation had quite actively done. It is difficult to say whether this change has occurred because of growing specialization and complexity or simply from a lack of effort among contemporary scientists. One way or another, lay persons today hardly ever get a glimpse of insight regarding the discoveries or theories for which the Nobel Prize is being awarded.

More dramatically, scientists (and engineers working on the borders of science) have become increasingly engaged in painting future situations of potentially apocalyptic impact, instead of further expanding the vision of a quiet, complex, and somehow dignified (almost Dantean) universe, accessible to the efforts of human understanding, a vision that had waned by the mid–twentieth century. By contrast, scientific research today obliges the historians and philosophers of our time to open their narratives and their visions to the dimension of the "Anthropocene," that is, to a dimension of time lasting from the emergence of *Homo sapiens sapiens* until his and her vanishing from Earth, caused by the negative ecological influence of human presence. Or think of the concept of "singularity" and the prediction of people working in the development of artificial intelligence, according to which we are no longer far away from the appearance of an algorithm-based intelligence superior to human intelligence, with the attendant risk of that superior intelligence wanting to terminate humankind.

Looking back "historically" from our worries of the early third millennium, we realize that some smooth balance between contingency (freedom of choice) and certainty (destiny) had existed, largely unnoticed and therefore not enough appreciated, during the nineteenth and early twentieth centuries, during the age of both the most ecstatic pathos of individual freedom and of the most unconditional belief in the truth-providing role of natural science. As a premise of epistemology, social change, and individual life, its two opposite dimensions and centers of energy, private liberty, and the objectivity of evolution hardly ever caused an impression of contradiction or tension. I do not believe, however, that the possibility is open for us to restore or to find our way back to that balance. All we can do at this point is sketch its emergence, historically, which may produce an unintentional discursive effect of irony, as the emergence of the balance in question may well have been part of the emergence of what historians today call the "historical worldview."

Now this reconstruction will make us aware of an intellectual reaction to contingency (and freedom) quite different from the (now lost) balance that had come with the historical worldview. It was a reaction practiced, without any political program or major institutional impact, by some late-eighteenth-century thinkers and artists, a reaction that has remained present as a peripheral possibility and potential, without ever being actively repressed. In concluding, I will refer to Denis Diderot's antinovel *Jacques le fataliste et son maître* as an illustration of that position and of its possible inspirational value (not more!) for our present-day situation.

III

If we try to understand and explain the emergence of the historical worldview, as it had firmly established itself by 1830, as an uncontested and truthful approach to the past, if we try to historicize the historical worldview by its own—historical—rules, we inevitably find ourselves referred to an obsession with contingency that began to manifest itself starting in the third quarter of the eighteenth century. During those decades and seemingly without any strong systematic reason, it became habitual among intellectuals (*philosophes*, in French, as the dominant language of the time) to observe themselves in all their acts of world observation. This shift had two major consequences for their epistemological practices, shifts that can be amply documented in contemporary texts.

In the first place, an observer observing herself in the act of world observation will quickly realize that the results of her observation (her respective experiences) will depend on the different points of view accessible to her, and as there always exists a potential infinity of such points of view, it follows that there will also be a potential infinity of representations (experiences) for each object of reference—a situation to which many intellectuals and artists reacted with great existential concern. In other words, it was this very change through which world observation first became a horizon of contingency—with all of the attendant psychic and cultural consequences. At the same time and with more historical specificity, a self-observing observer must also see, against the grain of the Cartesian dominance of mind and reason, that her experience is a product not only of the mind but of the mind together with the bodily senses. Thus the question arose how mind-based and sense-based components of world experience were possibly related.

Both questions triggered concerns and debates that dominated the intellectual scene of the late eighteenth century. It is quite easy to see in retrospect how two powerful (not to say drastic) reactions emerged and found strong institutional support after 1800 and became foundational for what was to become mainstream Western thought during the nineteenth and early twentieth centuries—although these reactions were at first not programmatically conceived of as "solutions." The second problem, the problem regarding the relation between sensual perception and mind-based experience in our world observation, was clearly bracketed in the work of the most influential thinkers of those years (I think of Hegel above all) and thus in the thinking of their students and readers. What, by contrast, absorbed the problem of contingency, polyperspectivism, and multiple forms of experience for each object of reference was the transition from a mirror-like, one-to-one pattern of world representation to a narrative principle of world representation, as we can trace it in the early nineteenth century.

From that time on, a person being asked, for example, what France was would show a tendency to answer with a history; descriptions of phenomena of nature began to show rudimentary traces of evolutionism; and in his *Phenomenology of Spirit*, the young philosopher Hegel chose the sequence of an individual human life as the form for his systematic conceptualization of "Spirit." How could this shift to narrative patterns (Michel Foucault referred to it as *historisation des êtres*) be a solution to the challenge of polyperspectivism and contingency? The answer is that narrative forms of discourse—independently of the intentions of those who operate them—have the elementary capacity of integrating multiple views regarding one and the same object of reference and of arranging them as a sequence. By 1830, this pattern had become the common matrix in Western culture for different branches of thought that occupied the decisive institutional spaces in education, politics, law, and even economics; it became the basis for the philosophy of history and for evolutionism in the sciences, for utopian forms of early socialism, and even for the practice of capitalism.

On the level of official institutional discourses, it provided a view of the world and its changes as being necessary—with sufficient distance between the institutions involved to never be experienced as tensions or contradictions. There was no actual political need at all, say, for the rising movement toward national independence in Italy (the Risorgimento), for the drive of the Prussian state toward dominance in what would become Germany, for Napoléon III's "Second Empire," and for the first social movements inspired by Karl Marx's philosophy to ever coordinate their claims of "necessity." At the same time, and this was the long-standing "balance" I have been referring to, the historical worldview seems to have been distant enough from all individual forms of experiencing life to leave them intact as a sphere of choice and independence that would not contradict the claims and concessions of "Liberty" so typical for nineteenth-century citizens. From a strictly philosophical angle, one obvious contradiction did exist: How could individual action be a behavior of freedom under the premise of "historical necessity"? This problem, however, was discussed in seminars of academic philosophy and not in everyday situations leading to practical decisions. Without any doubt, philosophy—and even more clearly, science—had provided a framework that successfully replaced religion as a comforting and reassuring horizon of individual life.

As I have already said, it was not before the late twentieth century that this balance, mainly caused by the transformation of private life from a field of contingency into a universe of contingency, lost its stability and thus its original function. In this situation, which is our situation, it may be worthwhile to return to the historical moment during the third quarter of the eighteenth century when contingency had first become an epistemological problem—and to an intellectual reaction that, instead of occupying central institutional spaces in Western culture, has always remained peripheral, without being actually repressed or eliminated. I am referring to figures like the French author Denis Diderot and the German philosopher of nature Georg Christoph Lichtenberg but also to Francisco Goya and Wolfgang Amadeus Mozart, who, without knowing of one another, and far from constituting a "school," showed similar structures of thought in their texts and aesthetic practice.

In the first place, none of them ever bracketed the question regarding the relationship between world appropriation through the mind and world appropriation through the senses. For Diderot, it rather triggered an almost lifelong, obsessive reflection that became part of what we have come to call eighteenth-century "materialism." If Karl Marx, a good fifty years later, would use this word to refer to the complex social conditions of human work, Diderot wanted to find out, as a "materialist," how each of the different senses of the human body made specific contributions to our understanding of the world and its objects. At the same time, he saw matter as containing a profound impulse of agency toward any kind of transformations that we can observe.

More importantly, from our point of view, Diderot never concentrated on "History" and the supposed regularities (or "laws") according to which these were supposed to change the world; this also meant that he did not participate in the absorption or neutralization of the problem of contingency through narrativization, as it would soon become central for the historical worldview. His worldview presupposed (not only for individual life) contingency as its one and basic condition, and his predominant practice of finding orientation was through individual judgment. This became particularly evident in his writing about contemporary painting and sculpture, where he quite provocatively abandoned all the values and rules inherited from classical antiquity in order to rely exclusively on his own intuitions and preferences. While Diderot seems to have enjoyed his independence (and in fact never complained about the absence of any "higher" orientation), we can recognize a certain affinity between his epistemological situation and our own contemporary intellectual and existential challenges coming from a universe of contingency.

Beyond this intellectual practice, as it is also manifest in his many philosophical treatises and in the entries that he contributed, as one of its two editors, to the monumental *Encyclopédie*, Diderot dedicated a complex yet enjoyable novel (often identified as an "antinovel") to the problem of contingency. I am referring to his text posthumously published under the title *Jacques le fataliste et son maître*, whose main narrative axis is the traveling conversation between an aristocrat, who wants to persuade himself of the existence of individual freedom, and his servant Jacques, who never ceases invoking destiny as a "book" in which every present and future event is already "written" and thus decided beforehand. Their dialogue is doubled by the interaction between a text-implicit reader, who constantly wants to know more about the protagonists and their circumstances, and a text-implicit narrator, who quite cynically insists on being the absolutely independent inventor and origin of everything that the book can possibly convey.

Over the course of *Jacques le fataliste*'s several hundred pages, it becomes clear that none of these both strange and fascinating protagonists coherently hold on to what would follow from their positions. The narrator all of a sudden confesses that the main orientation for him, instead of his own imagination, is the truth of what he is telling, whereas, at the very end, we read that he was simply relying on text fragments left behind by the English novelist Laurence Sterne. Jacques's master is not only occasionally tempted by fatalism as a philosophical position but the least able to control his own situations and future, while Jacques is the least willing to accept his everyday challenges and the entire trajectory of his life as inevitable. However, all of this does not mean that Diderot was leaning toward a one-sided recommendation in favor of contingency, freedom, and judgment.

Rather, we know that, as a materialist, he believed in the possibility of explaining all events and occurrences as necessary but was fully aware that this discourse, if at all, could only be an a posteriori option. In view of the future, he saw no way, even for a *fataliste*, to avoid contingency and choice. Of course, there is nothing philosophically earthshaking for us in the copresence of these two fundamental perspectives. It largely corresponds to our own contemporary situation in the universe of contingency—with natural science at the horizon, more competent than ever before in providing all retrospective explanations that we can possibly desire or imagine. What I want to insist upon is the simultaneity of the two approaches in the thinking of Diderot, who once, in a rather casual philosophical remark, wrote that "either everything is random—or nothing."[3] To accept this epistemological copresence as an existential condition may indeed be, if not a "solution," then at least a consolation for us, in the confrontation with the most dramatic challenges of our time.

We may try, individually and collectively, our best to minimize the effects of global warming, and we may develop the most plausible strategies to keep, under humanly acceptable control, the development of artificial intelligence. But in moments of depression and despair, I think it is preferable to assume (and to accept) that a possible end of humankind might be part of a larger evolutionary process that has always determined our behavior—rather than collectively accusing ourselves for actions whose impact we could not have possibly known while they happened. Serenity is certainly more livable than self-moralization—and perhaps even more reasonable.

NOTES

1. Being a native speaker of German and despite the definitions of "contingency" in most authoritative dictionaries of the English language, I cannot convince myself that German "*Kontingenz*" and English "contingency" are fully synonymous. "Contingency" always seems to include the connotation of being "contingent upon," which leads our attention to the circumstances that may explain the happening of an event or the existence of a phenomenon, whereas "*Kontingenz*" is free of a similar connection (which in German would be "*abhängig sein von*"). This said, I will use the word "contingency" as if it was fully synonymous with "*Kontingenz*" indeed.

2. Martin Heidegger, "The Age of the World Picture," in *The Question Concerning Technology and Other Essays*, trans. William Lovitt (New York: Harper Torchbooks, 1977), 115–54.

3. Jean Starobinski, *Diderot, un diable de ramage* (Paris: Gallimard, 2012), 318. For a more detailed analysis of Diderot's philosophy of contingency, I kindly refer the reader to my book *Prose of the World: Denis Diderot and the Periphery of Enlightenment* (Stanford, CA: Stanford University Press, 2021), esp. chap. 4.

Cosmopolitan Ethics as an Ethics of Contingency Toward a Metonymic Community

Thomas Claviez

INTRODUCTION

At a pivotal point in Amitav Ghosh's most recent novel, *Gun Island* (2019), the author has his main protagonist—a rare-books dealer by the name of Deen Datta—exclaim:

> The word "chance" hit me with such force that I lost track of what Piya was saying. Shutting my eyes I silently embraced the word, clinging to it as though it were my last connection with reality.
>
> Yes, of course, it was all chance, these unlikely encounters, these improbable intersections between past and present; that almost fatal accident that had brought me face to face with Rafi in the Ghetto: all of this was pure coincidence, of course it was. To lose sight of that was to risk becoming untethered from reality; chance was the very foundation of reality, of normalcy. There was absolutely no reason to imagine, as I had done, that such an encounter, in such a place, was outside of the range of the probable. Because no such thing existed; nothing was outside the

range of the probable—wasn't that why I had ensured myself against the possibility of living till the age of one hundred and three? Because that too might happen no matter how fractional the chances.[1]

Deen's musings—embedded in a cosmopolitan novel that narrates, among other things, the "improbable" connections between Deen, an old Indian manuscript, Venice, and the trajectory of Bengal fugitives—address a whole range of different layers: The first one emphasizes the relationship between reality and contingency, as Deen realizes that to deny contingency involves the risk of becoming "untethered from reality," an age-old problem that leads us back, as I will show, to Aristotle. The second one—let us call it a metaliterary one and one not unconnected to Aristotle—refers to the relationship between reality, literature, and questions of probability: If literature, as mimetic, is on the one hand designed to "mime" reality but, on the other hand, should be "probable" in order to not become, say, melodramatic (a genre usually defined as to narratively combine improbable contingencies), what does that tell us about the status of literature in general and its connection to reality—and, not least, about Ghosh's own novel? What, finally, might be the possible connections between a cosmopolitanism that, on the one hand, feels forced to acknowledge the improbable as the basis of a new reality but that, on the other hand, configures new—and maybe until now unheard of, and thus "improbable"—forms of community?

In what follows, I would like to readdress two questions that, in the extensive debates around the concept of cosmopolitanism that we have witnessed in recent years—if not decades—have not been exhaustively reflected upon and thus shed a new light on them through the prism of another neglected notion that figures so prominently in *Gun Island* (and, as I will show, in Ghosh's previous novels): that of contingency. The first question is: What is it specifically that distinguishes the idea of a "cosmopolitan community" from all other, traditional concepts of community? The second one is: How have we conceived of this distinction? Taking recourse to some of the classical philosophical texts on community—from Aristotle via Rousseau, Hobbes, and Locke to Tönnies and Heidegger—I will argue that (1) the main distinction between cosmopolitan and traditional concepts of community lies in the fact that the former not only makes the "outside," against which any of the latter have always defined themselves, disappear (or at least problematic) but that, moreover, (2) how we have defined this "outside"— usually through different notions of an/the other/Other—has led the debate into something like a dead end. It is here, I will argue, that resorting to the concept of contingency might offer the opportunity to veer off the trodden paths and to rethink a cosmopolitan community in terms that avoid the Same/Other but also the Universalism/Particularism dichotomies that have haunted the debate for quite some time. One, moreover, that takes, as Deen, contingency not only into account but that "tethers" it back to reality. Finally, I will argue that another neglected trope—metonymy—might help us gauge the implications and challenges of what would constitute a cosmopolitan "community of contingency," as well as what specifically literary forms it might take—or has taken.

TRADITIONAL CONCEPTS OF COMMUNITY: CLOSING OFF—AGAINST WHAT, EXACTLY?

> . . . for what ought not to be is what is false and what is not.
> —Aristotle, *Politics*, 103.

In his 2001 book with the programmatic title *Community: Seeking Safety in an Insecure World*, the sociologist Zygmunt Bauman gives us this tongue-in-cheek definition of a traditional community:

> Community is a "warm" place, a cosy and comfortable place. It is like a roof under which we shelter in the heavy rain, like a fireplace at which we warm our hands on a frosty day. Out there, in the street, all sorts of dangers lie in ambush; we have to be alert when we go out, watch whom we are talking to and who talks to us, be on the look-out every minute. In here, in the community, we can relax—we are safe, there are no dangers looming in dark corners. . . . In a community, we all understand each other, we may trust what we hear, we are safe most of the time and hardly ever puzzled or taken aback. We are never strangers to each other.[2]

Just how and why this snuggly feeling is ensured becomes clear in a passage a little later: This ideal community, which is paradoxically both "distinctive" and "indistinct" (or even "undistinguished"), in that it (a) distinguishes itself from all other groups around it but (b) does not evince any noticeable distinctions within itself, is characterized by the absence of—what, exactly? "There are no 'betwixt and between' cases left, it is crystal clear who is 'one of us' and who is not, there is no muddle and no cause for confusion—no cognitive ambiguity, and so no behavioral ambivalence."[3] Both of Bauman's citations should, however, give us pause: Just why should "all sorts of dangers" be related to "whom we are talking to and who talks to us?" Why should the "between and betwixt" cases immediately depend on the distinction between "who is 'one of us' and who is not?" Why should "cognitive ambiguity" be exclusively be caused by or result in "behavioral ambivalence?" All of the first terms suggest something like an epistemic insecurity, which can apply to all sorts of things, mostly contingencies we encounter that, according to a standard definition of contingency, "could have been otherwise." Just why they are then immediately transformed, or metonymically connected, to notions of "otherness"—the "stranger," the "not-us," and the "behavior" of "them"—remains a mystery. This mystery fiction—and such Bauman admits it to be ("It looks as if we will never stop dreaming of a community, but neither will we ever find in any self-proclaimed community the pleasures we savored in our dreams")[4]—is nothing else than the very topos that has drawn itself through almost all philosophical discussions revolving around the concept of community. And in almost all of those fictions the same phenomenon that we have discerned in Bauman reappears: Instances of contingency and concepts of otherness are immediately collapsed into each other and thus form—and here I come back to my first question—an imaginary "outside." But what is it exactly that this traditional community wants to close itself off against? Is it exclusively an "Other" of sorts? This question leads us back to Aristotle.

Aristotle opens his *Politics* with the following words: "The state is the highest form of community and aims at the highest good. How it differs from other communities will appear if we examine the parts of which it is composed."[5] I do not want to dwell on the fact that, right after this passage, Aristotle defines the microunit of the state as "founded upon the two relations of male and female, of master and slave,"[6] which already introduces certain forms of contingency; it is for a reason that John Locke devotes the entire first part of his *Two Treatises of Government*—"The Divine Right of Kings"—to meticulously taking apart this basic assumption upon which the entire edifice of Aristotle's concept of community rests.[7] Nor do I want to engage intensely with the highly problematic concept of a communal telos that informs Aristotle's thinking—though it might be important to keep in mind as to what it is that might potentially challenge or obfuscate this telos. But the entire famous passage where this telos is mentioned is worth quoting at length for other reasons:

For what each thing is when fully developed, we call its nature, whether we are speaking of a man, a horse or a family. Besides, the final cause and end of a thing is the best, and to be self-sufficing is the end and the best.

Hence it is evident that the state is a creation of nature, and that man is by nature a political animal. And he who by nature and not by mere accident is without a state, is either above humanity, or below it; he is the

"Tribeless, lawless, hearthless one,"

whom Homer denounces—the outcast who is a lover of war; he may be compared to an unprotected piece in the game of draughts.[8]

This figure of the *phaulos*, the warmongering outcast, and its role for Aristotle's philosophy have been much discussed, most recently by the French philosopher Jacques Rancière, who denounces it as an emblematic topos for an ethics of otherness along the lines of Giorgio Agamben and Emmanuel Levinas.[9] What I want to get at, however, is not his/her strange status as someone "either above humanity, or below it"[10] but rather two other facts: (1) that the *phaulos* "by nature, and not by mere accident, is without a state" and (2) given this nature is both "a lover of war" but on the other hand is compared to "an unprotected piece in the game of draughts." The first quotation indicates that the *phaulos* has taken a decision in this regard and is thus not tribeless by accident—that is, through contingency. This decision, however, makes him potentially dangerous on the one hand, vulnerable on the other: A "lover of war," he also resembles an "unprotected piece in the game of draughts." He is thus both the cause for potential contingencies (to others) *and* subject to them. Moreover, the fact that he is mentioned right after Aristotle introduces not only his concept of the teleological character of every single being but the logical conclusion that it is the state's task to ensure that each of its members reaches said "final cause and end," it becomes rather clear that the danger the outcast poses is that he might obstruct the achievement—individual or communal—of this end. "But he who is unable to live in society, or who has no need because he is sufficient for himself, must be either a beast or a god: he is no part of the state."[11]

Strangely enough, however, the problem is not the warmongering monstrosity of the *phaulos* per se, since Aristotle considers the "art of war . . . a natural art of acquisition, for it includes hunting, an art which we ought to practice against wild beasts, and against men who, though intended by nature to be governed, will not submit; for war of such kind is naturally just."[12] That is, not to be part of a community is unnatural, since those who defy being governed constitute a potential threat to community that then serves as a pretext to hunt those elements down, according to a (strange) logic that, on the one hand, considers war unnatural if waged by the outcasts but that, on the other, "naturalizes" the war waged on the former by the community.

Be s/he beast or god, there seems to be nothing at all "behaviorally ambivalent" in this outside/outcast that is Aristotle's *phaulos*: S/he is the warmonger exclusively and as such serves as a pivotal—if illogical—figure of legitimation for a community that is also characterized by another quality: self-sufficiency. That is why Aristotle warns again and again against a surplus economy and the barter that grows out of it. And again, he considers such barter to be barbarian and unnatural because it exposes community to contact with its "outside."[13] This argument is taken up with a vengeance by Ferdinand Tönnies in his (thinly disguised) rehash of Aristotle's *Politics* in *Community and Society*. What distinguishes this other "outside" from the bloodthirsty outsider is that it has to offer something else than bloodshed: goods that are missing in the community. This encounter might, however, expose us to contingencies that threaten to entangle us in "unnatural" dependencies, since the "proper" use of a shoe is to be worn and not to be exchanged.[14] I won't go into all the Marxian, Heideggerian, and Jamesonian implications of this example; suffice it here to say that the contingencies that the exposure to an outside offer need by no means be exclusively negative.

Rather strikingly, the very self-sufficiency that Aristotle so hails is one that introduces another form of contingency, in that it introduces otherness into the community: As he states, if "self-sufficiency is to be desired, the lesser degree of unity is more desirable than the greater,"[15] one of the reasons being that "that which is common to the greatest number has the least care bestowed upon it."[16] Ironically, this means that the common *telos*—the highest good of the community—would, according to this logic, be what gets the least attention, the reason being that, according to Aristotle, everyone takes more care of him- or herself than of said common telos. This, again, is because people do actually crave "external goods"; those, however, "come of themselves, and *chance* is the author of them, but no one is just or temperate by or through chance."[17] Again, we see that contingency interferes with the just as defined by Aristotle—with the telos that one should pursue.

That is, the pursuit of happiness through directed self-sufficiency stands in stark contrast to the vagaries of exposure to a contingent outside, a scenario in which chance manifests as the actual (and only) enemy of the telos. Even in cases where such contingencies prove advantageous, they go against a concept of "the good" that cannot but define itself in contrast to them.

However, at the end of his *Politics*, Aristotle finally has to admit that the *polis* has to integrate as much contingency inside itself ("there must always be in cities a multitude of slaves and sojourners and foreigners; but we should include only those who are members of the state, and who form an essential part of it"),[18] although (or maybe because) that very distinction threatens to collapse: "In an overpopulous state foreigners and metics will readily acquire the rights of citizens, for who will find them out?"[19] Already in one of its first formulations, in the mysterious fiction that seems to guarantee the possibility of distinguishing between them and us, "cognitive ambiguity" and "behavioral ambivalence" are right among us, and the snuggly romance of community evinces its first cracks.

CONTINGENCY RELOADED: FROM HOBBES VIA KANT TO HEIDEGGER

A specific form of contingency is also at the root of Hobbes's conception of the commonwealth: that of the perpetual war of all against all. The raison d'être for Hobbes's state is, seen in this light, rather simple: It serves to protect those who subscribe to its social contract from the potential anarchy and violence that is the "state of nature." Ironically, the only way to gain protection from the contingency of the wolves that surround us in this natural state is to subject ourselves to an overwolf called Leviathan, a subjection so total, as Hobbes sketches it, as to expose us almost totally to its unchecked power:

> Hereby it is manifest, that during the time men live without a common Power to keep them all in awe, they are in that condition which is called Warre; and such a warre, as is of every man, against every man. . . . The life of man, solitary, poore, nasty, brutish, and short.[20]

We should have reached the point, in the meantime, to realize that this constitutes a founding myth that simply naturalizes—in the sense that Roland Barthes gives it[21]—a state of affairs that never existed as such, one that, moreover, naturalizes contingency as something purely negative. And it is only on the basis of such a mythologized past that he then legitimizes the power of this awe-inspiring Leviathan, a power that must, consequently, be greater than that of all the other natural wolves put together in order to work:

> Sovereign Power . . . is as great, as possibly men can be imagined to make it. And though of so unlimited a Power, men may fancy many evil consequences, yet the consequences of the want of it, which is perpetuall warre of every man against his neighbour, are much worse. . . . And whosoever thinking Sovereign Power too great, will seek to make it lesse; must subject himselfe, to the Power, that can limit it; that is to say, a greater.[22]

This, however, creates two problems: (1) What is it that could possibly induce me to trust wolves who have signed a social contract? (2) My subjection and exposure to a power as great as the Leviathan's increase rather than diminish the "felt" contingency that the natural state offers. Or, as Roberto Esposito so perceptively puts it in his analysis of Hobbes in *Communitas*: "The state of nature is not overcome once and for all by the civil, but it resurfaces again in the same figure of the sovereign, because it is the only one to have preserved natural right in a context in which all the others have given it up."[23]

This is as much as to say that the contingency of the state of nature is overcome only by replacing it with an even larger and more threatening one; the processes of immunization that, again, Esposito uncovers and deconstructs in his book *Immunitas* simply do not work, because of the almost mathematical fact that, if we define contingency as forces that can only be overcome by forces stronger than them, *we are entering a spiral of immunizing strategies that can only aggravate the contingencies.*

Immanuel Kant's take on the problem does not differ from Hobbes's, in so far as he also identifies contingencies as the driving force behind man's evolution as a rational animal:

> The means which nature employs to bring about the development of innate capacities is that of antagonism within society, in so far as this antagonism becomes in the long run the cause of a law-governed social order. By antagonism, I mean in this context the *unsocial sociability* of men, that is, the tendency to come together in society, coupled, however, with a continual resistance which constantly threatens to break this society up.[24]

However, the fact that man has formed a "lawful" order through the state has simply transferred the problem of the war of all against all onto a higher level: that of nations now perpetually waging war against one another. That is one reason why Kant actually develops, in both "Idea for a Universal History from a Cosmopolitan Point of View" and "Perpetual Peace," the concept of both cosmopolitanism and hospitality and that of a League of Nations. There is, however, a problem located in his approach to transcend the nation-state, as it is based on the assumption that a state has the same rights as a single person, since to conquer it, and thus "to graft it unto another state . . . is to terminate its existence as a moral personality and make it into a commodity. This contradicts the idea of the original contract without which the rights of a people are unthinkable."[25] While this is in line with a long tradition of thinking the "body politic," it creates a clash with another assumption of his, which he makes in a footnote in "Perpetual Peace":

> It is usually assumed that one cannot take hostile action against anyone unless one has already been actively *injured* by them. This is perfectly correct if both parties are living in a legal civil state. For the fact that the one has entered such a state gives the required guarantee to the other, since both are subject to the same authority. But man (or an individual people) in a mere state of nature robs me of any such security and injures me by virtue of this very state in which he coexists with me. He may not have injured me actively (*facto*), but he injures me by the very lawlessness of his state (*statu iniusto*), for he is a permanent threat to me, and I can require him either to enter into a common lawful state with me or to move away from my vicinity. Thus the postulate on which all the following articles are based is that all men who can at all influence one another must adhere to some kind of civil institution.[26]

Here, an important difference between an individual and a state comes to the fore, and that difference pertains directly to the question of contingency as contiguity in space: While I, as a single person, certainly may politely or not so politely ask a stranger to remove him- or herself from my neighborhood, to comply with such a request might prove rather difficult in the case of states.

Moreover, the problem of the transfer from the state of war among individuals to that of nations does not solve the power problem inherent in the mathematical sum total of contingency: To ensure the enforcement of such a League of Nations, the specter of the Leviathan—this time on an international scale—looms at the horizon. That is, nations that do not play by the rules and threaten to continue to use violence need to be kept in check—or in "awe," as Hobbes puts it—by a sovereign whose power, as in the case of the single wolves, outrivals theirs.

While Heidegger actively tries to leave the enlightened paradigm—starting with Descartes and the assumption of a reasonable being—behind and tries to think Being as always also "Being-with," he is finally forced to countersteer the very contingency that the presumed "fallenness" of man and his exposure to the "Them" (*das Man*) creates. As the "Man" in the final analysis serves almost exclusively as an obstacle to the individual's potential for authenticity, he resorts to the very suspect notion of the "destiny" that is purely reserved for the "Schicksalsgemeinschaft."[27] Again, that is, an Aristotelian telos is being introduced, but, through another act of transference, this telos goes by the name of a "destined community":

> But if fateful Dasein, as Being-in-the-world, exists essentially in Being-with Others, its historizing is a co-historizing and is determinative for it as destiny [*Geschick*]: This is how we designate the historizing of the community, of a people. Destiny is not something that puts itself together out of individual fates, and more than Being-with-one-another can be conceived as the occurring together of several Subjects. Our fates have already been guided in advance, in our Being with one another in the same world and in our resoluteness for definite possibilities. Only in communicating and in struggling does the power of the destiny become free. Dasein's fateful destiny in and with its "generation" goes to make up the full authentic historizing of Dasein.[28]

The highly problematic implications of this passage in *Being and Time*'s notorious paragraph 74 have been intensely discussed. One rather "mundane" aspect that I would like to point out is that our fates cannot be "guided in advance" if we presumably live "in the same world"; it only can if we live in a very specific and circumscribed space—otherwise we would simply *all* share the same destiny. After all, we "fall" into, and eventually grow roots in, a very specific space/place, and we can share the "heritage" (that strange term that Heidegger draws out of the hat very late in *Being and Time*)[29] only with people that we "are-with" in this space/place. Again, I would like to emphasize that, all claims about him being the first to take Being-with seriously into account notwithstanding, Heidegger defines the "Man" as exclusively impedimental to the "authentic potential of being";[30] that is why, so I argue, he has to rein in the sheer contingency of Being-with by means of this dubious metaphor of a "destined community"—with all the rather unhealthy consequences this entails. Only by introducing it is he able to conceptualize what seems like an oxymoron within his own philosophy: an "authentic potential of being-*with*." Thus, while his attempt to take into account Being-with as an all-important aspect of Being might make him a pioneer in breaking with the heritage of the Enlightenment, his almost exclusively negative account as to what Being-with entails is still deeply rooted in it.[31] *Being and Time* is thus still in line with the story of the Enlightenment—a story that is told as the annals of one project: that of trying to overcome contingency. The question I would like to raise, however, is:

WHAT IS WRONG WITH CONTINGENCY?

The story of the Enlightenment—or rather, the story that the Enlightenment likes to tell about itself—is that human history is a succession of strategies to overcome contingencies, with each strategy proving allegedly more sophisticated than, and thus superior to, its predecessors.[32] In its neo-Kantian variety, this succession usually comprises polytheistic Myth, Monotheism, and finally syllogistic Reason. However, in face of the fact that the felt contingency of our contemporary world seems to reach ever higher fever pitches, it would seem that this human (his)story is one of a huge failure. Nor can this come as a surprise, after what has been said here: If the power to overcome contingency is only ever measured according to its superiority over the previous one, only more contingency is being created. But just why is it that contingency gets such bad press? After all, a contingency is not "bad" per se; just a short glimpse, for example, at our CVs will show that what they usually comprise is a list of contingencies beyond our control. And said lack of control is basically what is experienced as threatening. In order to exert control, the items in our CV are usually transcribed into a narrative—specifically when we tell someone our story or in autobiographies—in the process trying to make sense, retrospectively, of what doesn't make much sense: Our lives could have always also been different, and, as such, they are highly contingent.

This goes to show that storytelling itself is another strategy to overcome contingency, that is, to bring syntagmatic order into a tangled mass of single events and to introduce some kind of telos into it that turns the person I am now into the logical consequence of the items that constitute my life. This syntagmatic strategy has a name; it is closely connected to that of metonymy. I am referring here to the well-known distinction that Roman Jakobson makes in his famous essay "Two Aspects of Language and Two Types of Aphasic Disturbances." But let us first take a look at how the *Oxford Dictionary of Literary Terms* defines metonymy in contrast to metaphor: Metonymy "involves establishing relationships of contiguity between two things, whereas metaphor establishes relationships of similarity between them."[33] This implies that metaphor by default is not able to work with, or include, otherness. This shifts the problem of definition toward another term: contiguity. Contiguity is usually described as two things sharing the same space, being thus contiguous upon each other. While this sounds rather straightforward, it in fact opens up a can of worms. In his fifth book of *Physics*, Aristotle, in order to illustrate the concept of contiguity, uses the example of two books whose covers touch each other on a shelf.[34] This, however, is a misleading example, since it blurs the boundary between metaphor and metonymy, as the books do not only share a space and are contiguous upon each other but also share the similarity of being books—sharing a third, that is. However, adjacent to a book, contiguous with it, and sharing the same space, there could be anything from a microbe to a toaster to an aircraft carrier—the last admittedly being a rather rare coincidence. If we transfer this insight to literature, however, this would imply that I could use the microbe, the toaster, or the aircraft carrier to stand in for, and thus to figuratively represent, a book. Chances are that this would lead to a complete communicative breakdown, since nobody would and could possibly understand what I am trying to say when I replace the book—the tenor, in poetic jargon—with the vehicle of the toaster. While thus a radical metaphor might be highly difficult to decipher, a radical metonymy is both unthinkable and indecipherable, the reason being that the book and the toaster are not only contiguous but also contingent upon each other. Sheer spatial coincidence (or, for that matter, temporal succession), that is, cannot guarantee and is not enough to let the reader make the connection between them. Thus we have come from metonymy via contiguity to—contingency: a third and even more troublesome term.

This might explain a strange riddle in Jakobson's essay. There he states that "the researcher possesses more homogeneous means to handle metaphor, whereas metonymy, based on a different principle, *easily defies interpretation*. Therefore nothing comparable to the rich literature on metaphor . . . can be cited for the theory of metonymy."[35] Just why metonymy—which is usually connected to the more prosaic literary forms, while metaphor is usually connected to poetic genres—would "easily defy interpretation" is a question Jakobson does not address further. And indeed, whereas we have access to numerous metaphorologies, studies in metaphor, etc., nothing even remotely comparable exists with regard to metonymy. The fact that it "easily defies interpretation" encompasses two different realms: One is that—as my example of the toaster has shown—taken to its limit, it obfuscates communication. Moreover, interpretation is an exclusively metaphorical act, a fact Jakobson explains by noticing—and rightly so—that any metalanguage (and interpretation is nothing else) is based upon the premise of a similarity and thus is inherently metaphoric. What interpretation does is try to transform what is seemingly contingent in a text into something that is explicable and makes sense. This is how David Lodge, in his *Modes of Modern Writing*, explains this phenomenon:

> The solution would seem to lie in a recognition that, at the highest level of generality at which we can apply the metaphor/metonymy distinction, literature itself is metaphoric and nonliterature is metonymic. The literary text is always metaphoric in the sense that when we interpret it, when we uncover its "unity" . . . we make it into a total metaphor: the text is the vehicle, the world is the tenor. Jakobson himself, as we have already noted, observed that metalanguage (which is what criticism is, language applied to an object language) is comparable to metaphor, and uses this fact to explain why criticism has given more attention to metaphorical than to metonymic tropes.[36]

What is interesting to note here is that the metaphoricity of a text becomes relevant as its unity, for which the text is the vehicle and the world the tenor, which is as much as to say that the "unity" of the literary text stands in a metaphorical relation to an assumed unity of—the world. If we, however, consider the world to be not unitary, unified, but contingent, heterogeneous—would that change anything?

Well, yes and no. If we were to assume that the tenor is contingent, nonunified, and that a literary work—metonymical, contingent, and nonunified—were to reflect this aesthetically, this reflection of the metonymic character of the world by a similar character of the literary work would still be metaphoric, metaphoric in that we assume that there exists a relationship of similarity between the tenor and the vehicle. If we take this problem seriously, it amounts to the sheer fact that even if metonymy existed *either in the tenor or the vehicle*, we simply could not capture it by means of a metalanguage—it would have to remain as undecipherable as the toaster standing in for a book. Indeed, what any reader trying to make sense of such a metonymy would try to do is to find or forge a (metaphorical) connection between the toaster and the book—with different degrees of success, I would assume, considering the fact that he or she wouldn't even *know* that the toaster is actually designed to stand in for the book.

Thus, we are facing two conceptually distinct problems, which, however, are closely related: First of all, metonymy in itself is impossible; second of all, even if it were possible, we wouldn't be able to decipher or interpret it except via metaphor; otherwise, a communication breakdown would ensue. Strictly speaking, metonymy is nothing but a metaphoric (de)cipher(ment) of/for an unrepresentable contingency. One of the problems that would have to be pointed out, however, is that metonymy has always been collapsed into synecdoche—the principle of *pars pro toto*. This trope, however, is in fact nothing but a disguised metaphor, as the tenor (qua *toto*) simply becomes the third. All other relationships of the tenor and the vehicle listed for metonymy—such as name of the inventor or possessor for the invention or possession, the container for that which is contained, the modifier for modified, the effect for cause—also presume a third.[37] Metonymy is nothing else but the rhetorical strategy mirroring a way of thinking contingency of relationships that are not necessary—and could be different.

As far as the concept of a cosmopolitan community is concerned, this means that, in contradistinction to earlier times, we do conceive of our immediate neighbor not as "fatefully necessary," as he or she would have been in premodern times: More and more, we experience our neighbors, and all those who constitute our "community," indeed as contingent in the sense that all that connects us is that we are contiguous upon one another. Moreover, given the absence of a third that might actually explain—fatefully or rationally—why we happen to be neighbors, we are indeed contingent upon one another in a radical sense, sharing nothing but—space, a space that has become global. That is why for nationalists it is of utmost importance to describe this space as meaningful place (the "blood and soil" regime), because that provides meaning for what otherwise remains the empty contingency of and within space. In keeping with this logic, nationalist imperialism and colonialism will tend—indeed, have tended—to designate conquered or colonized spaces as "uninscribed" deserts or wildernesses, ready to receive the "imprint" of the colonizers.

I would thus argue that we would have to think cosmopolitanism along the lines of a community conceived of as metonymic. And there is a trilogy of books that exemplifies that—with the restrictions sketched out here as to the metaphoricity of any act of reading: It is Amitav Ghosh's Ibis trilogy.

HOW TO WRITE CONTINGENCY: THE IBIS TRILOGY AS "COSMOPOLITAN WORLD LITERATURE"

Ghosh's Ibis trilogy—which comprises *Sea of Poppies* (2008), *River of Smoke* (2011), and *Flood of Fire* (2015)[38]—reflects, in an exemplary way, the different facets of metonymy, contingency, and what I propose to call "metonymic communities." The latter is embodied, for example, in the group of protagonists that find themselves "exposed" (to use the term of Jean-Luc Nancy)[39] to one another aboard the ship that gives the trilogy its name: the *Ibis*. This group also constitutes what one could call a "destined community," one that indeed "shares the world," but in a very un-Heideggerian way, as the different "heritages" of that community, which the trilogy will unwind, show us the very contingency of history that already Aristotle pointed at to distinguish it from literature. While "classic" historiography, along the lines sketched by Hayden White (1973), tries to impose some generic structural markers onto the tangled mess of historical facts to give some sense and order to it, the Ibis trilogy unfolds history as just that: the erratic strivings of different political and economic powers, peoples, and effects of fateful (not destined) events and vectors that cross one another, with both benevolent or malevolent consequences arising out of these encounters.

These erratic encounters not only characterize the people thrown together aboard the *Ibis* but also the entire structure of the trilogy, in which the protagonists drift into and out of the narrative, with only a few of them staying in focus for long. And although one of the main personae aboard the *Ibis*—Deeti—claims to have previsions as to what is going to happen and accordingly builds her shrine,[40] the trilogy shows that the fateful encounter on the vessel spells quite different fates for the people involved. While one could be tempted to stylize the community among those who are forced onto the ship as a "cosmopolitan" one and to extrapolate the solidarity that starts to grow among some of them as an "ethics of cosmopolitanism," one has to keep in mind that all of this arises out of moments of contingency and crisis.[41] Indeed, the lascars on board the *Ibis* are defined exactly along the lines of a "contiguity in space": They have "nothing in common, except the Indian ocean; among them were Chinese and east Africans, Arabs and Malays, Bengalis and Goans, Tamils and Arakanese."[42] Not only, that is, is the community on board the *Ibis* contingent in the sense of it being "not necessary"; the storm that ends the vessel's voyage isn't, either.

The most striking moment of solidarity is, consequently, also one of the most ambivalent ones. As Paulette says: "On a boat of pilgrims, no one can lose caste and everyone is the same. . . . From now on, and forever afterwards, we will all be ship-siblings—jaházbhais and jaházbahens—to each other. There'll be no difference between us."[43] But this is only half of the story: It is not that differences magically disappear; some of the "pilgrims" aboard the *Ibis do lose their caste*. Neel is the most visible instance of this, and the loss is experienced as traumatic by him. It is important to retain this aspect of crisis and not simply to wave away any differences in a world that is constituted by them. They need to be acknowledged, not hidden under a romantic veil of Stoic equality. Differences do exist—and are acknowledged—but they are also subject to fateful changes through contingent forces.

That is why Chitra Sankaran's characterization of Ghosh's work as successfully "holding together a global, ecumenical perspective while focusing on highly individual, often contested and marginalized histories, such as refuges, Indian sepoys under the British Raj, the 'lower' caste Othered, and voiceless women" and thus counterpoising "vignettes of human drama that occupy these distinctive locales against epic backdrops that adumbrate global issues of capitalized 'History' without taking away the significance of either"[44] is only partially correct. The book does not hold together in its entirety. However, it shows that even capitalized "History" can by no means be defined as following a certain plan (a telos, or a destiny), as some Enlightenment philosophers would try to convince us. It could have been otherwise for both the people aboard the ship—and for "History" as a whole . . .

One could read Ghosh's trilogy as an extended commentary on the millennial concepts of human history as developed by Kant, Hegel, and Marx. In fact, it might also serve to explain a rather strange incongruence in one of Kant's central essays on cosmopolitanism. While in "Perpetual Peace" he strongly emphasizes the right to hospitality (even if only in its "conditional" form, as Jacques Derrida has pointed out)[45] and also insists that peaceful trade might further such an ethics, he is at the same time aware that even such a "conditional hospitality" might harbor its dangers. In a passage that seems almost prophetic in the face of the first Opium War that would start four decades later and that forms the main subject of Ghosh's trilogy, he writes:

> But to this perfection compare the inhospitable actions of the civilized and especially of the commercial states of our part of the world. The injustice which they show to lands and peoples they visit (which is equivalent to conquering them) is carried by them to terrifying lengths. America, the lands inhabited by the Negro, the Spice Islands, the Cape, etc., were at the time of their discovery considered by these civilized intruders as lands without owners, for they counted the inhabitants as nothing. In East India (Hindustan), under the pretense of establishing economic undertakings, they brought in foreign soldiers and used them to oppress the natives, excited widespread wars among the various states, spread famine, rebellion, perfidy, and the whole litany of evils which afflict mankind.
>
> China and Japan (Nippon), who have had experience with such guests, have wisely refused them entry, the former permitting their approach to their shores but not their entry, while the latter permit this approach to only one European people, the Dutch, but treat them like prisoners, not allowing them any communication with the inhabitants. The worst of this (or, to speak with the moralist, the best) is that all these outrages profit them nothing, since all these commercial ventures stand on the verge of collapse, and the Sugar Islands, that place of the most refined and cruel slavery, produces no real revenue except indirectly, only serving a not very praiseworthy purpose of furnishing sailors for war fleets and thus for the conduct of war in Europe. This service is rendered to powers which make a great show of their piety, and, while they drink injustice like water, they regard themselves as the elect in point of orthodoxy.[46]

We have to remember those words—as well as the following, often-quoted paragraph of Marx—when we read the Ibis trilogy:

> The bourgeoisie has through its exploitation of the world market given a cosmopolitan character to production and consumption in every country. To the great chagrin of Reactionists, it has drawn from under the feet of industry the national ground on which it stood. All old-established national industries have been destroyed or are daily being

destroyed. They are dislodged by new industries, whose introduction becomes a life and death question for all civilized nations, by industries that no longer work up indigenous raw material, but raw material drawn from the remotest zones; industries whose products are consumed, not only at home, but in every quarter of the globe. In place of the old wants, satisfied by the production of the country, we find new wants, requiring for their satisfaction the products of distant lands and climes. In place of the old local and national seclusion and self-sufficiency, we have intercourse in every direction, universal inter-dependence of nations. And as in material, so also in intellectual production. The intellectual creations of individual nations become common property. National one-sidedness and narrow-mindedness become more and more impossible, and from the numerous national and local literatures, there arises a world literature.[47]

However, while both Kant and Marx saw these developments as manifestations and symptoms of a millennio-teleological history unfolding itself along a predestined path,[48] Ghosh's works show that it is not only the local histories that seem to be at the mercy of an epic "History" writ large by either its winners or enlightened philosophers but that such "History" is itself prone to a highly contingent flow of time that does not seem to betray any destined direction—let alone a direction toward moral improvement or rational maturity.

Interestingly, both philosophers see at the root of their "driven" histories very similar "motors": For Kant, human development is driven by the antagonism embedded in his "unsocial sociability," as we have seen here; for Marx, it is the perpetual fight around the distribution of the means of production that propels human history. For both, then, the contingencies of antagonisms and clashes are what productively drive history, backbones that cease to exist once their respective histories have reached their millennial endpoints. It is thus quite telling to have Ghosh claim, in an interview, that "history itself is . . . in a novel . . . not very interesting, except in as much as it forms the background of an individual's predicaments."[49] Capitalized "History," I would argue, can only do so if it itself has features of a "predicament." It may be our task to realize and admit that the contingencies that drive it—and drive it into no specific direction—are here to stay, and a cosmopolitanism that admits to the challenges—as both crisis and chance—of those contingencies might be a more honest way to go about it. We might agree, then, that we are all "behaviorally ambivalent" in one another's eyes without necessarily being warmongering *phauloi* to one another. The warmongers of one of the first so-called free-trade wars—which was actually a drug war—were and are to be found elsewhere, as Ghosh's Ibis trilogy so convincingly shows. And, to come full circle, note one of the ironies of the quotation with which I began my essay: The protagonist of Ghosh's *Gun Island* actually mentions that he had insured himself "against the possibility of living till the age of one hundred and three." Insurances, as well as banks and other powerful and internationally acting agents, long ago accepted the existence of contingency, rather than in a futile manner trying to define it out of existence. What Ian Hacking and Rüdiger Campe, among others, have shown is that Deen's insight as to the radical contingency of reality is something that those big players—and, for that matter, literature—have long acknowledged.[50] While some Continental philosophers have started to take it into account, for many Hegel's dictum that the "sole aim of philosophical inquiry is to eliminate the contingent"[51] still holds true. Trying to claim that the elimination of contingency is possible and desirable brings philosophy close to questionable political ideologies whose pastoral concepts of power are built upon the exact same assumptions, as Simona Forti so powerfully argues in her book *New Demons*.[52]

CODA

Forti's book is, if anything, a call to "face" the contingencies that any life offers and not to subject oneself to power structures that seductively offer security and protection against them in exchange for obedience—a strategy as old as Hobbes's Leviathan. As we have changed the register from the philosophical to the political, a clarification might be in order. The notion of contingency should not be collapsed into or mixed up with another concept that has achieved notoriety through the works of Pierre Bourdieu and Judith Butler: that of precariousness.[53] Precarity—political, social, economic, or else—is, if anything, the structural solidification of a purely negative form of contingency at whose receiving end are clearly defined, powerless "victims." To be fired at will by an anonymous employer, to be beaten by a police officer because of the contingent color of your skin, or to be sexually assaulted are experiences encountered as (negatively) contingent by those who suffer them, and much would have to be said about the connection between the concept of contingency and that of agency (some of which I address in my second contribution to this volume). Such "contingencies," as mentioned here, are, however, the result of power constellations that actively create spheres of precariousness as structurally petrified—and, as mentioned, purely one-sided—regimes of negative contingency for clearly defined recipients, individuals, or groups. We have to keep in mind, in this regard, that for the perpetrator who commits atrocities or subjugates victims to such contingencies and "useless suffering," they are emphatically *not* contingent, and not useless, either. That is, the contingent freedom of choice—a perpetual thorn in both Kant's and Hegel's philosophies—is unilaterally abolished for one side and unilaterally withheld from the other. What I am arguing for is emphatically not that we simply and quietly accept such contingencies created through the intersections of power, acquiescence, and alleged security but that we are aware that the one-sided elimination and abolition of contingency might, politically speaking, serve as a legitimization to *create such structural spheres of precarity.* I think we are all aware—and again, Ghosh's trilogy brilliantly illustrates this—that one man's security and another woman's precarity are not purely contingent but, in most cases, metaphorically connected through a (powerful) third. The questions to be addressed, then, are: (1) At whose "mercy" are we? And (2) do we have the contingent freedom and ability to react to our choices and take responsibility for both our freedom and our actions?

NOTES

1. Amitav Ghosh, *Gun Island* (London: John Murray, 2019), 201.
2. Zygmunt Bauman, *Community: Seeking Safety in an Insecure World* (Oxford: Polity, 2001), 1–2.
3. Bauman, *Community*, 12.
4. Bauman, *Community*, 5.
5. Aristotle, *Politics*, trans. Benjamin Jowett (Mineola, NY: Dover, 2000), 7.
6. Aristotle, *Politics*, 7.
7. John Locke, *Two Treatises of Government*, ed. Peter Laslett (Cambridge: Cambridge University Press, 2015), 161–264.
8. Aristotle, *Politics*, 28.
9. Jacques Rancière, *On the Shores of Politics* (London: Verso, 2007), 27.
10. Rancière, *On the Shores of Politics*, 135.
11. Aristotle, *Politics*, 29. That is why I think Simona Forti is mistaken to evoke this figure in connection with the concept of evil, when she writes: "The freedom of the tyrant is absolute, making it comparable to godly freedom, but its lack of

restraint—its leonine ferocity and elementary, animal compulsiveness—drags him on to the level of the beast. This is the same as what Aristotle observed about those who make themselves similar to beasts or gods by living outside the polis, the political community." Simona Forti, *New Demons: Rethinking Power and Evil Today*, trans. Zakiya Hanafi (Stanford, CA: Stanford University Press, 2015), 144. First of all, the tyrants responsible for the Holocaust and the Gulag emphatically are part of the community; second, I think that the *phaulos* is an indication of the xenophobia that characterizes both Aristotle's philosophy and Nazi ideology—and thus a victim rather than the potential perpetrator that Forti makes him out to be. On this, see Thomas Claviez, *Aesthetics and Ethics: Otherness and Moral Imagination from Aristotle to Levinas and from "Uncle Tom's Cabin" to "House Made of Dawn"* (Heidelberg: Winter, 2008), 59–71.

12. Aristotle, *Politics*, 40.

13. Aristotle, *Politics*, 41ff.

14. Aristotle, *Politics*, 41. Interestingly, Aristotle claims that surplus economy is "unnatural" because it is a "mode by which men gain from one another" (46). Just what is wrong about such a possibility escapes me. Aristotle's isolationist self-sufficiency goes as far as to exclude sea commerce: "It is argued that the introduction of strangers brought up under other laws, and the increase of population, will be adverse to good order (for a maritime people will always have a crowd of merchants coming and going), and that intercourse by sea is inimical to good government" (269).

15. Aristotle, *Politics*, 56.

16. Aristotle, *Politics*, 57.

17. Aristotle, *Politics*, 259; my emphasis.

18. Aristotle, *Politics*, 266.

19. Aristotle, *Politics*, 267.

20. Thomas Hobbes, *Leviathan*, ed. Richard Tuck (Cambridge: Cambridge University Press, 2016), 88.

21. Roland Barthes, *Mythologies*, trans. Annette Lavers (London: Paladin, 1972), 140–47.

22. Barthes, *Mythologies*, 144–45.

23. Roberto Esposito, *Communitas* (Stanford, CA: Stanford University Press, 2010), 30.

24. Immanuel Kant, "Idea for a Universal History with a Cosmopolitan Purpose," in *Kant: Political Writings*, ed. Hans Reiss (Cambridge: Cambridge University Press, 1991), 44. And he adds: "Without these asocial qualities (far from admirable in themselves) which cause the resistance inevitably encountered by each individual as he furthers his self-seeking pretensions, man would live an Arcadian, pastoral existence of perfect concord, self-sufficiency and mutual love. But all human talents

would remain hidden for ever in a dormant state, and men, as good-natured as the sheep they tended, would scarcely render their existence more valuable than that of their animals. The end for which they were created, their rational nature, would be an unfulfilled void. Nature should thus be thanked for fostering social incompatibility, enviously competitive vanity, and insatiable desires for possession or even power. Without these desires, all men's excellent natural capacities would never be roused to develop. Man wishes concord, but nature, knowing better what is good for his species, wishes discord" (45). A rather strange idea from today's point of view . . .

25. Immanuel Kant, "Perpetual Peace: A Philosophical Sketch," in *Kant: Political Writings*, ed. Hans Reiss (Cambridge: Cambridge University Press, 1991), 94.

26. Kant, "Perpetual Peace," 98n.

27. Martin Heidegger, *Being and Time*, trans. John McQuarrie and Edward Robinson (New York: Harper Perennial, 2008), 368ff.

28. Heidegger, *Being and Time*, 436.

29. Heidegger, *Being and Time*, 390ff. From my point of view, the sudden introduction of this concept basically contradicts Heidegger's entire argument about the "fallenness" of Dasein; moreover, he explicitly excludes the Man from partaking in it: "The 'they' evades the choice [to become part of authentic historicality]. Blind for possibilities, it cannot repeat what has been, but only retains and receives the 'actual' that is left over, the world-historical that has been, the leavings, and the information about them that is present-at-hand" (443).

30. Heidegger, *Being and Time*, 307–16.

31. On this debate, see David Egan, "Das Man and Distantiality in *Being and Time*," *Inquiry* 55 (2012): 289–306; William F. Bracken, "Is There a Puzzle about How Authentic Dasein Can Act? A Critique of Dreyfus and Rubin on *Being and Time*, Division II," *Inquiry* 48 (2005): 533–52; Hubert Dreyfus, "Interpreting Heidegger on das Man," *Inquiry* 38 (1995): 423–30; Taylor Carman, "On Being Social: A Reply to Olafson," *Inquiry* 37 (1994): 203–23.

32. The millennialism inherent in such philosophical happy-ending stories can be traced from Condorcet's 1795 *Sketch for a Historical Picture of the Progress of the Human Mind*, through the philosophies of Kant and Hegel, into neo-Kantian approaches. It is only in the twentieth century—and the works of Max Weber, Nietzsche, Heidegger, and Adorno—that Enlightenment optimism receives a first and massive blow and that this utopian story gets a dystopian makeover. See Richard J. Bernstein, *The New Constellation* (New York: Polity, 1991), 31–57.

33. Chris Baldick, *Oxford Dictionary of Literary Terms*, 3rd ed. (Oxford: Oxford University Press, 2008), 206.

34. Aristotle, *Physics Book 5–8*, trans. Philip H. Wicksteed and Francis M. Cornford (Cambridge, MA: Harvard University Press, 1934), 3, 227, b 2.

35. Roman Jakobson, *On Language*, ed. Linda R. Waugh and Monique Monville-Burston (Cambridge, MA: Harvard University Press, 1995), 132; my emphasis.

36. David Lodge, *Modes of Modern Writing* (London: Edward Arnold, 1977), 109. However, just why this process would be reserved to literature and not apply to nonliterature is something that Lodge never explains.

37. Wallace Martin, "Metonymy," in *Princeton Encyclopedia of Poetry and Poetics*, 4th ed., ed. Roland Greene (Princeton, NJ: Princeton University Press, 2012), 876–78.

38. Amitav Ghosh, *Sea of Poppies* (London: John Murray, 2008); Amitav Ghosh, *River of Smoke* (London: John Murray, 2011); Amitav Ghosh, *Blood of Fire* (London: John Murray, 2015).

39. Here is how Nancy describes "exposure": "We 'resemble' together, if you will. That is to say, there is no original or origin of identity. What holds the place of an 'origin' is the sharing of singularities. . . . I do not rediscover myself, nor do I recognize myself in the other: I experience the other's alterity, or I experience alterity in the other together with the alteration that 'in me' sets my singularity outside me and infinitely delimits it." Jean-Luc Nancy, *The Inoperative Community*, trans. Peter Connor et al. (Minneapolis: University of Minnesota Press, 1991), 33–34.

40. "I don't know . . . I just know that it must be there; and not just the ship, but also many of those who are in it; they too must be on the walls of our puja room. But who are they? said the puzzled child. I don't know yet, Deeti told her. But I will when I see them." Ghosh, *Sea of Poppies*, 9.

41. That is why it seems rather strange to have Martha Nussbaum claim that a cosmopolitan literature's "appeal to world citizenship fails . . . because patriotism is full of color and intensity and passion, whereas cosmopolitanism seems to have a hard time gripping the imagination." Martha Nussbaum, "Patriotism and Cosmopolitanism," in *For Love of Country* (Boston: Beacon, 1996), 15.

42. Ghosh, *Sea of Poppies*, 13.

43. Ghosh, *Sea of Poppies*, 328.

44. Chita Sankaran, introduction to *History, Narrative, and Testimony in Amitav Ghosh's Fiction*, ed. Chita Sankaran (Albany: SUNY Press, 2012), xv.

45. Jacques Derrida, *Of Hospitality: Anne Dufourmantelle Invites Jacques Derrida to Respond* (Stanford, CA: Stanford University Press, 2000).

46. Kant, "Perpetual Peace," 106–7.

47. Karl Marx, "The Communist Manifesto," in *The Marx-Engels Reader*, ed. Robert C. Tucker (New York: Norton, 1978), 476.

48. One would, however, have to point to a very strange incongruence in Kant's two essays that have, in my view, up to now only been insufficiently addressed, namely, that, in spite of his alleged belief in a teleological development of human-

kind toward a shared reason, almost all of the instances he mentions as possible models for achieving Perpetual Peace, a League of Nations, or hospitality are located in the past. Furthermore, he is basically forced to admit that one instance of this rational trajectory—the founding of states—has, in fact, made things worse, since the natural state—not unlike Hobbes's—has not been superseded but simply transported from the individual to the state level—with even more precarious consequences than the one before.

49. Sankaran, "Diasporic Predicaments," 1.

50. Ian Hacking, *The Taming of Chance* (Cambridge: Cambridge University Press, 1990); Rüdiger Campe, *The Game of Probability*, trans. Ellwood H. Wiggins Jr. (Stanford, CA: Stanford University Press, 2012).

51. Georg Wilhelm Friedrich Hegel, *Lectures on the Philosophy of World History*, trans. H. B. Nisbet (Cambridge: Cambridge University Press, 1975), 28.

52. Simona Forti, *New Demons: Rethinking Power and Evil Today*, trans. Zakiya Hanafi (Stanford, CA: Stanford University Press, 2015).

53. Pierre Bourdieu, "La précarité est aujourd'hui partout," in *Contre-feux. Propos pour servir à la résistance contre l'invasion néo-libérale* (Paris: Liber-Raisons d'Agir, 1998), 95–101; Judith Butler, *Precarious Life: The Powers of Mourning and Violence* (London: Verso, 2016).

Dumb Luck
Jacques Derrida and the Problem of Contingency

Michael Naas

He was too tired to appreciate the irony, or coincidence, or whatever it was. There were too many ironies and coincidences. A shrewd person would one day start a religion based on coincidence, if he hasn't already, and make a million.

—Don DeLillo, *Libra*

While all invitations, without exception, are exceptional, that is, contingent, and so worthy of surprise, some invitations, like this one from Thomas Claviez, are more contingent and thus more surprising than others. Were it not, in fact, for another very unexpected chance invitation to speak a couple of years ago in Paris, not on the philosophical work of Jacques Derrida, which would have made a certain amount of sense, but on the literary work of the American novelist Don DeLillo,[1] I would never have met one of Thomas Claviez's students, who was then kind enough to suggest that I be invited to speak to you here in Bern. It was thus a chance encounter, itself the result of a long series of chance encounters, that was at the origin of this invitation and, as a result, of my desire to try to say something about what I cannot help but call, in a rather strange English idiom, the "dumb luck" that has brought me here today to Bern.

As you may know, the expression "dumb luck," like its quasi-equivalents "blind luck," "sheer luck," or "pure luck," is typically used to describe a good or fortunate occurrence that arrives completely by chance, without any planning or preparation, in a purely gratuitous, unmerited, or undeserved way. Like beginner's luck, dumb luck suggests a stroke of good fortune that has come unexpectedly and without effort; unlike beginner's luck, dumb luck can, if one is really lucky, keep on happening, against all odds and in defiance of all logic.

As for the word "dumb" in the expression "dumb luck," it no doubt refers to this innocence, this lack of planning, skill, preparation, deliberation, foresight, or intelligence. For if, as it is sometimes said, we "make our own luck" through planning, preparation, hard work, educated guesses, strategy, cunning, knowledge, and so on, all those things that allow us to create opportunities that look in retrospect like good luck or that allow us to take advantage of what fortune or chance has offered us, dumb luck seems to require no such preparation, skill, or intelligence. Dumb luck happens or befalls those who, at least with respect to the good thing or the stroke of good fortune in question, have none of these attributes. In short, dumb luck is always the good fortune of the completely clueless.

Yet there is, perhaps, a bit of dumb luck lodged within the expression *dumb luck* itself, since "dumb" also means, of course, to be lacking not in intelligence but in the ability to speak, to be without a voice, that is, to be mute, *aphonos* in Greek, *aphone* in French, *stumm* in German. Some of you may recognize this meaning of the term "dumb" from a song of almost fifty years ago (1969)—or the movie of 1975—that spoke of a certain arcade game aficionado named Tommy who was celebrated in the rock opera that bears his name as "a deaf, dumb, and blind kid / who sure played a mean pinball."[2]

But this relationship between luck or good fortune and dumbness as speechlessness can already be found in one of the West's first and most fabled tales about fortune. You may recall the story told by Herodotus of Solon, who is asked by the Lydian king Croesus whether he has "'ever seen a man more blest [*olbiōtatos*] than all his fellows,'" "supposing himself," Herodotus interjects, "to be blest beyond all men."[3] To this question, Solon famously responds that "the whole of man is but chance [*pan esti anthrōpos symphorē*]" and that one must wait to see whether a man ends his life well before calling him blessed.[4] Aristotle, in the first book of the *Nicomachean Ethics*, recalls this story and suggests that we must "obey Solon's warning, and 'look to the end,'" for "only when a man is dead can one safely call him blessed as being now beyond the reach of evil and misfortune"—and even then we must be careful, Aristotle cautions, since the actions or conditions of children can retrospectively transform a man's happiness or blessedness even after death.[5] Dumb luck, Aristotle seems to suggest, is not just a personal but a family, even an intergenerational, affair, a lesson he might have also learned from Herodotus. Indeed later in the same book of his *Persian Wars*, Herodotus recounts what eventually happened to Croesus, a story that—though there is no etymological link and no play on words that I can make out—brings dumbness and luck together into a single story, dumbness, luck, life and death, and (as will be crucial for me here) kinship or inheritance, in this case the relation between fathers and sons. Explaining what "befell Croesus" in the wake of his encounter with Solon, Herodotus tells us that Croesus, the Lydian king, had two sons, one of whom—we are not even given his name—was born "dumb," that is, *aphōnos*.[6] Croesus did everything he could to cure his son of his affliction, going so far as to inquire from the oracle at Delphi about a remedy. But the answer he received back from the priestess was not encouraging: She said that it would be better that this son's voice not be heard in the palace, better that he remain dumb, she said, for "luckless [*anolbōi*] that day shall be when first thou hearest him speaking." And so it came to pass that when the Persians overtook the Lydians and stormed the palace, "a certain Persian, not knowing who Croesus was, came at him with intent to kill him." Overcome by the "misfortune [*symphorēs*]," Croesus was "past caring, and would as soon be smitten to death as not; but this dumb [*aphōnos*] son, seeing the Persian coming, in his fear and his grief broke into speech and cried, 'Man [*anthrōpe*], do not kill [*mē kteine*] Croesus!'" "This was the first word he uttered," says Herodotus, "and after that for all the days of his life he had power of speech."[7] Hence the very first words of Croesus's until then speechless son save Croesus from an immediate death only to deliver him over into the hands of Cyrus, who condemns him to burning upon a pyre. As he thus stands upon that pyre, Croesus recalls for all to hear "how divinely inspired was that saying of Solon, that no living man was blest [*mēdena einai tōn zōontōn olbion*]."[8] Hearing these words of Croesus on the brink of death, Cyrus goes back on his purpose and has the fire put out, for he considered that he, "being also a man [*anthrōpos*], was burning alive another man [*allon anthrōpon*] who had once been as fortunate [*eudaimoniēi*] as himself."[9]

Having thus first been saved by his previously mute son's first words, Croesus is subsequently saved by his own words, or by Solon's, saved as a testament, as it were, to the chance or the contingency, the *symphorē*, that mankind or *anthrōpos*, the whole of *anthrōpos*, as Solon says, the whole life of mankind, essentially *is*. It is a story of dumb luck, with several twists and turns all revolving around words spoken on the threshold of death, words spoken between generations, between fathers and sons, not unlike, let me say in passing, the story of the Who's Tommy, Tommy who actually *becomes* deaf, dumb, and blind after witnessing the death of his father, who had been presumed dead in World War II but who returns—severely burned—only to be killed by Tommy's uncle. The life of *anthrōpos* is indeed a life of chance, a life of contingency, right up to the very end—and even, for Aristotle, beyond the end. While *anthrōpos* can thus speak of this contingency, he—he or she—remains utterly at a loss for words, *aphonos*, when confronted with it. Dumb luck—inseparable from its contrary, its twin, complete and utter misfortune—is the plight of *anthrōpos*, but it is a plight that *anthrōpos* no doubt shares with all other living beings, a plight that he too has thus inherited. In short, dumb luck is in the very DNA of *anthrōpos* as a living being, passed on not only from one human generation to the next but from one species to another—an inheritance at the origin not just of what happens in life but, perhaps, of life itself. Dumb luck, chance, is perhaps the very logic of the living.

It so happens that when I began to think about contingency in order to write this essay, I was in the process of translating into English Jacques Derrida's unpublished seminar of 1975–1976 entitled *Life Death*, *La vie la mort*.[10] Approximately four hundred pages in length, delivered over the course of fourteen two-hour sessions, the seminar looks at the relationship between life and death in Nietzsche, Heidegger, Freud, and—perhaps most surprising and interesting—the Nobel Prize–winning geneticist François Jacob, whose book *La logique du vivant*, *The Logic of the Living*, had appeared just a couple of years before. It is a rather surprising book for Derrida to be reading but one that becomes central to the seminar. What I would like to do is to give you some sense of how Derrida reads Jacob in order to understand the role played by "contingency" in Derrida's thinking of life and death—life, death, inheritance, and, once again, dumb luck.

The *Life Death* seminar is, of course, hardly the only and not even the first place Derrida treated the question of luck, chance, or contingency—terms I am not distinguishing for the moment. This question is at the heart of several works, from *Dissemination* (1972) and *The Post Card* (1980) through two essays from 1988, "Telepathy," which looks at Freud's changing views on telepathy in the 1920s and 1930s, and "My Chances," which revolves around psychoanalysis and the famous swerve or *clinamen* of Democritus, the dumb luck, as it were, that would be at the origin of the universe and that Plato will have treated with what Derrida calls a symptomatic silence—a silence, a muteness, rather than, say, as in the *Timaeus*, an ordering *logos* with regard to the Demiurge's ordered creation of the universe.[11] But that is just the beginning of a very long list of Derrida's works on the question of contingency from very early on right up to *Rogues* in 2003.[12] Even when the theme is not central, it constantly makes an appearance, in one guise or another, indeed to such an extent that one could say that Derrida spoke, in the end, of nothing but contingency, that, for example, the very notion that a letter *may not* arrive at its destination was simply a way of suggesting that contingency—that a certain dumb luck—is the very condition of possibility of every event. In many early works, Derrida seems to suggest that throughout the Western philosophical tradition one of the names of this contingency of the letter has been "writing." Whereas speech, under the control, or the putative control, of some authority, some father or master, would be able to assure the proper arrival or inheritance of that speech, would be able to ensure receipt by a proper recipient, by a legitimate or lawful heir, as Plato suggests in the *Phaedrus*, the history of the notion of writing from Plato onward will have been the history of a contingency that makes it possible for a letter, for a message, always *not* to arrive at its destination, that is, for it not to arrive at *any* destination—since that is always possible—or for it to arrive at the *wrong* destination, the wrong address. Derrida then goes on to demonstrate in one work after another that, however much speech tries to oppose itself to writing, it too is contingent in just the way writing is, susceptible in its structure to the same dumb luck and so open to the same abuses, the same severing of the word from intention, of the voice from logos, of the son from the father. Though it may have taken the contingent invention of writing to point this out, to expose this risk, dumb luck will have always already haunted speech as well as writing. It is in this context, I think, that we should read this passage from *Of Grammatology*, a work published already more than fifty years ago, where Derrida speaks of an "absolute contingency." The passage comes from a section of that work entitled "The Supplement of (at) the Origin"—this notion of supplement, as we will see, being central to Derrida's reading some ten years later of François Jacob. Derrida writes:

> Thus . . . the absolute *alterity* of writing might nevertheless affect living speech, from the outside, within its inside: *alter it* [for the worse]. Even as it has an independent history . . . writing marks the history of speech. Although it is born out of "needs of a different kind" . . . although these needs might "never have occurred," the irruption of this *absolute contingency* determined the interior of an essential history and affected the interior unity of a life.[13]

The irruption of absolute alterity, the contingency of alterity, *alters*, says Derrida. Something that may always *not* have taken place, something from the outside, the invention of writing, for example, ends up altering from within "an essential history," "the interior unity of a life." Writing comes from the outside as an absolute alterity to alter the inside—like a mutation, perhaps, but a mutation that inscribes not just this or that particular characteristic but something like dumb luck as the very law of mutation itself.

With this passage from *Of Grammatology* in mind, let me now turn, as promised, to Derrida's seminar of 1975–1976, *Life Death*, which I wish to read not only because of what Derrida says there about life, death, and contingency in conjunction with François Jacob but also because of the way Derrida *rethinks* key philosophical terms and oppositions such as necessity and contingency, the human and the nonhuman, or life and death, by means of Jacob. Let me begin, then, with a passage from *Life Death* where Derrida makes explicit reference back to the very work I just quoted, *Of Grammatology*. The context is Derrida's analysis of the notion of *program* in François Jacob's *The Logic of the Living*, an analysis that aims to show that, despite Jacob's claims to have avoided a philosophical, metaphysical conception of life by means of the notion of program, he has in fact repeated, reproduced, or reinscribed metaphysical notions of teleology, of life and death, within it. Here is Derrida in *Life Death*:

> Some ten years ago, in *Of Grammatology*, in a chapter near the beginning that is titled (already, one might say, by coincidence, prescience, or an almost subjectless teleology) "The Program," I recalled that, and I quote, "the contemporary biologist speaks of writing and *pro-gram* in relation to the most elementary processes of information within the living cell." The point there was not, however, to reinvest the notion or the word *program* with the entire conceptual machine of logos and its semantics but to try to show that the appeal to a non-phonetic writing

in genetics had to or should involve and incite an entire deconstruction of the logocentric machine rather than a return to Aristotle.[14]

I will return to this notion of *program* in just a moment, but I wanted to begin here so as to help explain why Derrida finds François Jacob's *The Logic of the Living*, that is, a work written by a geneticist and not a philosopher, a legitimate object of critique. The problem is not just that Jacob, though this alone would warrant scrutiny, uses philosophical language to describe his own scientific project and the projects of others. The real problem is that Jacob claims throughout *The Logic of the Living* that by speaking of the living, of living beings rather than of life, he is avoiding all the trappings and false problems of Western metaphysics. Derrida will go on to show that Jacob not only does not avoid such a metaphysics but falls in line with the most traditional aspects of it, reinscribing a notion of teleology in his conception of living beings and projecting a problematic humanism into the hierarchization of those living beings. Despite all his protestations to the contrary, Jacob's notion of program returns us, Derrida will ultimately claim, to Aristotle, to the logocentric machine that Jacob in 1970 should have been trying to deconstruct rather than reaffirm and so reinscribe.

But how does Derrida come to this conclusion in his seminar? Let me begin with that notion of program. Central to *The Logic of the Living* is the relationship Jacob establishes between two programs or two kinds of program, which are distinguished in large part, as we will see, on the basis of contingency. The first of these is the genetic program, the program of DNA, a program we share with other living beings, indeed with all other living beings. The second program is the institutional, cultural, cerebral, mental program that has set human beings—our dumb luck—apart from all other living beings. Now these two programs or two kinds of program—and, let me underscore, "program" is Jacob's word—correspond to two kinds of memory. The first, the memory of the genetic program of deoxyribonucleic acid, is characterized by Jacob as rigid or inflexible, a memory that works by mere repetition or retranscription of the genetic code—the notion of "code" being Jacob's as well. The second form of memory, that which is found in the institutional or mental program, is more flexible and capable of being transformed, or rather, capable of transforming itself, since it, unlike the genetic program, learns from experience. Derrida writes of this opposition between an inflexible genetic program, on the one hand, and a flexible, transformative institutional program, on the other:

> We should thus conclude from this that the mental (institutional) program has a relation to the outside, that it learns from experience, that it lets itself be transformed, whereas the genetic program forms a closed, deaf [*sourd*] system, purely endogenous, impervious to the kind of change that Jacob calls, with this very suspect word, "deliberate."[15]

We can see Derrida here beginning to cast suspicion upon Jacob's use of philosophical terms and categories with a long and cumbersome tradition. According to Jacob, the institutional program is able to change because of deliberate, by which he means *free, conscious*, interventions from the outside, whereas the genetic program, which is closed, deaf, says Jacob, can have no such interventions from without. But the opposition is clearly not so simple, as Jacob acknowledges. Derrida continues:

> When Jacob says that the genetic message does not allow the slightest intervention from the outside, he immediately has to clarify the meaning of that formulation. Of course there are interventions from the outside: it is just that, between the cause coming from the outside to transform the program and the effect in or on the program there is no relationship of resemblance, no conscious or knowing correlation. It is this heterogeneity and this relationship of non-knowing or non-consciousness that Jacob calls contingency.[16]

Derrida then goes on to quote a long passage from *The Logic of the Living* where Jacob argues that this genetic program, "made up of a combination of essentially invariant elements," can indeed change—mutate—but without "the slightest concerted intervention from without," that is, without any deliberate or conscious intervention from without. Derrida cites Jacob:

> Whether chemical or mechanical, all the phenomena which contribute to variation in organisms and populations occur without any awareness [*en toute ignorance*] of their effects; they are unconnected with the organism's need to adapt. In a mutation, there are "causes" which modify a chemical radical, break a chromosome, invert a segment of nucleic acid. But in no case can there be correlation between the cause and the effect of the mutation. Nor is this contingency limited to mutations alone. It applies to each stage in the formation of an individual's genetic

inheritance, the segregation of the chromosomes, their recombination, the choice of the gametes which play a role in fertilization and even, to a large extent, to the choice of sexual partners. There is not the slightest connection between a particular fact and its consequences in any of these phenomena. Each individual program is the result of a cascade of *contingent events*. The very nature of the genetic code prevents any deliberate change in program whether through its own action or as an effect of its environment. It prohibits any influence on the message by the products of its expression. The program does not learn from experience.[17]

Unlike the institutional, cerebral program, therefore, the genetic program—deaf, dumb, and blind, a bit like Tommy, one might say—does not learn from experience, though it does, of course, change, mutate. These mutations are thus, for Jacob, like unintentional copying errors that, once introduced, get faithfully transmitted from one generation to the next, faithfully but blindly, unknowingly, dumbly transmitted, endlessly transmitted, since, as Jacob underscores, the genetic program does not learn from experience.

Hence the genetic program is characterized by contingency, by "causes"—a word Jacob puts in quotation marks—that come from outside in the form of mutations in a wholly unplanned, unpredictable, nondeliberate, unconscious way. The genetic program thus seems to be identified here with all those things typically associated with contingency and exteriority in the metaphysical tradition, for example, a certain automaticity, signifiers, that is, the elements of code, divorced from signifieds, signs divorced from their meaning, and so on. This would thus seem to be, at least on its surface, an enormous break with the Western metaphysical tradition inasmuch as Jacob would appear to be identifying life—the code or program of life, the very workings of DNA—with contingency or chance, with signifiers or codes divorced from signifieds or meaning. There where philosophers and theologians have located an ordering *logos*, a meaningful teleology, sometimes even a creative breath, Jacob will have placed—or so it seems—a certain contingency, a kind of dumb luck.

But let's return to the other program, the institutional or cerebral or mental program. That is the program whereby, according to Jacob, information is passed on from one human generation to the next not in a contingent, nonintentional, blind way, as it is in the genetic program, but knowingly or deliberately through human culture and institutions. This program, the institutional program, came on the scene through evolution or through a mutation in the genetic program, but this mutation or break was so radical that what resulted was a completely new form of memory and program, the institutional program of the human. Indeed so radical was this mutation that the cerebral, mental program has been able to free itself from the rigidity of the genetic program by means of institutions that can deliberately and selectively pass on information from one generation to the next. In fact, with the discovery of the workings or the mechanisms of DNA in the middle of the twentieth century, it became possible for humans to intervene in the very processes of heredity, to manipulate and change both mankind's own genetic program and that of other living beings. "For two thousand million years or more," says Derrida, citing Jacob, heredity has not allowed "the slightest concerted intervention from without," and "all the phenomena which contribute to variation in organisms and populations" have occurred "without any awareness of their effects."[18] The institutional program is thus the supplement to the genetic program that today allows humankind to alter even the genetic program; chance can be replaced by deliberate, internal planning; trial and error, experience in the breeding of animals and plants and humans, can be replaced by knowledge, by cause and effect. While changes have occurred throughout the whole evolutionary process in the form of mutations, these have been due "entirely to chance," that is, they have come from the outside without any deliberation, without any correlation between cause and effect; in short, they have come completely blindly, either in the form of a happy accident, dumb luck, or, on the other side, a monstrous and deadly mutation. Dumb luck and groping in the dark can thus today be replaced by enlightened knowledge of DNA and the processes of reproduction. Here is how François Jacob near the end of his *Logic of the Living* envisions the possibility of mankind actually controlling the evolutionary process through the genetic program:

> With the accumulation of knowledge, man has become the first product of evolution capable of controlling evolution. Not only the evolution of others, by encouraging species of interest to him and eliminating bothersome ones, but also his own evolution. Perhaps one day it will become possible to intervene in the execution of the genetic program, or even in its structure, to correct some faults and slip in supplementary instructions. Perhaps it will also be possible to produce at will, and in as

many copies as required, exact duplicates of individuals, a politician, for instance, an artist, a beauty queen or an athlete. There is nothing to prevent immediate application to human beings of the selection processes used for race-horses, laboratory mice or milk cows.[19]

Jacob can therefore claim that modern genetics will have, in effect, resolved the long-standing debate within biology over whether acquired characters can be inherited. The institutional program not only allows humankind to learn from experience but to transmit "acquired characters."[20]

Jacob thus makes it all sound rather hopeful, even triumphant; planning and deliberation can vastly improve human lives and the lives of other living beings. Of course, one need not look very far into twentieth-century history to see how easily this dream of controlling the evolutionary process, of being able to select out certain debilitating diseases or characteristics, for example, can turn into a eugenics nightmare.[21] Were Jacob to have known about the possibilities opened up by new gene-editing technologies such as CRISPR, his enthusiasm would have perhaps been even more unfettered and our trepidation or call for caution even more warranted.

That, then, is how Derrida understands the relationship, the opposition, in Jacob between the genetic program and the institutional program. While the first is rigid, exposed to contingency coming from the outside, the second is deliberate, controlled from the outside, as it were, by human planning. How, then, does Derrida go about questioning this relation or this opposition? He begins—and this is a strategy, a logic, that one can find operating in all of Derrida's work, from beginning to end—by asking whether the least metaphysical of the two sides of the opposition, the side that has been traditionally put down, denigrated, or repressed, can be so readily separated or distinguished from the good, valued, elevated side. In this case, he begins by asking whether the institutional program, that is, the more valued program, the human program, the one that is now promising to control, manipulate, and transform in a deliberate way the genetic program, is really as deliberate as all that, that is, whether there is not a kind of "contingency" built into it as well. Having cited Jacob on the opposition between the two programs, the rigid, inflexible genetic program and the flexible, deliberate cerebral-institutional program, Derrida concludes: "In order, then, for the genetic program, when described in this way, to be opposed in a pertinent fashion to the mental, cerebral-institutional program, one would need to be certain that the same thing cannot be said about this latter. But can't the same thing be said about it?"[22] He then continues—and this is, recall, written in 1975–1976:

> If there is one generally accepted tenet of a certain number of theoretical breaks in what I call, just to say it quickly for now, modernity, it is that causality in the order of, let us say, "cerebral-institutional" programs (psychical, social, cultural, institutional, politico-economic, and so on) has exactly the same style, in its laws, as the causality that Jacob seems to want to reserve for genetic programs, namely [—I am this time quoting Jacob while applying his phrase to "institutional" programs—] "all the phenomena which contribute to variation in organisms and populations occur without any awareness of their effects." Similarly, the heterogeneity between causes and effects, the non-deliberate character of changes in the program, in a word, everything that places subjects from within the system in a situation of being unconscious effects of causality, everything that produces effects of contingency between an action coming from the outside and the internal transformations of the system—all of this characterizes the non-genetic program as well as the genetic program.[23]

Hence Derrida suggests that, despite or in addition to all the seemingly deliberate planning, all the supposed freedom operating in the institutional, cerebral program, there are—as we have learned from psychoanalysis, psychology, sociology, economics, and so on—all kinds of nondeliberate, unconscious, that is, in Jacob's lexicon, "contingent" effects that come from the outside and so cause the program either to repeat itself or to change in ways and according to processes that are beyond the control of any of its actors. What Jacob calls contingency could thus well be thought in terms of dumb luck, that is, in terms of a chance occurrence that is not planned, that is dumb in the sense of unintelligent but also in the sense of having no meaning, no *logos* or language, no unfolding essence embedded within it.

Derrida thus appeals to certain insights from the "social sciences" in order to question Jacob's claim about the noncontingency of the institutional program. What remains for him now is to use the insights of "philosophy" to diagnose the reasons why Jacob would make such a claim in the first place. I continue the quote:

> [But] where does Jacob get the notion that, outside the genetic system and the genetic programs, changes in program are deliberate, essentially

deliberate? Where does he get this notion if not from an ideologico-metaphysical opposition that determines superior or symbolic programs (with humanity at the very summit of these) on the basis of meaning, consciousness, freedom, knowledge of the limit between the inside and the outside, objectivity and non-objectivity, etc.[24]

Derrida is arguing, in short, that there is a latent metaphysical humanism in Jacob's work that has caused him to oppose the institutional, cerebral program to the genetic one on the basis of attributes such as deliberation and freedom. This is no doubt one of the reasons, let it be said in passing, why Derrida would declare himself throughout his work to be skeptical of this notion of freedom, using it sparingly and almost always strategically, as a way to oppose what is rigidly predetermined. In an interview from some twenty-five years later, published in 2001 in *For What Tomorrow*, Derrida says in the context of a discussion regarding science and, then, genetic engineering—and there is surely *no coincidence* in this:

> I rarely use the word "freedom." . . . On certain occasions, I will defend freedom as an excess of complexity in relation to a determinate machine-like state. . . . But this word seems to me to be loaded with metaphysical presuppositions that confer on the subject or on consciousness—that is, on an egological subject—a sovereign independence in relation to drives, calculation, the economy, the machine.[25]

Hence Derrida in the *Life Death* seminar criticizes Jacob's claim that the institutional program changes because of the free, deliberate, conscious choices or decisions of its actors, because of actors who are working freely, as it were, from the outside to transform it. The institutional program changes—mutates—not because of the fully deliberate choices or decisions of free, rational actors but, to a large degree, because of those nondeliberate, unconscious, in Jacob's words "contingent causes" coming from outside the system like mutations within DNA.[26] The cultural, cerebral, institutional program is thus, just like the genetic program, influenced or transformed through contingencies that are beyond the freedom, consciousness, and intentions of any of the so-called actors within the program. Taking the terms of the genetic program—unconsciousness, nondeliberation, lack of freedom, contingency, and so on—and applying them to the institutional program, Derrida can claim, contra Jacob, that the human is not the master of his own program, that is, of the institutional, cerebral program, despite all appearances to the contrary. This does not mean, of course, that we simply need to abandon notions of freedom, deliberation, and so on, but it does suggest that we use them with more circumspection. It means that the institutional program cannot be rigorously distinguished from the genetic program on the basis of contingency and freedom, for Jacob's distinction or, rather, opposition between the two programs seems to be itself conditioned or subtended by a "generalized contingency" that marks and determines, in different ways and to varying degrees, both programs. Derrida concludes this passage:

> Here again, as you see, the opposition between the two programs cannot be rigorous, and this seems to me to be due to the fact that, for lack of reelaborating at once the general notion of program and the value of analogy, we leave these marked by a logocentric teleology and a humanist semantics, by what I will call a philosophy of life.[27]

But in speaking here of a "logocentric teleology" and a "philosophy of life" Derrida seems to be suggesting something else, something more. What Jacob says about the genetic program—namely, that it is a program of contingency, of exteriority—seems to be contradicted by the suggestion of a certain teleology within that program, not any kind of divine plan or "intelligent design," to update Derrida's critique, but an unfolding logos nonetheless. In other words, after having suggested that the institutional program is itself conditioned by nondeliberate, unconscious, contingent elements—all those elements that Jacob had attributed to the genetic program—Derrida is now suggesting that there is a concealed or surreptitious teleology behind Jacob's own understanding of the genetic program. While Jacob's characterization of DNA as code looked like a break with the metaphysical tradition, it was in the end completely consistent with it insofar as that code was understood logocentrically or phonocentrically, that is, as the unfolding of a logos or of some predetermined design or plan. For this understanding of heredity as a program passing along information from one generation to the next is perfectly consistent with the Aristotelian model whereby a logos, a kind of predetermined plan or design, is transmitted. Had Jacob considered the genetic code from a nonphonocentric point of view, his understanding of the workings of DNA might have been very different, more radical, and more in line with what the last fifty years have shown about how DNA actually works.[28] Derrida is thus suggesting that within even the genetic program there is, for Jacob, no real chance, for a teleology is secretly guiding its development.

Hence the institutional, cerebral, mental program is not nearly as conscious or deliberate as Jacob thinks, and Jacob thinks the way he does and opposes the institutional program to the genetic one because of a metaphysical humanism that has caused him to attribute freedom and deliberation to the institutional program in an explicit fashion and a logos and telos to the genetic program in an implicit but no less decisive way. Whereas a certain contingency or chance, a certain dumb luck, conditions, on Derrida's account, both the genetic program and the institutional program, making it impossible to distinguish the two with attributes such as contingency, on the one hand, and freedom, on the other, Jacob has infused both programs with the humanistic and teleological assumptions that characterize the institutional program. The point, then, for Derrida is not to attribute everything to dumb luck; it is, rather, to show that the part played by dumb luck can never be completely excluded or ruled out. In other words, a certain dumb luck always haunts the best-laid plans and programs of mice, men, and milch cows.

Derrida will go on in the *Life Death* seminar to demonstrate just how Jacob's teleological humanism determines his discourse with regard to what he, Jacob, calls two "supplements" to the genetic program, namely, sexuality and death. For according to Jacob, sexuality and death were not always part of the living; they were acquisitions, the result of mutations that happened at a certain point in time, mutations that then came to define—and this will be the point of Derrida's critique—the essence of the living, as if these mutations, these supplements, had somehow occurred with a view to this essence.

With regard to sexuality, Derrida demonstrates how Jacob defines the living, what is most living about the living, in terms of a capacity for self-reproduction, a capacity that is most fully realized or embodied in certain higher organisms and most particularly in humankind. Other living beings, bacteria, for example, reproduce but do not reproduce *themselves* and so fall short of this essence of living beings. A series of mutations within the genetic program will have thus one day produced a supplement in the form of the capacity for self-reproduction that then came to define, as it were, the living itself, as its essence and its telos. By defining the living in terms of self-reproduction, Jacob ends up attributing a kind of "interiority" to a genetic program that *seemed* to be understood solely in terms of exteriority and contingency. That interiority then takes the form of an internal essence or capacity, the capacity to self-reproduce—notions that seem to reinscribe the most classical philosophical terms and concepts. Derrida writes:

In other words, not only does Jacob not break purely and simply with the philosophical discourse on essence but he ends up returning, with this essence of life as tendency and capacity for reproduction, not only, I would say, to essence but to the essentiality of essence, the origin and end of essence as a dynamics and energy of being, that which gives the power and actuality of being, maximal being, and which assures—from the inside, and that is the essence of essence, namely, to have one's principle of being in oneself and not in some accident come from outside—assures from the inside its own production, that is, its re-production. From this point of view, it is not just difficult to claim that, for Jacob, there is no essence of life; indeed, quite to the contrary, he seems to be saying, in a traditional way, that life is the essence, the capacity to produce-reproduce oneself from the inside (intrinsic property), that it is, in this sense, more essential than the non-living that it integrates into it, into its being living.[29]

Derrida's claim regarding this surreptitious essence of life is perhaps even clearer with regard to death. Just as bacteria do not reproduce sexually, that is, just as they do not, on Jacob's account, require a relation to an other, to a second, in order to reproduce themselves, so they do not die—despite the fact that they are living. According to Jacob, bacteria do not die but simply disappear or get diluted or wither away. They do not die in any real or essential sense insofar as "death" comes to them only from the outside as a contingency or an accident. There are thus living things that disappear but do not die in the true sense of the word, and then there are living beings, higher organisms, that do die in a more genuine sense of the term because their death is "internal" to their essence. Derrida summarizes:

> This description leads Jacob to posit that in this system of simple reproduction of the bacterium neither sexuality nor, *as a result*, death are essential constituents, and that, therefore, as a result, they come as supplements, as if from the outside. It is this link between sexuality and death, on the one hand, and this value of the outside, [on the other,] that I wish to insist on. For Jacob there is no bacterial sexuality because fission is produced within an organic individual and such fission excludes or does not need the intervention of another individual, another individual system, another program. For the same reason, there is no death because death does not come from inside; it consists of a dilution of identity, of

the entity, says Jacob, through the simple disappearance and exhaustion of the reproductive capacity.[30]

If bacteria die, it is thus only because of something that happens from the outside; what they die is, therefore, only a contingent death, a semideath, as opposed to the noncontingent death of animals such as human beings, animals that reproduce sexually and have death "within" them, that is, as part of their essence.

It thus seems that the "inside," in conformity with a long metaphysical tradition, is the place of both "real life," life in accordance with the essence of life, and "real death," life and death in the full sense of these terms. It is this relation between true life and true death that explains why, for Jacob, the bacterium can have neither. Derrida thus sees Jacob slowly reinscribing an inside within the genetic program, a program that he had earlier seemed to characterize in terms of exteriority and contingency alone. Evolution will thus have been moving not simply toward greater and greater "complexity" but, through what would seem to be a latent humanism, toward a certain "essence of life."

One can see here how Derrida's understanding of the logic of the supplement, a logic whose workings Derrida carefully demonstrates in *Of Grammatology* (1967), *Dissemination* (1972), and elsewhere, is here being deployed to help read Jacob. For Jacob, the supplement of sexuality or of death comes to certain living beings from outside the genetic program and only then is inscribed on the inside as what is essential for living beings in general. Derrida says in a passage that should remind us of what we heard him say earlier in *Of Grammatology* regarding the absolute contingency of writing:

> One would thus have to admit, for sexuality as well as for death, that these two "inventions," supervening from the outside, quasi-accidentally, consist in bringing inside, in inscribing as an internal law, the very thing that comes from the outside. That which the supplement brings in from the outside is an internal supplement, such that all these oppositions that Jacob takes up with such confidence (necessary/contingent, internal/external, organism/milieu, etc., and as a result non-sexuality/sexuality, life/non-life) break down, and this forces him, without ever reflecting upon this law, to make either formally contradictory statements or empirical approximations in which the conceptual sharpness of certain claims gives way or dissipates or loses its edge.[31]

As in *Of Grammatology*, what is assumed to come from the outside is *in fact* operating already on the inside—be it writing or spacing or difference. The outside is already operating within in such a way as to contaminate or alter the purity of our distinctions. Without having to affirm, contra Jacob, that bacteria really do reproduce sexually or really do die—claims that would simply extend an already suspect "essence" of life and death to other living beings—Derrida is able to show through an analysis of Jacob's own discourse that the human cannot be distinguished from the nonhuman, just as the institutional program cannot be distinguished from the genetic program, in the terms that Jacob believes. Derrida thus suggests that another logic, a logic beyond Jacob's logic of the living, would be required to think these relations:

> I do not want to conclude from all this that there has always already been sexuality or death or that, according to the simple reversal, there will have never yet been sexuality or death, but rather that if "science" or "philosophy" must speak of sexuality or of death, the oppositions positive/negative, more/less, inside/outside, along with the logic of the either/or, of the *and* [*et*] or of the *is* [*est*], no longer suffice.[32]

In other words, there is no *pure* inside or outside, no uncontaminated or unbroached inside. What seems to be on the outside is always already working from within, the contingent within what appeared to be noncontingent, contingent death within what appeared to be a noncontingent, essential death, and so forth. At the very least, these oppositions are no longer as stable as Jacob would like to think. Derrida continues—and note in what follows the very strong claim about not just bacteria or humankind but "every living system":

> All this might appear somewhat trivial, but I am citing Jacob here in order to underscore that this structural opening of every living system makes untenable those statements about bacteria not dying because death comes to them from the outside or about death in the proper sense of the term having to be inscribed in the organism, etc. It also makes untenable all the simple oppositions between inside and outside that subtend what the book says both about sexuality and mortality as accidents come from the outside that come to be inscribed within. Supplementarity is inscribed in the very definition of every system, every living or non-living system.[33]

This reference to the "structural opening of every living system" should provoke us to return, once again, to *Of Grammatology*, where Derrida writes: "Archē-writing, first the possibility of speech, then of the 'graphy' in the narrow sense of the term . . . this trace is the opening of the first exteriority in general, the enigmatic relation of the living to its other and of an inside to an outside: spacing [*l'espacement*]."[34]

If there is an analogical relation between the living being or the genetic code and the text—or a relation that is more than an analogy, more than a model—it is to be found *not*, as Jacob thinks, in the fact that in both cases there is a code or a message or information that is being transferred or conveyed, for that is still a logocentric conception of the text; it is to be found, rather, in this "structural opening to an outside." Compare what was just said in *Life Death* regarding the "structural opening of every living system," that is, the structural opening of every living system to an outside and to everything that comes along with that outside, that is, as he says in *Of Grammatology*, "the enigmatic relation of the living to its other and of an inside to an outside"—compare all that to the following from *Life Death*:

> Whenever one speaks of textuality, the value of relations of force, of differences of force, an economic agonistics, will there be just as irreducible. Just like the opening to the outside of every textual system at the very moment it re-marks itself and re-inscribes itself. Re-production itself implies this agonistics.[35]

The originary opening of a "putative" inside to an outside—that is what links the text to the genetic program. And that is what links the program, every program, I think, to dumb luck or to chance. Indeed it is this opening of an inside to an outside, this originary opening of the inside to the outside, of essence to contingency, that determines almost everything in Derrida, everything from invention and decision to the event and the future.

For Derrida always and everywhere tried to give a chance to chance, to give chance its chance, to give dumb luck a certain place at the limits of certainty and language. For without chance, without dumb luck, there would be no mutation or invention, no decision and no future, only repetition and death.[36] Without reducing, not in the least, the importance of analysis, understanding, knowledge, and so on, Derrida wanted to leave a certain space for the dumb luck that makes an event or a genuine decision possible, that prevents the horizon of the future from determining all decisions in the form of a program. Whereas Jacob understands the origin as what controls the future development of an organism, and of humankind especially, Derrida, by locating a certain contingency within this development, opens the future up to the radically unknown. This is evident in the way Derrida reads and interprets the final lines of *The Logic of the Living*, which gives us the metaphor or the image of a Russian doll, the image par excellence, it seems, of inside and outside, of a series of insides inside other insides or outsides outside other outsides. Here is how Jacob concludes *The Logic of the Living*: "Today the world is messages, codes, and information. Tomorrow what analysis will break down our objects to reconstitute them in a new space? What new Russian doll will emerge?"[37]

It seems like a perfectly appropriate, unobjectionable way to conclude. The history of science has shown us that there are certain ruptures or breaks, epistemic shifts, if you will, changes in models that resemble the discovery of a new, more complex, more powerful Russian doll within the Russian doll we already know, that is, within the prevailing model with which we have been working. But Derrida thinks that Jacob concedes or betrays too much through this analogy. For while Jacob is willing to admit—for how could he not—that we do not know exactly what the next scientific model, that is, what the next Russian doll, will look like, his image seems to suggest that he already knows that whatever this new model will be it will at least look like a Russian doll, and *that*, for Derrida, is perhaps already to assume too much. Derrida says right near the very end of his analysis of Jacob:

> It is perhaps presuming a lot about this resemblance to what we know today to say that this will still be a "Russian doll," something bearing enough of a resemblance, however "new" it may be, to a Russian doll. Note that a Russian doll that would "emerge," as he says, is itself already rather new and rather monstrous compared to what we know. He wants it to come out of a shell in which it is enclosed by a series of nested shells that are predictable in their overall structure, and yet he wants it to emerge, discontinuously, that is to say, to come out all at once, but from the sea.[38]

For Derrida, the future cannot be thought along the lines of a Russian doll within a Russian doll, that is, as something as yet invisible that will nonetheless resemble in its general form what has come before. The future cannot be mastered or controlled, envisioned, foreseen, or shown, *montré*, in this way. It must always have, as the future, a "monstrous" form, that is, a deformed or unformed form, unpredictable, unforeseeable, a form, if that is still the appropriate term, that would emerge all at once not from another, similar Russian doll but from the sea—a sea monstrosity, then, like Proteus, perhaps, the monster that never appears as such but always in different monstrous forms. As Derrida writes in an often-cited line right near the end of the exergue of the book to which I have returned several times already, namely, *Of Grammatology*:

> The future can only be anticipated in the form of an absolute danger. It is that which breaks absolutely with constituted normality and can only be proclaimed, presented, as a sort of monstrosity [*sous l'espèce de la monstruosité*]. For that future world and for that within it which will have put into question the values of sign, word, and writing, for that which guides our future anterior, there is as yet no exergue.[39]

So the Russian doll, an image of insides and of resemblance par excellence, simply will not suffice. The future is not *inside* the present in any way. It is out there, ready to emerge, as if from the sea, as a sort of monstrosity, *sous l'espèce* of monstrosity, that is, according to a kind or species of monstrosity, a kind or species that, as monstrosity, has no known kind or species. And that is exactly what Derrida argued, in effect, already back in 1966 at the end of "Structure, Sign, and Play," initially presented at a conference at Johns Hopkins University in Baltimore and subsequently published some fifty years ago in *Writing and Difference*. Once again he speaks at the very end of a text of species that go beyond species, of monstrosity, though also—for these are inseparable—of dumbness or dumb luck. Derrida writes:

> Here there is a kind of question, let us still call it historical, whose *conception, formation, gestation,* and *labor* we are only catching a glimpse of today. I employ these words, I admit, with a glance toward the operations of childbearing—but also with a glance toward those who, in a society from which I do not exclude myself, turn their eyes away when faced by the as yet unnamable which is proclaiming itself and which can do so, as is necessary whenever a birth is in the offing, only under the species of the nonspecies [*sous l'espèce de la non-espèce*], in the formless, mute [*muette*], infant, and terrifying form of monstrosity.[40]

By calling this terrifying form of monstrosity formless, *informe*, mute, *muette*, and infant, *infante*, Derrida is alluding to the fact that the Latin *infans* means not only child or childlike but speechless or inarticulate, *infans*, derived from a negation and the Greek *phēmi* ("I speak"). We are thus back to the dumbness of dumb luck in terms of what is mute, unspeaking, either because there is, as with the infant, an undeveloped capacity or because, as with the Who's Tommy, that capacity has been subverted or destroyed through some kind of trauma that takes our breath, or takes our voice, away—a trauma that could be the trauma of birth or of death, a chasm, in either case, that opens up experience or tears a gaping hole within it, leaving us—our dumb luck—open-mouthed before it, agape before the absolute contingency of it all.

Now I began by speaking of my own dumb luck in having been invited here to Bern because of a conference devoted to the work not of Jacques Derrida but Don DeLillo. To mark or to celebrate that chance, that contingency, let me conclude by briefly recalling a moment in a DeLillo novel that revolves around speech, silence, and dumb luck. The novel is titled *The Names*, and it traces an American archaeologist and linguist from the plains of Kansas who becomes fascinated by a strange language cult in Greece, a cult that goes by the name of *Ta onomata*, that is, the Names. The archaeologist's fascination for this cult is attributable in large part to a great failure in his own childhood, his inability to speak in tongues in a Pentecostal church where his parents were both members, that is, his inability to partake in a glossolalia that would give him access to something like an absolutely new or original language, something like the language of God. The archaeologist thus tracks this language cult from Greece all the way to India, into the Thar, the Great Indian Desert, where he confronts a female cult member who is trying to starve herself to death. "Thick-lipped, broad, utterly silent for weeks," the woman spends "almost all her time sealed in one of the thatched silos" in the desert.[41] Sealed up in the silo, sealed up in silence, speechless, mute, *aphone*, dumb, *stumm*, agape before a death that is coming upon her, her mouth open but her lips sealed, the woman never speaks in the novel, but she does have a name; this figure from DeLillo's novel *The Names* has a name even if she does not have a voice, and that name—wouldn't you know it, my dumb luck—is Bern.

NOTES

1. The epigraph to this essay is from Don DeLillo, *Libra* (New York: Viking, 1988), 79.

2. The Who, "Pinball Wizard," lyrics by Pete Townshend (London: Polydor, 1969).

3. Herodotus, *The Persian Wars*, trans. Alfred D. Godley (Cambridge, MA: Harvard University Press, 1990), I.30.

4. Herodotus, *The Persian Wars*, I.32.

5. Aristotle, *Nicomachean Ethics*, trans. Harris Rackham (Cambridge, MA: Harvard University Press, 1982), I.x.1–5.

6. Aristotle, *Nicomachean Ethics*, I.85; see also I.34.

7. Aristotle, *Nicomachean Ethics*, I.85.

8. Aristotle, *Nicomachean Ethics*, I.86.

9. Aristotle, *Nicomachean Ethics*, I.87.

10. Jacques Derrida, *Life Death*, trans. Pascale-Anne Brault and Michael Naas (Chicago: University of Chicago Press, 2020); Jacques Derrida, *La vie la mort*, ed. Pascale-Anne Brault and Peggy Kamuf (Paris: Éditions du Seuil, 2019).

11. Jacques Derrida, "Telepathy," trans. Nicholas Royle, in *Psyche: Inventions of the Other*, ed. Peggy Kamuf and Elizabeth Rottenberg (Stanford, CA: Stanford University Press, 2007), 1:227–61; Jacques Derrida, "My Chances / Mes chances: A Rendezvous with Some Epicurean Stereophonies," trans. Irene Harvey and Avital Ronell, in *Psyche: Inventions of the Other*, see esp. 1:362.

12. See Jacques Derrida, *Rogues: Two Essays on Reason*, trans. Pascale-Anne Brault and Michael Naas (Stanford, CA: Stanford University Press, 2005): "It is indeed on the side of chance, that is, the side of the incalculable *perhaps*, and toward the incalculability of another thought of life, of what is living in life, that I would like to venture here under the old and yet still completely new and perhaps unthought name 'democracy'" (5).

13. Jacques Derrida, *Of Grammatology*, trans. Gayatri Chakravorty Spivak (Baltimore, MD: Johns Hopkins University Press, 1976), 314; my emphasis of "*absolute contingency.*"

14. Derrida, *Life Death*, 23; see Derrida, *Of Grammatology*, 9.

15. Derrida, *Life Death*, 18.

16. Derrida, *Life Death*, 19.

17. François Jacob, *The Logic of Life: A History of Heredity*, trans. Betty E. Spillman (New York: Random House, 1973), 3. Cited at Derrida, *Life Death*, 19. The French title of Jacob's book is *La logique du vivant*, literally "The Logic of the *Living*." Since both Jacob and Derrida distinguish between *la vie* (life) and *le vivant* (the living, living beings), I refer to Jacob's book throughout by this more literal title.

18. Jacob, *The Logic of the Living*, 3–4; cited at Derrida, *Life Death*, 19.

19. Jacob, *The Logic of the Living*, 322.

20. Jacob, *The Logic of the Living*, 3.

21. Dawne McCance, in her work *The Reproduction of Life Death: Derrida's "La vie la mort"* (New York: Fordham University Press, 2019), draws out even more

explicitly the consequences of the assumptions of biologists such as Bernard and Jacob to control or dominate nature and the assumption of mankind as the one animal capable of manipulating both his own genetic code and that of other animals.

22. Derrida, *Life Death*, 19.

23. Derrida, *Life Death*, 19. Derrida says in a similar vein on the very next page: "if anything has been learned from what are today called the structural sciences, it is the possibility of affirming that systems linked to language, to the symbolic, to cerebral memory, etc., also have an internal functioning or an internal regulation that escapes deliberation and consciousness and enables the effects that come from the outside to be perceived as contingencies, heterogeneous forces that need to be interpreted, translated, assimilated into the internal code in an attempt to master them. And it is when this attempt fails that 'mutations' are produced, mutations that might take all kinds of forms but that signal in each case a violent intrusion from the outside, necessitating a general restructuring" (20).

24. Derrida, *Life Death*, 19.

25. Derrida, Jacques and Roudinesco, Elisabeth. *For What Tomorrow…: A Dialogue*. 48.

26. This is, to be sure, a surprising use of the word 'contingency,' as Derrida himself notes: "The apparent paradox is to be found in the chiasm by which Jacob places contingency on the side of the greatest internal rigidity, on the side of the most constraining necessity of reproduction, whereas, along the other line of the chiasm, contingency, the effect of contingency, is limited even though freedom and deliberation are there predominant." Derrida, *Life Death*, 20. For Jacob, contingency is *opposed* to freedom, not, as it frequently is, associated with it.

27. Derrida, *Life Death*, 20.

28. For this notion of a 'nonphonetic' writing within genetics, one that Jacob completely ignores, see again McCance, *The Reproduction of Life Death*, 31.

29. Derrida, *Life Death*, 88.

30. Derrida, *Life Death*, 88.

31. Derrida, *Life Death*, 88.

32. Derrida, *Life Death*, 88. Derrida can then argue that certain somewhat rare and exceptional facts about bacterial reproduction and death support his argument and call into question the purity of Jacob's distinctions: "No matter the frequency or rarity of these phenomena, no matter their partial character (without cellular fusion, etc.), they nonetheless signal, just by being possible, that such things can always happen to the 'pure' bacterium as a model of reproduction without sexuality and without death, pure inside or pure outside, pure inside of living reproducibility or pure surface able to receive death only from the outside as contingent" (113).

33. Derrida, *Life Death*, 126.

34. Derrida, *Of Grammatology*, 103.

35. Derrida, *Life Death*, 124.

36. Dawne McCance says this well: "The genetic 'text' cannot be encompassed by 'the model' . . . without effacing or ignoring nonappropriable differences in favor of some desired homogeneity. Jacob's definition of reproduction as the transfer of an identical program to the following generation leaves little room for—even attempts to exclude—differences, random and unpredictable variations. Ostensibly, for him, to eliminate, or assimilate, ungraspable differences would be to reduce the risk, the chance, involved in reproduction (the eugenicist's dream). Yet as Derrida has it, 'If there is no risk, there is only death.'" McCance, *The Reproduction of Life Death*, 30–31. McCance is citing here Jacques Derrida, "Nietzsche and the Machine (Interview with Richard Beardsworth)," trans. Richard R. Beardsworth, in *Negotiations: Interventions and Interviews, 1971–2001*, ed. Elizabeth Rottenberg (Stanford, CA: Stanford University Press, 2002), 248.

37. Jacob, *The Logic of the Living*, 324; cited at Derrida, *Life Death*, 136.

38. Derrida, *Life Death*, 136.

39. Derrida, *Of Grammatology*, 5.

40. Jacques Derrida, "Structure, Sign, and Play in the Discourse of the Human Sciences," trans. Alan A. Bass, in *Writing and Difference* (Chicago: University of Chicago Press, 1978), 293.

41. Don DeLillo, *The Names* (New York: Vintage, 1989), 290.

The Apophatic Community
Ethics, Contingency, Negation

Viola Marchi

When I pronounce the word Silence, I destroy it.
—Wisława Szymborska

If there is one thing we know about ethics, at least since Aristotle, is that it is not an exact science.[1] It is clear that we cannot base our ethical decisions on an a priori intellectual intuition or deduce ethical norms of action by drawing on axiomatic knowledge. Even an inductive method, which, rooted in the particularity of the situation, would seem best suited to approach ethical matters, is still not sufficient for moral reasoning. Let us begin with the quite obvious observation that, if a rule of conduct is to be of any use and have any validity, as Kant reminds us, it has to be "universalizable," that is, applicable to a plurality of constantly new, singular, contingent circumstances. But here's the rub: If we can move from the concrete to the abstract and thus formulate a general norm by stripping the situation at hand of all that is contingent and accidental, we cannot as easily reverse the process and apply the norm thus obtained back to the plurality of new situations and events. Whereas I can subsume the particular under the universal, by stripping it of its contingent qualities, I cannot apply my general rule back to the plurality of circumstances by simply reintroducing contingency and difference *as such*. And this is because, each time, I would be dealing with *different* differences and contingencies. There remains, in other words, a basic untranslatability between the singular, embodied lived experience and universalizable, general norms. As Aristotle puts it, ethical deliberations "depend on particular circumstances, and the decision lies with perception."[2] In order to decide, the general norm has to be suspended, and one needs to start back again from perception, the particular, and its sensible aspects. Very concisely put: Whereas, in ethical matters, I can perhaps try to *induce* necessity out of contingency, I certainly cannot *deduce* contingency from necessity. Ethics, therefore, becomes a matter of practical negotiation between two theoretically irreconcilable realms, a practical knowledge that, for Aristotle, is geared toward the cultivation of virtue through experience. The "common ground," so to speak, in which the process of ethical mediation can take place is that of *ethos* itself, as the social customs, habits, values, character, or "spirit" of a community.

But what happens when community stops functioning as a (necessary) bulwark against contingency and becomes itself contingent? And what are the ethical implications of such a shift, from what Miranda Joseph has aptly defined as "the romance of community"[3] to what I'd like to call "a community without ethos?"[4] These are the questions that I will pursue in what follows, focusing specifically on Jean-Luc Nancy's and Maurice Blanchot's now classic texts on community.

Still today, in fact, almost forty years after the fact, no philosophical approach to community can afford to ignore what Jacques Derrida defined as the "seismic event"[5] that, in the early 1980s, shook and permanently altered the landscape of the theoretical investigation of this problematic and ambiguous notion. What I am referring to is the publication of Jean-Luc Nancy's *The Inoperative Community* in 1983 and of Maurice Blanchot's prompt reply, appearing later that same year, *The Unavowable Community*. Derrida identifies the disruptive power of these texts in the "new logic" they employ, characterized by the "necessarily contradictory and undecidable statements that organize these discourses and give them their paradoxical force."[6] To this strategy of thinking corresponds, at the level of writing, what one could call a new "poetics," one centered around "the necessity of these 'apparently contradictory' statements . . . an event that opens up a world in which we must today, now, write in this way, and deliver ourselves over to this necessity."[7] A necessity that, again somewhat paradoxically, is determined by the utter contingency that comes to define Nancy's and Blanchot's understandings of community, stripped of all references to an identity or even to a generic "something in common"—apart, perhaps, from the sheer chance event of being-together—that would lend a reason to the existence of the community itself.

Taking my cue from Derrida's admittedly nebulous assessment, I will try to inquire into this logic and poetics of community. I will argue that the pictures of community offered by Nancy and Blanchot are articulated through the recourse to apophaticism as a philosophical method and style of writing, a strategy they derive, first of all, from their profound engagement with the work of Georges Bataille. My central claim is that, in both thinkers, the apophatic strategy signals the attempt at thinking community nondialectically and, more specifically, outside of a dialectic of the "proper." However, while Nancy seems to reject mediation altogether, Blanchot moves toward the formulation of a nondialectical mediation, in which apophaticism works as the point of departure to tease out the affirmative potentialities of a thinking of the negative that does not take the form of a logical or ontological negation. The essay concludes by proposing an ethics of contestation (or of nonpositive affirmation) as the fundamental counterpart to an idea of community that evades the traps of dialectics and does not annihilate or sublate contingency.

APOPHATICISM AS METHODOLOGY: NEGATING THE PROPOSITIONAL

Let me begin by offering at least a few words of clarification on this unusual methodological choice. If I borrow the concept of apophaticism from theology it is because I want to argue that Nancy's and Blanchot's texts actually carry the trace of a mystic discourse that goes far beyond the well-known controversial discussion on the relationship between deconstruction and negative theology. Whereas both negative theology and apophatic mysticism are connected to the so-called *via negativa*, the former is usually associated with *theoria*, in the sense of a speculative doctrine linked by its Greek etymology to ideas of vision and contemplation. Mysticism, on the other hand, derives from the Greek root *muo* (or *mu*), meaning "to close," and "therefore denotes the practice of closing one's eyes or of closing one's lips."[8] Whereas theology can be defined as the systematic study of concepts of god, mysticism is rooted in the experiential and linked to a textual tradition concerned with the paradoxical task of giving linguistic articulation to the experience of contact with the ineffable. Therefore, the texts belonging to this tradition often exhibit a strong self-reflexive character, directly pointing to their own textuality and to the problems connected with representational language as such.

As to the "ineffable," the main characteristic of the god of apophatic mysticism is that the divine is so radically nonanthropomorphic, so utterly transcendent and wholly Other, that it is often indiscernible from "nothing." For this reason, the alterity of the divine is irreducible to language and to thought, and this theme is stylistically reflected in the recurrent use of oxymoron and synaesthesia, logically articulated through a series of iterative negations, unsolvable contradictions, and paradoxes. In the context of this limit experience, and in the confrontation with the utter nothingness of the divine, the possibility of knowledge is not simply negated but rather transformed into a process of unknowing and undoing of the realm of the intelligible. As Denys Turner succinctly puts it in *The Darkness of God: Negativity in Christian Mysticism*, "*apophasis* is a Greek neologism for the breakdown of *speech*,"[9] as language turning on itself at the moment in which thought is confronted with what undermines it and with a theoretical excess that cannot be grasped or eliminated.

As a method of reasoning, apophaticism proceeds by what Eugene Thacker calls "ascending negations."[10] In contrast to the deductive, top-down approach of the cataphatic, apophaticism is characterized by a bottom-up perspective based on an inductive method, moving from the multiplicity of the sensible toward an impossible unity that actually results in the dissolution of both the self and the divine. In ontological terms, this process could be described as the attempt to reach pure substance by progressively stripping it of all its attributes and relations, only to discover that this substance is, effectively, *nothing*.

A last distinction that I would like to briefly address, in order to get a glimpse into the main operation of apophasis and its underlying logic, is the one that opposes it to cataphasis. It is essential to point out that cataphasis should not simply be understood in terms of an affirmative discourse on the divine. By considering the obvious fact that for something to be un-said (as is the case in apophaticism) something must be said first, it is easy to see how apophasis and cataphasis are not mutually exclusive rhetorical strategies but rather two moments of the same process. However, as Turner explains, the processual relation that exists between apophasis and cataphasis cannot be defined as a movement of negation and affirmation, as a "no" opposed to a "yes." Most importantly, even if the positive and negative moments are by definition intertwined and part of the same conceptual movement, this does not lead to a final dialectical resolution. Admittedly, apophasis itself introduces a third step, that of the "negation of negation." What we need to keep in mind, however, is that this process allows neither for synthesis nor for the formation of absolute concepts or concepts of the absolute. As Turner explains, the "negation of negation is not a third utterance, additional to the affirmative and the negative, in good linguistic order; it is not some intelligible synthesis of affirmation and negation; it is rather the collapse of our affirmations and denials into disorder."[11] While negative propositions or negative images can also belong to texts that are essentially cataphatic, the fundamental element that characterizes apophaticism is "the strategy of *negating the propositional*" itself and "the *negation of imagery*."[12] In other words, the use of negative propositions and images in apophaticism ultimately results in the negation of the text, and every linguistic instance of un-saying reflects, at a broader level, the movement of a text un-saying itself.

JEAN-LUC NANCY'S ECSTASY

It is while Nancy is teaching a course on the work of Georges Bataille and its political implications that Jean-Christophe Bailly solicits his intervention on the topic of "Community, Number" for a special issue of the journal *Aléa*.[13] In Nancy's own words, the goal of his work on Bataille and the political was that of "researching, very precisely, the possibility of a hitherto unheard-of resource that would avoid fascism and communism as much as democratic or republican individualism."[14]

Despite its seemingly anecdotic quality, this circumstance is of fundamental importance to give us access to the central concerns of *The Inoperative Community*, as it helps identify the specific historicopolitical circumstances Nancy's contribution is attempting to respond to. Furthermore, if we consider the role that Bataille plays in it—so central that the text often takes the form of a close reading, a commentary, almost a glossary of Bataille's work—it becomes apparent that, in order to reconstruct the background of the question, one needs to turn to the relationship between the two thinkers.

The background out of which the question emerges is constituted by the great totalitarianisms of the twentieth century, and the content of the question itself has, as its kernel, the problem of rethinking community after communism. However, as the reference to "democratic or republican individualism" in the previous quotation suggests, there is an ulterior political challenge faced by Nancy in the 1980s and, one could infer, in conjunction with the rise of neoliberalism.

The bleak situation Nancy is confronting is represented by a sphere of the political that appears to be dominated both by a logic of absolute necessity as well as by a dichotomous rationale that has reduced the realm of the possible to either the unbridled individualism of contemporary capitalist democracies or to a conservative and nostalgic return to community as an ideal that, taken to its most radical extremes, might contain within itself the seeds of new forms of totalitarianism. The atomistic conception of contemporary liberal society, therefore, is for Nancy as dangerous and misguided as certain positions that understand community in organicistic terms and as an instance of communion and fusion of "egos into an Ego or a higher We."[15] They both feature in *The Inoperative Community* as figures of "immanentism," understood by Nancy as a synonym for "totalitarianism" and as the fundamental stumbling block that obstructs every possibility for thinking community.

Yet one should be aware that the use of the term "totalitarianism" in Nancy does not limit itself to the specific regimes that would usually fit under that category: Fascism and communism (the last one in its blatant historical failure) are totalitarian just as much as the radical individualism and self-centeredness of contemporary democratic societies. By positing "immanentism" (which is not immanence) and "totalitarianism" (which is not a particular totalitarian regime) as synonyms, Nancy points to their direct relation to a "work of death." As he states: "The fully realized person of individualistic or communistic humanism is the dead person."[16]

The references to Hegel's *Phenomenology of Spirit*—to the "'we,' that is a single Ego,"[17] to the "work [*Werk*]" of each and all as the substance of community ("*das Tun aller und jeder*"),[18] and to the "fully realized person" that clearly echoes Hegel's "actually realized individuality"[19]—are here too structural and pervasive to be ignored. First of all, they are essential for beginning to understand at least a facet of the meaning of the notion of "worklessness" and the stress that both Nancy and Blanchot place on this term. The self-conscious individual is constituted in the *Phenomenology* through work, as the unfolding into the world of one's self-expression, culminating in the coordination and unanimity of the action of all and each in the "self-conscious community."[20] Against this background, we can better see how the "work" of community Nancy's critique is attempting to "unwork" is, in fact, as Andreas Wagner suggests, that of the "supposition of a (to-be-expressed) identity immanent to the community" that would lead to the "political project of unfolding of that identity."[21]

If individualism and communitarianism, in their extreme form of immanentism, are the fundamental impediments to thinking community—as well as very concrete and deadly historical weapons—and if the central philosophical problem is posed by a dialectical mechanism of community formation that continues to subtend virtually every account of this concept, the question we are left with is: Why Bataille? What kind of philosophical and linguistic tools could such a controversial and, at least at the time, mostly ignored author have to offer in view of such a radical rethinking of community?

For Nancy, Bataille is, first of all, the one that "has gone farther into the crucial experience of the modern destiny of community."[22] Not only did he go "through the ordeal of seeing communism betrayed,"[23] but he could never separate his intellectual engagement with the topic of community from his very personal commitment to the actual lived experience of groups such as Acéphale, Contre-Attaque, and the Collège de Sociologie.

It is in the late 1930s, and in conjunction with the painful realization of the failure of the communist experience, that, according to Nancy, Bataille's "uneasiness concerning the political"[24] gives rise to two contradictory directions in his thought: a "revolutionary impulse," on the one side, still linked to the climate of the October Revolution, and a "fascination with fascism," on the other. The reason for this unsustainable contradiction resides in Bataille's dreadful diagnosis—whose prescient foresight, as we have seen, Nancy was recognizing in the 1980s and that seems even clearer to us today—of the very concrete risk that liberal democracies would eventually revert into fascism. Fascism, in Bataille's view, is not simply an ideology that could somehow be fought and eradicated. It is, rather, "one of the recourses of capitalism," arising out of "the already established, stifling reign of society."[25]

Bataille's attempt to fight the individualistic paradigm and its authoritarian outcomes takes the form of an impossible task, based on the misappropriation of the enemy's main tools: myth, the sphere of the sacred, and the sacrificial paradigm (with sacrifice as both metaphoric fantasy and programmatic element of the Acéphale group). The failure of this controversial intellectual path is what, according to Nancy, led to Bataille's "final withdrawal from thinking community,"[26] after having "thought it *to the limit*—at and to its limit, and at the limit of his thought."[27] The reaching of the limit, however, has not exhausted the question; on the contrary, what Bataille "had to think at his limit is what he leaves for us to think in our turn."[28] While in this passage Nancy is clearly indicating the necessity to start from but also move beyond Bataille's reflections on community, his insistence on the notion of the limit is also a clear reference to Bataille's own thought, deeply preoccupied with the possible ways to access an experience of the impossible—what he calls "inner experience" and what Blanchot will refer to as "limit-experience"—and with the consequent limits of language and philosophy as appropriate means to describe and conceptualize it.

In his rather vitriolic analysis of Blanchot's *The Unavowable Community*—published under the title *The Disavowed Community* in 2014, namely, thirty years after their first exchange—Nancy identifies the decisive point of contrast in their approaches to Bataille. While Blanchot "sought to return to the prewar Bataille,"[29] Nancy was more interested in the writings of the postwar period. The choice to concentrate on two different periods of Bataille's life and work is, in Nancy's view, the main reason for their different approaches to community.

In the last years of the war, in its immediate aftermath, and up until the mid-1950s—that is, in the period that interests Nancy—Bataille is working on three main projects, apparently unrelated and covering disparate fields: the unfinished and fragmentary *Atheological Summa*,[30] the treatise of political economy *The Accursed Share*, and the book on *Eroticism*. The *Atheological Summa* displays Bataille's lifetime interest in the foundational texts of apophatic mysticism, which exhibit, according to him, a fundamental, albeit admittedly bizarre, similarity with Nietzsche's work, both in terms of the content of what they are seeking to communicate as well as their writing methods and strategies.[31] The main aim of the project is to articulate what I have previously referred to as "inner experience" or "limit-experience," namely, a mysticism without God, "an apophatic aporia that he called 'the impossible,'"[32] through a language that is necessarily negative, nonrepresentational, and fragmentary.

A few years later, in 1949, Bataille publishes *The Accursed Share*, his treatise on political economy. The book argues for a shift from what he calls the perspective of "restricted economy" to that of a "general economy." As he puts it in the introduction to the first volume, this change of perspective, as "the overturning of economic principles—the overturning of the ethics that grounds them," would accomplish "a Copernican transformation," namely, "a reversal of thinking—and of ethics."[33] In his Nietzschean attempt at "transvaluation," Bataille's main target is the principle of utility that has come to saturate the entire social field, dictating the status and the very content of every possible relation. His "Copernican revolution" thus consists in the overturning of the asymmetrical relations that obtain, within the contemporary political and economic landscape, between economic utility and "expenditure," bourgeois accumulation and useless consumption.

The mid-1950s saw the publication of *Eroticism* (1956), an eclectic study on the notions of taboo, transgression, and the mystical experience. The erotic experience, in the form of a desire that undoes and dispossesses the self, features as the privileged point of access to the impersonal, affective field that Bataille calls "continuity of being," in contrast to the discontinuity that reigns in the world of individuals, society, and work. The "impersonal fullness of life itself,"[34] preceding the processes of individuation and subsequently absorbed into the discontinuity that characterizes the personal, the social, and the everyday, can only be approached through an affirmative form of desire that is "assenting to life even in death."[35] However, the mystical experience leading from discontinuous to continuous being, in Bataille's specific understanding of the terms, does not culminate in a final fusional unity. On the contrary, the immediate contact with the impersonal field remains unattainable and can only be elliptically glimpsed through those moments in which "the ceaseless operation of cognition is dissolved."[36]

In the same way in which the final fusional stage is fundamentally unattainable, the erotic/deadly/mystical "pathless ecstasy he seeks cannot be given an itinerary"[37] and does not follow a proper movement of transcendence. Conversely, Bataille's inner experience can be best characterized as an inverse (non)trajectory leading toward a "base materialism." As Thacker rightly suggests in *Starry Speculative Corpse*, pointing to the intimate relation that connects the seemingly divergent theoretical interests that occupy Bataille in the postwar period:

> Bataille's mystical writings are not simply a ventriloquizing of these earlier mystical authors, and neither are they about the existentialist crisis of the modern subject; for Bataille this type of darkness runs the gamut from the most basic forms of "base materialism" and inorganic matter, to the planetary and almost cosmic cycles of production, accumulation, and expenditure.[38]

Rejecting a transcendent and divine beyond, Bataille links his idea of the mystical experience to his proposal of an economy of expenditure and intransitive, nonreciprocal gift giving[39] against capitalist accumulation and appropriation. In so doing, he reverses the trajectory of the mystical path from an ascent toward the divine to a descent into "base materialism," from the illumination of divine knowledge to a plunging into the darkness of "unknowing" in the double sense of a *non-savoir* (as the struggle of a thought of excess that inevitably ends up crashing against the constraints of conceptual thinking) and of *l'inconnu* (as the openness toward the unknown of a time to come and as chance, namely, what comes to lacerate the illusory unity and coherence of a self and of "a world in principle unified and stripped of all accidents").[40]

When understood in these terms—as a nonfusional, life-affirming, immanent exit from the self, following the movement of an affirmative desire that is rigorously objectless, aimless, and unintentional in the phenomenological sense—it becomes clear how the inner experience Bataille is talking about in fact has nothing to do with interiority. As also Nancy argues, "the 'inner experience' of which Bataille speaks is in no way 'interior' or 'subjective,' but is indissociable from the experience of this relation to an incommensurable outside. Only community furnishes this relation its spacing, its rhythm."[41] By progressively snatching the self from its self-positing, the inner experience opens up the possibility of what Bataille refers to as "ecstatic communication" (and, of course, no possibility of communication is given once fusion is achieved).

Bataille's notions of ecstasy and communication, all developed out of his heterodox, Nietzschean approach to the literature of mysticism, are arguably the central elements from which Nancy's thought on community departs. Communication, in fact, as Nancy repeatedly reminds us, is not something that happens among subjects, locked up in their "autarchy of absolute immanence,"[42] in the same way that speech "is not a *means* of communication."[43] Speech is communication itself, and communication is always ecstatic, or, more precisely, ecstasy is the primary, necessary condition for the possibility of communication as such. Speech, then, does not proceed from the interiority of a subject outward toward the other subjects; rather, it is articulated at the limit, at the point of what Nancy calls *clinamen*, an inside/outside that only exists as exposure. For these reasons, for Nancy as for Bataille, "the question of community is henceforth inseparable from a question of ecstasy. . . . *Community, or the being-ecstatic of Being itself*? That would be the question."[44]

Bataille's ecstatic experience—and the ensuing descent into base materialism—is also a struggle against the language of philosophical reason (and, in particular, Hegelian dialectics) through the means offered by the language of apophatic mysticism. The aimless goal of this strategy "is not to avoid the paradox, nor to attempt to resolve it, but to embrace it and force the reader to think it in all its contradiction."[45] And aimless writing, in opposition to writing as the creation of the work (as instrumental communication and instrument of representation), is, in fact, one of the main paradoxes around which many of Bataille's texts articulate themselves and that brings him to a fragmentary, "antigeneric" form of writing. "The paradoxical problem of *Guilty*," for instance, "is how to write (a) desire (without object) aimlessly or how to write without end and without why."[46]

As previously mentioned in reference to the relation between apophasis and cataphasis, understood as part of the same movement of a text that simultaneously writes and deletes itself, Bataille's writing and thought remain suspended within the unsolvable tension between meaning and its dispersion, at those points where "descriptive language becomes meaningless at the decisive instant when the stirrings of transgression itself take over the discursive account of transgression."[47] This apophatic tension between writing and its own erasure is echoed in Nancy's assessment of Bataille's work in terms of a movement of inscription and exscription.

In the article "Exscription," Nancy describes Bataille's texts as "stretching writing to its bursting point, the excess of what makes writing: that is to say what simultaneously inscribes and exscribes it."[48] The play of inscription and exscription Nancy is describing refers to a movement that occurs at the very limits of the text, in that relational space of exposure as the articulation of the inside/outside, which is also the space that allows for the "compearance," distribution, and sharing of singular beings. Writing is understood here as operating on the threshold, or at the point of exposure, between language, as the locus of inscription of intelligible signification, and its outside, as the exscription of meaning. In exscribing meaning, Bataille's texts open onto his own "'life' or 'cry'"[49] as they take place outside writing and within "lived experience," another of Bataille's central notions.[50] This outside, however, as Nancy specifies, "is not that of a referent to which signification would refer."[51] It is, conversely, "entirely exscribed into the text," "as the infinite retreat of meaning by which each existence exists."[52] Thus textuality, in Bataille's hands, at least from Nancy's point of view, takes place at the level of exposure and of existence itself, as the very condition of a language suspended at the nexus between the immateriality of meaning and the materiality of writing as praxis, of life, of the body, and of Bataille's inarticulate cry.

It is here, I think, that we should locate Nancy's idea of "literary communism." In "Myth Interrupted," Nancy attributes to literature or writing a primary role in the interruption of the myth of community—the founding narrative of communal origin—which he specifically understands as "the proper figuration of the proper."[53] The interruption of the myth of community can be interpreted as what suspends the drive to communion and the centripetal force that gathers singularities toward a center. Conversely, the voice of this interruption, which Nancy identifies with literature or writing, is itself the voice of a community "exposed to its own dispersion,"[54] as a speech that does not give substance to the proper of community but that "puts into play nothing other than being *in* common."[55]

Therefore, whereas myth, in Nancy's understanding, inscribes itself at the heart of community in a movement that appears to be purely affirmative or cataphatic, closing up the space of exposure and congealing singularities into an image of fusional unity, writing operates according to a double, apophatic movement. First, it interrupts the myth of community by inscribing and writing itself over it. Then it exscribes itself, erasing its own figuration and opening itself up to "lived experience," in a movement akin to apophaticism's "strategy of *negating the propositional*" and as "the *negation of imagery*,"[56] in the undoing and unsaying of what Nancy calls myth's "proper figuration of the proper."

One of the recent collections of essays on Nancy's philosophy—titled *Nancy Now* and published in 2014—opens with a short prelude by Giorgio Agamben called "The Silhouette of Jean-Luc Nancy." In the prelude, Agamben attempts a delineation of Nancy's philosophical trajectory and—significantly for our discussion of apophaticism—attributes to him the epithet of "ferocious mystic"[57] who "stubbornly remains in contact, in the dark and blinding night where all medium and all representation are wrecked."[58] Identifying Nancy, first and foremost, as a thinker of touch, Agamben argues that "what defines the very character of touch in relation to the other senses is that it lacks a medium or an exterior milieu. . . . The flesh is simultaneously the medium and the subject of touch,"[59] understood at the same time as "im-mediate" contact and as beyond all representation. It is in "this absence of representation, this ruin of the medium"[60] that Agamben locates the core of Nancy's thought.

This description bears striking similarities to what Thacker refers to, in connection to the discourse of mysticism, as "immediation," in the sense of a positive relation to a negative term, namely, the negative divinity,[61] or to what Simon Critchley calls, in his critique of *Being Singular Plural*, Nancy's "thought of pure mediation,"[62] a mediation without medium or mediator that Critchley directly links to Nancy's project of "rewriting" Heideggerian ontology.

In fact, as Nancy already suggests in "The Inoperative Community" and as he later bluntly admits in "The Confronted Community": "Bataille had not made possible for me to touch on a new and unprecedented politics. On the contrary in many respects he had made political possibility as such even more remote."[63] The main problem that Bataille's work arguably poses to him is that, in Nancy's eyes, it still maintains, even if only as a residue, the structure of subjectivity he is so determined to do away with.[64] This is the reason why he turns to Heidegger instead and to *Dasein*, which, in its being-toward-death, "is something other than a subject."[65]

Yet I would argue that there is another fundamental aspect of Bataille's work that proves troubling for Nancy, namely, the fact that, in the end, "it is as though the communication of each being with NOTHING were beginning to prevail over the communication between beings."[66] It is interesting to refer again, in this regard, to Thacker's "Dark Media," as it might give us a better sense of this central difference that distances Bataille's and Nancy's thought of mediation and, more broadly, of community. As Thacker states:

> Whenever Bataille speaks of communication or mediation, his reference is always that of the mystical tradition of the *via negativa*; for him mediation and communication always imply the dissolution of sender and receiver, leaving perhaps only the message that is the gulf or abyss between them.... These movements flow out into an external existence: there they lose themselves, they "communicate," it would appear, with the outside (*le dehors*).[67]

Thus, while in Nancy's thought of mediation, as Agamben also suggests, what is dissolved is the medium itself, at that point of exposure (and touch) where inside/outside, interior/exterior become indistinguishable, in Bataille it is possibly only the medium that effectively subsists through the process of mediation, while both sender and receiver vacate their positions and enter into a relation that is always open *by* and *to* a third term, an "outside." Whereas community, as experienced by Bataille, is "neither a work to be produced, nor a lost communion, but rather . . . space itself, and the spacing of the experience of the outside, of the outside-of-self,"[68] in Nancy's ontological account of being-with as a brute fact of existence, "there is no other, no outside, in distinction to which a 'common' of this community could be delineated."[69]

On the one hand, this surely attests to Nancy's attempt at thinking community as inclusiveness, against the exclusionary mechanisms of an identity that can constitute its belonging only in its difference to (and rejection of) an other. On the other hand, however, it also points to the dangers, which many have recognized, of political ineffectiveness and quietism. For instance, according to Roberto Esposito, despite the clear merit of having opened up a fertile and necessary discussion on community in completely new terms, Nancy's discourse remains fundamentally "politically untranslatable." As he argues, it "is as if the absolute privilege assigned to the figure of the relation [*relazione, rapporto*] would erase the most relevant content . . . and thus, with it, also its potential political meaning."[70] In words that are closer to our analysis, Nancy's thought of "immediation" (Thacker) or "pure mediation" (Critchley), as lack of a "medium or an external milieu" (Agamben), ends up erasing not only the content of the relation, as Esposito rightly argues, but, it also seems to me, to consign the *there* of *Dasein* to an already saturated space where the relation, being always already given and originary, is also immutable and, in Esposito's parlance, "immune" to the possibility of different articulations.

In this sense, I agree with Critchley's critique that reads Nancy's project of a coexistential analytic as falling back into the Western philosophical tradition's classic move, namely, that of collapsing the ethical into the ontological. More specifically, what Nancy's gesture implies, according to Critchley, is "the suppression of ontic plurality and multiplicity"[71] in favor of "ontological otherness *überhaupt*,"[72] with the consequent subordination of the political understood as a field of mutable, contingent, and antagonistic relationality. It is under these presuppositions that Critchley moves to his final, and to my mind most significant, objection to Nancy:

> Nancy's conception of being-with risks reducing intersubjectivity to a relation of reciprocity, equality and symmetry, where I rub shoulders or stand shoulder to shoulder with the other, but where I do not *face* him. That is, I do not see in the other person that dimension of surprise, separateness or secrecy that continually defies my attempts at comprehension and appropriation.[73]

The Levinasian undertones of Critchley's position are evident, yet I believe one need not necessarily embrace the tenets of an ethics of transcendence and radical alterity to be able to see the significance of this remark. What is problematic in Nancy's version of what we could call an "ethical ontology" of the Heideggerian matrix is the exclusive emphasis on the discourse of the "with" that, from Critchley's point of view, ends up in the "*flattening of the structure of ethical experience.*" "Perhaps I am never fundamentally 'with' the other," argues Critchley. "Perhaps I am also 'without' the other . . . in a relation that demands my *acknowledgement* because it exceeds the limits of my knowledge."[74]

As both preliminary conclusion and exploratory guideline, I suggest starting from and slightly twisting Critchley's proposal, in light of the previous analysis of Bataille and of the discussion of Blanchot to follow. The suggestion Critchley advances is to shift the focus from the "with" to the "without," as what always already subtends the relation with the other. "It is therefore a matter," he argues, "ontologically, ethically, politically—not of thinking without the 'with,' but of thinking the 'without' within this 'with.'"[75]

Or, perhaps, I should like to suggest, the question is not that of thinking the "without" within the "with," as Critchley encourages us to do. Perhaps what we need to think is the *out* of the "with-out" itself—the "otherwise than with," as it were—as a way to move beyond Nancy's "pre-positional" ontology and toward a more "adverbial" understanding of community, in as much as it *modifies* the relation not by attaching properties to it but in the play of its degrees and modes.

MAURICE BLANCHOT'S SECRET

How do we start thinking the *out*? To tackle this problem, I would like now to turn to *The Unavowable Community*, Blanchot's response to Nancy, published in the autumn of 1983 only a few months after *The Inoperative Community*. As far as the relationship between the two texts is concerned, the game is played out, as we have seen, around the figure of Bataille and around the choice to concentrate on two different periods of his life and work. As a matter of fact, Blanchot's text opens with an indirect yet quite obvious reproach to Nancy's choice to focus on Bataille's postwar production:

It is clear that (approximately) between 1930 and 1940, the word "community" imposed itself on his research [Bataille's] more than during the following periods, even if the publication of *La Part Maudite* and, later, of *L'Erotisme* (which gives precedence to a certain form of communication) prolongs nearly analogous themes which however cannot be subordinated to what came before (there would be others as well: the unfinished text of *La Souveraineté*, the unfinished text on the *Theorie de la Religion*).[76]

This preliminary decision, then, determines the different Bataillean themes that will inform Blanchot's study on community, namely, what he calls "the principle of incompleteness"[77]—and that Bataille in "The Labyrinth" (1935–1936) refers to as the "principle of insufficiency"[78]—and the controversial experience of Acéphale (1936–1939) that Nancy, on the other hand, preferred to overlook because, as he argues, Bataille himself recognized that phase as "a failure."[79]

By considering Acéphale—published review, secret society, religious sect, and subversive political cell—as "the only group that counted for Georges Bataille,"[80] Blanchot introduces at the core of his discourse on community the motif of secrecy and of the "unavowable" that gives the title to his book. Before trying to inquire more closely into Blanchot's "secret," let us begin by saying that, if the experience of the specific community of Acéphale and its operations remain wrapped up in "mystery,"[81] the choice of the name immediately brings us back to the force of the negative as both the avoidance and impossibility of positive definitions. As the famous illustrations by André Masson, accompanying many of the pieces published in the review, show, the alpha privative in *Acéphale* takes the form of a headless man. While, on the one hand, Masson's sketch can be interpreted at many different levels, thus producing a surplus and proliferation of meanings, on the other, and almost paradoxically, the image's polysemic character seems in fact to point toward the dispersion of "meaningfulness" itself. This is a significant point that requires further clarification.

First of all, it is difficult not to read Bataille's and Masson's decapitated man in connection to the sketch of the "Mortal God" appearing on the title page of Hobbes's *Leviathan* and thus in reference to a community that will emerge from the destruction of the absolute political power of the "head" of the state. In this sense, the image can be further interpreted as an allusion to what Derrida calls, in reference to Freud's thesis of the "primal horde" in *Totem and Taboo*, "the mythical moment of the father's murder"[82] as the origin of the social bond. The scene of the primal killing, as the foundation of the communitarian relation, brings out another level of significance of the acephalic body, namely, its link to the sacrificial paradigm that directly emerges from the field of myth.

As we have seen, it is exactly at this problematic juncture that Nancy abandons Bataille's work and actively strives to "interrupt" the mythical scene by resorting to literature or writing. Bataille, on his part, elects myth as the primary tool in the struggle against fascism (as an endeavor to fight the enemy on its very ground) and against, as mentioned, the dry rationalism of capitalist societies and the individualism of liberal democracies.

During the brief span of time that circumscribed the fleeting existence of the community of Acéphale, the sacrificial paradigm might have even figured, at a certain point, as a real possibility, to be performed during one of the society's nocturnal meetings "in a 'sacred' place near a tree struck by lightning."[83] In any case, whether actually planned, merely imagined, or pure and simple provocation, sacrifice remains, in the words of Blanchot, "an obsessive notion for Georges Bataille."[84] Here explicitly opens up the substantial gulf that distances Nancy's and Blanchot's approaches to Bataille. While the former dismisses Bataille's thought of sacrifice as "a disastrous puerility" leading to his final "withdrawal from the communitarian enterprise,"[85] the latter places the notion at the core of the "secret" of Bataille's community, linking it to the semantic constellation of the gift as abandonment, as what "commits the abandoned being to giving without any return in mind, without any calculation and without any safeguard even for his own giving being."[86]

In *The Disavowed Community*, Nancy interprets Blanchot's deployment of "abandonment" as a reference to his own text "Abandoned Being," first published in 1981. While that is certainly the case, Blanchot's formulation of sacrifice as "without return" also strongly echoes Derrida's essay on Bataille "From Restricted to General Economy." In that text Derrida attributes to Bataille a "Hegelianism without Reserve," in the sense that for him Bataille is one of the rare figures that, despite his limited access to the Hegelian oeuvre, mediated mainly through the work of Kojève, "takes it seriously."[87] If "taken one by one and immobilized outside their syntax, all of Bataille's concepts are Hegelian." Derrida argues that one needs also to "grasp the rigorous effect of the trembling to which he submits these concepts, the new configuration into which he displaces and reinscribes them."⁸⁸ In the frame of this movement of dislocation of the Hegelian system, the "sacrifice without return" constitutes, for Derrida, Bataille's "laughter" in the face of the dialectic:

> The notion of *Aufhebung* (the speculative concept par excellence, says Hegel, the concept whose untranslatable privilege is wielded by the German language) is laughable in that it signifies the busying of a discourse losing its breath as it reappropriates all negativity for itself, as it works the "putting at stake" into an *investment*, as it *amortizes* absolute expenditure; and as it gives meaning to death.⁸⁹

Against the calculation of interests, the amortization of loss, the reappropriation of what is given, and the extraction of surplus value offered by dialectical synthesis, useless expenditure, or "the sacrifice without return and without reserve," becomes in Bataille "the absolute sacrifice of meaning."⁹⁰ It is in these terms that we should read my previous comment about the polysemic character of Masson's image actually pointing to the dispersion of meaningfulness itself, while also keeping in mind that what Bataille is after is not mere senselessness. What he is looking for is, rather, a way out of a discourse that can conceive of meaning only in its integrity and in its movement of reappropriation, and—as he argues in "The Sacred Conspiracy," the opening and programmatic article of the first issue of *Acéphale*—of human life "as the head of, or the reason for, the universe."⁹¹

Of course, Blanchot is not blind to the fact that Bataille's sacrificial fantasies turned out to be nothing more than a "mere parody,"⁹² although what I think we should read in this term is not just a reprise of Nancy's "disastrous puerility" but another reference to Bataille's "laughter" and to his own ironic reading of Hegel as the "Sage" in "Hegel, Death, and Sacrifice."⁹³ What essentially distinguishes Bataille's founding sacrifice from the mythical murder of the Freudian horde is, for Blanchot, the very idea of "execution," which, by defining sacrifice as the carrying out of a task, would end up *producing* the community *through* and *as* the labor of a "work."⁹⁴ Conversely, sacrifice as gift and absolute abandonment "founds the community by undoing it."⁹⁵

As Derrida warned us, Blanchot offers us here the first of a long series of "'apparently contradictory' statements"⁹⁶ that will constitute the new logic and poetics of his discourse on community. Two questions arise at this point. The first question goes out to Blanchot: What does it mean, exactly, to "found" community by "undoing" it? The second question, on the other hand, will have to be addressed back at Derrida: Why would Blanchot's contradictory statements be only "apparently" so? And if the contradiction is only apparent, what are we supposed to find beneath it?

Let us interrogate Blanchot first by considering his description of the "community of monks," working here as a formal model for community in general. "The monks divest themselves of what they have, and indeed of themselves, to impart it to the community," says Blanchot, "which in turn makes them again the owners of everything, with God as guarantor."[97] The monks thus transfer their property ("what they have") and their "proper" ("themselves") onto the community only as a way to secure them and get them back in the form of a universal, as the sharing of a property. It is against this rationale that Blanchot tries to think the experience of Acéphale, namely, against a mechanism in which the abandonment of one's "proper" to the community is a merely transitory stage whose goal is to finally return each and all members to their proper self through the attribution of the quality of belonging.

What he sees in Bataille's sacrificial abandonment is an idea of community in which what is "transferred"—or given absolutely, without any expectation of a return—is only a "nothing to give"[98] because it cannot be in any way proper to, or reappropriable by, the individual and because, strictly speaking, there is no proper as such there to give. The possibility of such a community thus takes in Blanchot the form of "the shared experience of that which could not be shared, nor kept as one's own, nor kept back for an ulterior abandonment"[99] simply because it is not a property and, as such, escapes appropriation on both the individual and collective level. On this ground, we can now begin to approach the meaning of the contradictory claim of founding community by undoing it: It is only by "unworking" the mechanism of the dialectic (that is, by undoing the community that emerges as its product) that we can open the possibility for a different understanding of the communitarian experience.

Yet as any of his readers might anticipate, Blanchot is not one to give away the game—the secret—too easily. As a matter of fact, now that we think we have started unraveling the contradiction of "founding by undoing," we merely find ourselves stuck with "the shared experience of that which could not be shared." More than the neutralization of the question or a paralyzing undecidability, Blanchot's text performatively presents us with a movement of thought in which the settling of the contradiction only seems to imply the necessity of stepping into another one.

Does this mean that Blanchot's effort of "unworking" the dialectic of community—at least as far as my reading goes—is just falling prey to the same movement he is trying to undo? If we take Nancy's opinion on the matter, this, before any other, is *The Unavowable Community*'s main flaw. It is already Blanchot's choice of the title for the first part of his book—"The Negative Community"—that alerts Nancy to this possibility. According to him, the negativity Blanchot attributes to the community will have to develop, by necessity, into something else that, although "it will certainly not be possible to think of as a positivity . . . will not escape the 'negative' either" and "will operate a form of sublation [*relève*]."¹⁰⁰

Let us look at the following passage in which Nancy gives us a more detailed description of what he considers to be Blanchot's essentially dialectical movement of thought:

> Indeed it seems that Blanchot, both here and elsewhere, mostly proceeds by a negation of negation (for which the "neuter" becomes the form?) that has the traits of the dialectical *Aufhebung* while subtracting the moment of "synthesis." . . . If the first negation is found in separation (solitude), the second is found in reunion (whether this is separation of or with [*d'avec*] self or from the other, since both terms are themselves produced through separation). Where Hegel constantly seems to propose a third moment, the unity of the two in the third (say, the child or the State, in any case, society, or with Hegel "ethical idea in action"), Blanchot steps back [*se tient en retrait*] by proposing "neither separation nor reunion." However, this neither-nor is not simply positing a nothing between the two. Rather, it is the movement of their simultaneous conjunction and disjunction—*coincidentia oppositorum* (another trace of romantic-idealism).¹⁰¹

The first element worthy of our attention—also because Nancy strangely phrases it in the form of a question, certainly aware of forcing the issue here—is the interpretation of Blanchot's neuter as the result of a negation of negation, that is, as the product of a dialectical *Aufhebung* that simply holds back the moment of synthesis.

The second point to be stressed is the fact that, by recognizing the first stage of Blanchot's movement of negation of negation in "separation" or "solitude," and by understanding it in terms of alienation (namely, as a "separation of or with [*d'avec*] self or from the other"), Nancy argues that Blanchot further negates this stage by "lifting up" the contradiction in the moment of "reunion." Instead of proposing a third, synthetic moment in his otherwise perfectly developed dialectic, Blanchot, in "a sleight of hand" almost bordering on willful "deceit," "tries hard to make us admit" that the "paradox of a conjunction of opposites (presence/absence, gathering/dispersal) is not at all illusory and, on the contrary, refers to the most profound necessity—in fact the thesis (if one can call it thus) of the community."[102]

The hostile tone of Nancy's analysis, barely hidden behind a veil of ironic contempt, is certainly not difficult to spot, and one could go as far as to say that it traverses *The Disavowed Community* as its most striking stylistic feature.[103] In any case, whether Blanchot is trying to "deceive" his readers or whether he simply falls short of his goal, the result of his pseudodialectics is, for Nancy, a "neither . . . nor" negative structure that maintains the opposites in a relation that is, at one and the same time, both conjunctive and disjunctive and that ends up in the unity of opposites, a *coincidentia oppositorum*. In other words, Blanchot's community would be graspable in the ultimate correspondence of the opposed determinations of which it consists, namely, in its constitutive contradictory character.

But is this actually the case? Is Blanchot's solution to the problem of community to be found in a paradoxical (dis)conjunction of opposites, that is, in the contradictions of a community that, despite holding back the moment of synthesis, still effectively mimics the movement of a dialectical progression? Or is the contradiction only "apparent"?

Before following Derrida's lead on this, I would like to point to Nancy's reference to the *coincidentia oppositorum* that, even before signaling Blanchot's "romantic-idealism," is in fact a notion that arises out of the very field of apophatic mysticism that has provided the ground for our readings up to now. First introduced as a term in *De docta ignorantia* (1440) by Nicholas Cusa, whom Nancy explicitly mentions,[104] the idea of the unity of opposites is based on an approach to the divine that relies on a paradoxical "learned unknowing" that directly influenced Bataille's own development of the theme.[105] The reason for this necessary *docta ignorantia* lies in the confrontation between the absolute infinity of the divine and our less than perfect capacity for knowledge and understanding. As absolutely infinite, as the One that contains everything within itself, God cannot be thought, for Cusa, but in terms of a unity of opposites, a *coincidentia oppositorum*.[106]

Yet if we really want to attribute to Blanchot's thought a reliance on some kind of unity of opposites, the real predecessor we would have to go back to is the first "to speak in the neuter singular,"[107] the philosopher after which "everything changes because with him everything begins":[108] Heraclitus the Obscure.

What, according to Blanchot, *changes* with Heraclitus is the drastic shift in perspective that cuts off Being at the root and consigns the world to a movement of incessant becoming. What *begins* is a new language of philosophy, a manner of speaking and writing that opens onto the world of things. Heraclitus's perpetual flux strips the *logos* itself of the possibility of an *arkhē*, as the immutable principle that would be able to escape becoming. Heraclitus's anarchic *logos* does not impose itself on the world of things; it does not manage, organize, or hierarchize their relations. According to Blanchot, "what is language for Heraclitus, what speaks essentially in things and words . . . is Difference itself."[109] A difference that remains unsayable because it is the source of all that is (or, better, *becomes*) and of all speech: an ungraspable, formless, and restless *an-arkhē* that very much behaves like Heraclitus's fire.

To return to our central concern, namely, to Nancy's reading of Blanchot's thought of community as a dialectical contradiction falling back into a unity of opposites, let us note that, within Heraclitus's continuous flux and "other *logos*," the principle of contradiction does not hold. That is, if a contradiction consists in a *coincidentia oppositorum* (A= ¬A) or in the attribution of two opposing predicates to the same entity at the same time (community is neither/both "separation" nor/and "reunion"), then the problem, with Heraclitus as well as with Blanchot, actually lies with "at the same time." In other words, for both of them, there is no "now" in which the opposites could actually coexist, that is, be present simultaneously.

It is in this sense that I suggest interpreting Derrida's allusion to the "apparently contradictory" character of Blanchot's statements. The Heraclitean incessant movement of becoming and the exclusion of the order of the present, also at the core of Blanchot's notion of the disaster, always in transit "from the 'not yet' to the 'no longer,'"[110] deactivates the very possibility of thinking the contradiction, let alone the *simultaneous presence* of opposites.

Therefore, more than based in contradictions, Blanchot's discourse might be better understood in terms of aporias. As Dennis King Keenan notes, the "'not yet' of the aporia interrupts the presentation or recognition of the identity (the 'at the same time') of the contradictories insofar as it is discovered that the moments of aporia are not 'at the same time.'"[111] The disaster, in which the "*Aufhebung* turns inoperable, ceases,"[112] revolves around these aporetic moments that, however, do not imply mere undecidability or a suspension of the opposition. Rather, they introduce an instance of disjunction, as a difficulty in passage (*a-poros*) from one term to the other and as the exit from the processual becoming-identical of contradictories.

If the main difference between Nancy's and Blanchot's treatment of community originates in their diverging approaches to Bataille, Blanchot also offers us an alternative trajectory, approaching Levinas rather than Heidegger. Whereas Nancy goes toward Heidegger's ontology, Blanchot finds his complement to Bataille in Levinas's moral philosophy, which, refusing the very idea of an ethics of reciprocity, foregrounds instead the radical asymmetry inherent to every ethical encounter and the ensuing call for an infinite, nonmutual responsibility.

It is through Levinas, in fact, that Blanchot reads Bataille's "principle of insufficiency." This leads him away from a dialectic of recognition, already challenged by Nancy, and, by introducing a fundamental dissymmetry in the relation with an irreducible other, Blanchot tries at the same time to avoid the risk of flattening the "with" into a relation of reciprocity or, as Critchley puts it, a rubbing of the shoulders. The obliquity of the relation Blanchot envisages, however, is not simply a result of its irreciprocity but also of its being a relation that, as we saw in the case of Bataille, never leads to fusion but disrupts the logic of dialogue and copresence through the opening of an "outside."

While Blanchot "places brackets around the terms 'ethics' and 'God' and hence holds back from the metaphysical affirmation of the Good beyond Being,"[113] what draws him to Levinas is certainly the relation the latter institutes between the Other and language. In a movement similar to what I have tried to configure as the relation between the apophatic and the cataphatic, inscription and exscription, the creation of the work (*oeuvre*) and worklessness (*désoeuvrement*), Levinas's ethics is in fact traversed by the difficult tension between the Saying (*le dire*) and the Said (*le dit*). This tension between the prelinguistic ethical encounter that founds language, on the one hand, and linguistic expression, on the other, results in the philosophical attempt to give a propositional account of what is at the very foundation of the possibility of language itself.

However, as Bruns argues, in Blanchot, as opposed to Levinas, "the other speaks not from an inaccessible height but from the outside, outside the 'speech of power.'"[114] At play, more than Levinas's noncognizable, absolute transcendence of *autrui*, is a certain "strangeness between man and man," an "experience in which the Other, the Outside itself, exceeding any positive or negative term," cannot be thought "either in terms of transcendence or in terms of immanence."[115] Rather, the "non-isomorphic field" in which the relation articulates itself would be the space of the neutral, "if it is well understood that the neutral does not annul, does not neutralize."[116]

The space of the neuter, which does not cancel out but rather exceeds affirmation and negation, the positive and the negative, can be understood here as an attempt to resist the very real possibility that "the Other man who is '*autrui*' also risks being always Other than man, close to what cannot be close to me: close to death, close to the night, and certainly as repulsive as anything that comes to me from these regions without horizon."[117] Blanchot's decisive insight thus concerns the essential ambiguity both of the relation, where the "other man" is always exposed to the peril of becoming "other than man," as well as of affirmation and negation. If, as Paolo Virno has highlighted, a linguistic negation can easily turn into a concrete means for the annihilation of the other, as with the "Nazi lieutenant, who says 'nonhuman' with reference to the old, weeping Jewish man,"[118] the positive, in Blanchot's eyes, can be no less pernicious, in its assertive relation to the realm of truth, to what can be known, and, as its etymology indicates, posited, presupposed, fixed in a definition.

This is the main reason, I would argue, that brings Blanchot to substitute a schema of recognition with a principle of "contestation." As he states: "A being does not want to be recognized, it wants to be contested."[119] Now, how are we to read this term? We could certainly interpret it in a Levinasian sense, as a rejection of the dialecticity implicit in a relation of recognition and as the approach of the Other coming to disturb and contest the tranquil identity of the Same and calling it to responsibility. But I believe this would miss the deeper point. Contestation, in fact, is also a notion that Blanchot derives from the work of Bataille, halfway between political stance and "limit-experience." As Blanchot explains, Bataille's "inner experience," which "cannot be distinguished from contestation,"[120] has offered him the model of "an affirmation, for the first time, that is not a product (the result of a double negation), and that thereby escapes all the movements, oppositions and reversals of dialectical reason."[121] Or, in the words Foucault uses in "Preface to Transgression," contestation in Blanchot "is this philosophy of non-positive affirmation," which "does not imply a generalized negation, but an affirmation that affirms nothing, a radical break of transitivity."[122]

Let us try to clarify this complex and, once again, almost paradoxical formulation: Contestation is an affirmative movement that escapes the dialectic, but it is an affirmation that is nonpositive and that, ultimately, affirms nothing. What I think is really at play in Blanchot's nonpositive affirmation is, on the one hand, an *affirmation of what is nonpositive*, in the sense of not posited, fixed, or immobilized, namely, of "Difference itself," as it speaks in language while making language speak. On the other hand, to "affirm nothing" does not mean to "affirm nothingness" but rather to let everything *positively escape affirmation*, linked as it is, in its etymological derivation in the Latin *firmare*, to the halting of a movement, to an action of enclosing, and to the firm grasp exercised over an object of knowledge.

AN ETHICS OF NONPOSITIVE AFFIRMATION

We can now begin to better understand the claim I advanced at the beginning of this essay, concerning Blanchot's deployment of the negative as what does not determine or annihilate but rather contains affirmative potentialities while putting itself at risk in language in the attempt to deactivate the mechanism of the proper itself.

In his analysis of Blanchot's fiction and its use of negative modifiers, or "unwords," Shane Weller concludes, in stark contrast to Nancy's reading, that Blanchot's writing articulates an "experience of estranged negativity"[123] that actually divests the dialectic of its driving force in a movement of dislocation that approximates Bataille's abandoning sacrifice. Weller interprets Blanchot's use of negation as a "high risk strategy" dictated by the attempt "to try to speak of that which resists articulation"[124] and that "preserves the adjectival force at the expense of the nominal."[125] Taking our cue from Weller, I would like now to briefly look at some instances of "unwording" we encounter in *The Unavowable Community*. What is really at stake in formulations such as "sharing of what cannot be shared,"[126] "transmission of the untransmittable,"[127] or "knowledge of what cannot be known"?[128]

I argue that, more than the preservation of the adjectival against the nominal, as Weller suggests, Blanchot's linguistic negativism in *The Unavowable Community* seems to follow the exact reverse path: In the relationship between the nominal form and the negative modifier, what is effectively subtracted is the possibility of a positive predication. Blanchot's nonpositive affirmation thus takes the form of a contestation of, and a resistance to, the attribution and the self-attribution of properties. Most crucially, what is negated in all these cases is the "proper" of the nominal itself, leaving us with a "knowledge" and a "sharing" that have at their core nothing else than their own nonproperty of "unknowability" and "unsharability."

Now, what do the notions of contestation and nonpositive affirmation, that I have developed out of Blanchot's thought on community, have to do with a concrete, ethical practice? Are they not empty paradoxical formulations that remain—to return to Esposito's words here—politically and ethically untranslatable? I would actually claim that, if anything, the "sharing of what cannot be shared" might be a very good approximation of what constitutes the ethical demand as such, since the injustice, the violence, and the suffering inflicted upon the other are exactly, and paradoxically, what *cannot* yet what *needs* to be shared. In this sense, the notion of contestation might help us frame an ethics of commitment and collective testimony (from *con-*, "together," and *testare*, "to witness") in which the ground for a nondialectical mediation is offered not by the unified and exclusionary ethos of the community but by a plurality of multiple voices, articulated from their highly contingent (and contiguous) standpoints. In the same way, to suspend the possibility of a positive predication, far from being a mere shallow exercise in political correctness, can effectively work as a political strategy that allows for the constitution of a different idea of community, one not grounded upon or arrogantly arrogating for itself its own "proper."

What I claim, albeit in different ways, Nancy's and Blanchot's texts pass on to us—after having thought it to the limit, and at the limit of (their) thought—is the difficult task of finally finding a way to disjoin the seemingly indissociable connection that ties community to the "proper," at a moment in which every invocation of community functions as a call to the self-righteous and violent defense of the proper (of various types of identities, territories, cultures, or even civilizations) and in which every defense of the proper (as property, ownership, and as exclusive and autochthonous rights and privileges) finds its justification in the moral undertones the notion of community continues to carry.

NOTES

1. This essay's epigraph is from Wisława Szymborska, "The Three Oddest Words," in *Poems New and Collected, 1957–1997*, trans. Stanisław Barańczak and Clare Cavanagh (New York: Harcourt, 1998), 261.

2. Aristotle, *Nicomachean Ethics*, trans. Harris Rackham (Cambridge, MA: Harvard University Press, 1982), 1109 b.20.

3. Miranda Joseph, *Against the Romance of Community* (Minneapolis: University of Minnesota Press, 2002).

4. Viola Marchi, "Ethics, Interrupted: Community and Impersonality in Levinas," *SPELL* 32 (2015): 143–58.

5. Jacques Derrida, *The Politics of Friendship*, trans. George Collins (London: Verso, 2005), 47n15.

6. Derrida, *The Politics of Friendship*, 47n15.

7. Derrida, *The Politics of Friendship*, 47n15.

8. John R. Hinnells, ed., *The Routledge Companion to the Study of Religion* (London: Routledge, 2005), 307.

9. Denys Turner, *The Darkness of God: Negativity in Christian Mysticism* (Cambridge: Cambridge University Press, 1995), 20.

10. Eugene Thacker, *After Life* (Chicago: University of Chicago Press, 2010), 40.

11. Turner, *The Darkness of God*, 22.

12. Turner, *The Darkness of God*, 35.

13. Jean-Christophe Bailly et al., eds., "La communauté, le nombre," *Aléa* 4 (1983), special issue.

14. Jean-Luc Nancy, "The Confronted Community," trans. Jason Kemp Winfree, in *The Obsessions of Georges Bataille: Community and Communication*, ed. Andrew J. Mitchell and Jason Kemp Winfree (Albany: SUNY Press, 2009), 21.

15. Jean-Luc Nancy, *The Inoperative Community*, trans. Peter Connor et al. (Minneapolis: University of Minnesota Press, 1991), 15.

16. Nancy, *The Inoperative Community*, 13.

17. G. W. F. Hegel, *The Phenomenology of Spirit*, trans. Michael Inwood (Oxford: Oxford University Press, 2018), 86.

18. Hegel, *The Phenomenology of Spirit*, 187.

19. Hegel, *The Phenomenology of Spirit*, 181.

20. Hegel, *The Phenomenology of Spirit*, 177.

21. Andreas Wagner, "Jean-Luc Nancy—A Negative Politics?," *Philosophy and Social Criticism* 32, no. 1 (2006): 93.

22. Nancy, *The Inoperative Community*, 16.

23. Nancy, *The Inoperative Community*, 16.

24. Nancy, *The Inoperative Community*, 16.

25. Nancy, *The Inoperative Community*, 17.

26. Nancy, *The Inoperative Community*, 17.

27. Nancy, *The Inoperative Community*, 25.

28. Nancy, *The Inoperative Community*, 25.

29. Jean-Luc Nancy, *The Disavowed Community*, trans. Philip Armstrong (New York: Fordham University Press, 2016), 12.

30. Meant as a collection of some of his writings, Bataille worked on it until his death, without ever finalizing the arrangement of the content. Of the five volumes that were supposed to constitute the *Summa*, Bataille published only *Inner Experience* (1943), *Guilty* (1944), and *On Nietzsche* (1945); *Pure Happiness* and *The*

Unfinished System of Non-knowledge were never completed. In 2001, Stuart Kendall, in a careful reconstruction of what the two remaining volumes might have looked like, published *The Unfinished System of Non-knowledge*, ed. Stuart Kendall, trans. Michelle Kendall and Stuart Kendall (Minneapolis: University of Minnesota Press, 2007).

31. On Bataille's insistence on this bizarre coupling, see Amy Hollywood, "Bataille and Mysticism: A 'Dazzling Dissolution,'" *Diacritics* 26, no. 2 (1996): 74–85.

32. Jeremy Biles and Kent L. Brintnall, eds., *Negative Ecstasies: Georges Bataille and the Study of Religion* (New York: Fordham University Press, 2015), 6.

33. Georges Bataille, *The Accursed Share: An Essay on General Economy*, vol. 1, trans. Robert Hurley (New York: Zone, 1988), 25–26.

34. Georges Bataille, *Eroticism*, trans. Mary Dalwood (London: Penguin, 2012), 91.

35. Bataille, *Eroticism*, 11.

36. Georges Bataille, *The Accursed Share: An Essay on General Economy*, vols. 2–3, trans. Robert Hurley (New York: Zone, 1989), 208.

37. Hollywood, "Bataille and Mysticism," 79.

38. Eugene Thacker, *Starry Speculative Corpse* (Alresford: Zero, 2015), 35–36.

39. See Georges Bataille's discussion of the *potlatch* in "The Notion of Expenditure," in *Visions of Excess: Selected Writings, 1927–1939*, trans. Allan Stoekl with Carl R. Lovitt and Donald M. Leslie Jr. (Minneapolis: University of Minnesota Press, 1985), 116–29.

40. Maurice Blanchot, *The Infinite Conversation*, trans. Susan Hanson (Minneapolis: University of Minnesota Press, 1993), 209.

41. Nancy, *The Inoperative Community*, 18.

42. Nancy, *The Inoperative Community*, 4.

43. Nancy, *The Inoperative Community*, 31.

44. Nancy, *The Inoperative Community*, 6.

45. Hollywood, "Bataille and Mysticism," 82.

46. Hollywood, "Bataille and Mysticism," 83.

47. Bataille, *Eroticism*, 275.

48. Jean-Luc Nancy, "Exscription," trans. Katherine Lydon, *Yale French Studies* 78 (1990): 60.

49. Nancy, "Exscription," 63.

50. On this notion, see Benjamin Noys, *Georges Bataille: A Critical Introduction* (London: Pluto, 2000), 5–14.

51. Nancy, "Exscription," 64.

52. Nancy, "Exscription," 64.

53. Nancy, *The Inoperative Community*, 54.

54. Nancy, *The Inoperative Community*, 62.

55. Nancy, *The Inoperative Community*, 65.
56. Turner, *The Darkness of God*, 35.
57. I would like to point out here the parallelism between Agamben's choice of the adjective "ferocious" and Bataille's famous affirmation in "The Sacred Conspiracy": "WE ARE FEROCIOUSLY RELIGIOUS." Georges Bataille, "The Sacred Conspiracy," in *Visions of Excess: Selected Writings, 1927–1939*, trans. Allan Stoekl with Carl R. Lovitt and Donald M. Leslie Jr. (Minneapolis: University of Minnesota Press, 1985), 179.
58. Giorgio Agamben, "The Silhouette of Jean-Luc Nancy," in *Nancy Now*, ed. Verena Andermatt Conley and Irving Goh (Cambridge: Polity, 2014), xi–xii.
59. Agamben, "The Silhouette of Jean-Luc Nancy," xi.
60. Agamben, "The Silhouette of Jean-Luc Nancy," xi.
61. Eugene Thacker, "Dark Media," in *Excommunication: Three Inquiries in Media and Mediation*, ed. Alexander Galloway, Eugene Thacker, and McKenzie Wark (Chicago: University of Chicago Press, 2014), 107.
62. Simon Critchley, *Ethics-Politics-Subjectivity: Essays on Derrida, Levinas, and Contemporary French Thought* (London: Verso, 1999), 248.
63. Nancy, "The Confronted Community," 21.
64. See Nancy, *The Inoperative Community*, esp. 23.
65. Nancy, *The Inoperative Community*, 14.
66. Nancy, *The Inoperative Community*, 22.
67. Thacker, "Dark Media," 136.
68. Nancy, *The Inoperative Community*, 19.
69. Wagner, "Jean-Luc Nancy," 113.
70. Roberto Esposito, "Community, Immunity, Biopolitics," trans. Michela Russo, *Política común* 3 (2012): n.p.
71. Critchley, *Ethics-Politics-Subjectivity*, 250.
72. Critchley, *Ethics-Politics-Subjectivity*, 249.
73. Critchley, *Ethics-Politics-Subjectivity*, 251.
74. Critchley, *Ethics-Politics-Subjectivity*, 251.
75. Critchley, *Ethics-Politics-Subjectivity*, 252.
76. Maurice Blanchot, *The Unavowable Community*, trans. Pierre Joris (Barrytown, NY: Station Hill, 1988), 4.
77. Blanchot, *The Unavowable Community*, 5.
78. Georges Bataille, "The Labyrinth," in *Visions of Excess: Selected Writings, 1927–1939*, trans. Allan Stoekl with Carl R. Lovitt and Donald M. Leslie Jr. (Minneapolis: University of Minnesota Press, 1985), 172.
79. Nancy, *The Disavowed Community*, 12.
80. Blanchot, *The Unavowable Community*, 13.
81. Blanchot, *The Unavowable Community*, 13.

82. Derrida, *The Politics of Friendship*, 47.

83. Allan Stoekl, introduction to *Visions of Excess: Selected Writings, 1927–1939*, trans. Allan Stoekl with Carl R. Lovitt and Donald M. Leslie Jr. (Minneapolis: University of Minnesota Press, 1985), xx.

84. Blanchot, *The Unavowable Community*, 15.

85. Nancy, *The Inoperative Community*, 17.

86. Blanchot, *The Unavowable Community*, 57–58n6.

87. Jacques Derrida, "From Restricted to General Economy: A Hegelianism without Reserve," in *Writing and Difference*, trans. Alan Bass (London: Routledge, 2001), 319.

88. Derrida, "From Restricted to General Economy," 320.

89. Derrida, "From Restricted to General Economy," 324.

90. Derrida, "From Restricted to General Economy," 324.

91. Bataille, "The Sacred Conspiracy," 180.

92. Blanchot, *The Unavowable Community*, 14.

93. Georges Bataille, "Hegel, Death, and Sacrifice," *Yale French Studies* 78 (1990): 9–28.

94. See Blanchot, *The Unavowable Community*, 58n7.

95. Blanchot, *The Unavowable Community*, 15.

96. Derrida, *The Politics of Friendship*, 47.

97. Blanchot, *The Unavowable Community*, 15.

98. Blanchot, *The Unavowable Community*, 15.

99. Blanchot, *The Unavowable Community*, 15.

100. Nancy, *The Disavowed Community*, 15.

101. Nancy, *The Disavowed Community*, 35.

102. Nancy, *The Disavowed Community*, 35.

103. As Philip Armstrong points out in the introduction to Nancy's *The Disavowed Community*, the book "lies open here like an open wound ... everywhere characterized by this sense of exposure and susceptibility, liability and vulnerability" (xiii).

104. Nancy, *The Disavowed Community*, 15.

105. In 1931–1932, Bataille attended Alexandre Koyré's lectures on Nicholas Cusa's *De docta ignorantia* at the École Pratique des Hautes Études. Interestingly enough, the course on Cusa was followed, in 1933–1934, by one on Hegel's philosophy of religion still taught by Koyré. See Rodolphe Gasché, *Georges Bataille: Phenomenology and Phantasmatology*, trans. Roland Végső (Stanford, CA: Stanford University Press, 2012), 239; and Stuart Kendall, *Georges Bataille* (London: Reaktion, 2007), 90.

106. See Dermot Moran, "Nicholas Cusa and Modern Philosophy," in *The Cambridge Companion to Renaissance Philosophy*, ed. James Hankins (Cambridge: Cambridge University Press, 2007), 182.

107. Blanchot, *The Infinite Conversation*, 299.

108. Blanchot, *The Infinite Conversation*, 89.
109. Blanchot, *The Infinite Conversation*, 89.
110. Maurice Blanchot, *Vicious Circles: Two Fictions and "After the Fact,"* trans. Paul Auster (Barrytown, NY: Station Hill, 1985), 60.
111. Dennis Keenan King, *Hegel and Contemporary Continental Philosophy* (Albany: SUNY Press, 2004), 51.
112. Maurice Blanchot, *The Writing of the Disaster*, trans. Ann Smock (Lincoln: University of Nebraska Press, 1995), 40.
113. Simon Critchley, *Very Little . . . Almost Nothing* (London: Routledge, 1997), 96.
114. Gerald L. Bruns, "Blanchot/Levinas: Interruption (On the Conflict of Alterities)," *Research in Phenomenology* 26 (1996): 146.
115. Blanchot, *The Infinite Conversation*, 71.
116. Blanchot, *The Infinite Conversation*, 71.
117. Blanchot, *The Infinite Conversation*, 72.
118. Paolo Virno, *Multitude: Between Innovation and Negation*, trans. Isabella Bertoletti, James Cascaito, and Andrea Casson (Los Angeles: Semiotext(e), 2008), 187.
119. Blanchot, *The Unavowable Community*, 6.
120. Blanchot, *The Infinite Conversation*, 208.
121. Blanchot, *The Infinite Conversation*, 209.
122. Michel Foucault, "Preface to Transgression," in *Language, Counter-memory, Practice: Selected Essays and Interviews*, ed. Donald F. Bouchard, trans. Donald F. Bouchard and Sherry Simon (Ithaca, NY: Cornell University Press, 1977), 36.
123. Shane Weller, "Voidance: Linguistic Negativism in Blanchot's Fiction," *French Studies: A Quarterly Review* 69, no. 1 (January 2015): 32.
124. Weller, "Voidance," 45.
125. Weller, "Voidance," 44.
126. Blanchot, *The Unavowable Community*, 15.
127. Blanchot, *The Unavowable Community*, 18.
128. Blanchot, *The Unavowable Community*, 127.

Other Others

Ethics 2.0 and the Problem of the "Unsynthesizable"

Commonality versus Individuality
An Ethical Dilemma?

Étienne Balibar

More than ever these days, we find ourselves caught in a debate about ethics where the values of "communitarianism" and of "individualism" are opposed. On one side, with more or less substitutability, such values as solidarity, belonging, fraternity, recognition; on the other side, such values as utility or personal agency, self-entrepreneurship, and self-achievement. On both sides there are notions of rights, duties, interests. Before entering the debate, which I would like to historicize and problematize, allow me to propose a terminological convention. I will place the simple defense of each orientation in the realm of *moral discourses* (and doctrines), and I will preserve the category "ethics" for more complex, reflexive positions, in which it is a question of constructing the value of the individual from *within* the idea of the community, in relation to its existence, and conversely. This will lead me, in my conclusion, to insist on the importance, in these matters, of thinking always in *relational terms.*

I pursue a threefold objective. First, I want to delineate a genealogy of the opposition itself, showing its *metapolitical* character (which generally is a specificity of ethics, when it tries to provide politics with foundations or representations of its ends, therefore entering with politics into a constitutive circular relation). Second, I want to ask in which sense this opposition is typically "modern," by invoking classical "narratives" of the construction of modernity, such as Max Weber's (for whom "individualism" is typically a juridical invention) and Karl Marx's (for whom it is essentially a consequence of the development of economic structures: capitalism and the market).[1] Third, I want to see if a confrontation between Marx and Foucault helps us understand the question. Apparently, they fall right into the antithetic pattern, with Marx the "socialist" on the communitarian side and Foucault the Nietzschean aesthete on the individualist—even the hyperindividualist—side. Nevertheless, Marx and Foucault have several things in common, to begin with, their critique of the "empirical-transcendental doublet" of modern bourgeois anthropology, which serves as a foundation for the various institutions mediating the social and moral tensions between the principles of liberty and equality. On this basis, it should be possible to show that Marx's communism is not just a patriotism of the national community displaced and Foucault's individualism a variety of libertarian anarchism.

I shall discuss these issues in two moments, each divided into three parts, to begin with the question of the "abstract individual" and conclude on the question of the "ontology of relation."

FROM "CIVIC-BOURGEOIS UNIVERSALISM" TO CONFLICTUAL VISIONS OF CITIZENSHIP

In my perception, the question of the abstract individual is a direct correlative of the emergence of an ideological and institutional formation which I call civic-bourgeois universalism (as expressed in the great *Declarations of Rights* and the constitutions of the American and the French revolutions at the end of the eighteenth century). In analyzing its structure, I rely mainly on two authors who diverge on essential points but are both *institutionalists*: Hegel (in the 1820 *Philosophy of Right*) and Arendt (particularly in her analysis of the crisis of the nation-state and the rights of man).[2] For them, the individual who appears as a bearer of rights and a potential citizen is not naturally "given"; he needs to be constructed historically through the work of institutions. It is in this framework that we can understand the crucial articulation of what Arendt calls "the right to have rights," with its two sides: an active participation in the public sphere and a more passive subjecthood coinciding with the acquisition of legal personality. Since Locke's *Second Treatise of Government*, this double aspect has been philosophically reflected in the category of "self-ownership" of the individual.[3] This legal and social construction becomes philosophically expressed in what Foucault has called the "empirical-transcendental doublet" as an instrument to reduce anthropological differences and subject them to the abstraction of the universal subject.[4] Importantly, reducing is not erasing: Anthropological differences (of culture or "nationality," race, gender, age, morality or "character," etc.) are not *suppressed* or *ignored* by a philosopher like Kant (the key reference here), but they are *particularized* and inscribed in the realm of empiricity (the various modes of articulation of "nature" and "culture" in the history and geography of mankind). This in turn makes it possible to subject them to the universality of human *moral* nature (defining the transcendental subject, common to all humans, who is also the bearer of rights and the agent of absolute morality). This speculative articulation acquires a practical function, when it comes to devising the institutional forms that prescribe the transformation of individuals into citizens (particularly *pedagogy*), which simultaneously emphasize (or categorize) differences and valorize—through imposing as a norm—the features of the abstract individual.[5]

A second look at this complex dialectic shows that we can express the abstraction in a symmetric manner. An abstract individual (who is essentially defined in moral and juridical terms, what Hegel after Locke will call "the person") is represented as a formal member of an abstract community (the body politic, or community of citizens), but each of these two abstractions also needs to acquire a "concrete" form of existence. For the community of citizens, this is essentially provided when citizenship is equated with *national* membership and the normative character that is imposed on all members is represented as national or even "ethnic" identity.[6] For the individual, this is provided by *conditions of normality*, which command the practical use of the various differences (for example, gender differences) in the social processes with a civic function: education, work, judiciary procedures, etc. I will come to this more precisely in my second part.[7]

We must now pause to examine different genealogies that have been proposed for this grand narrative, which lies at the core of the "sociological tradition" since the early nineteenth century: indicating how individual "subjects" became isolated as such, detached from their constitutive memberships, therefore at the same time *alienated* and *liberated* (we might speak paradoxically of an "alienating autonomy").[8] Why are there rival genealogies?

Because one, best illustrated by Max Weber, emphasizes the *legal determination*, whereas the second, best illustrated by Marx, emphasizes the *economic determination*. The first essentially characterizes the abstract individual as a legal subject, whereas the second derives its properties from the notion of "*Homo economicus.*" In the Weberian genealogy, as very clearly explained by Catherine Colliot-Thélène, the decisive moment is provided by the emergence of "subjective rights" for the individual, which are rooted in the state's *monopoly of legislation* (and not only "monopoly of violence").[9] In the Marxian genealogy, "private owners" of themselves (who can become contractors of their own capacities, especially their "labor power") are historically released from their membership in closed, self-sustaining communities, through the dissolving effect of market relations (both internal and external). Importantly, this *production of the abstract* in history affects both the "capitalist" and the "proletarian" subject because they are both contractors with equal formal rights (which, of course, in Marx's explanation, serve to implement a highly dissymmetric power relation). We seem to have yet another "doublet," which materially underpins the philosophical construction of the anthropological doublet.

Leaving aside a closer discussion of Max Weber's genealogy (which would be just as important), I want to qualify the (common) representation of Marx's genealogy as purely "economic" (if not economicist), which I have just reproduced. In fact, Marx's account is more complex (and more dialectical) because it includes an essential *juridical moment* in its construction of the capitalist social relation. This emerges when (essentially in volume 1 of *Capital*, chapter 2, "The Process of Exchange") Marx analyzes a formal structure (one could see it as the great "structuralist" moment in *Capital*) where the relationship of *exchange among equivalents* (commodities incorporating the same amount of "social labor") is mirrored in a *contractual relationship among persons* (the owners of the commodities), which have the same formal properties. Each of them is at the same time an "image" of the other and the practical complement without which it would not work. Accordingly, there is a "fetishism of persons" just as there is a "fetishism of commodities," both of them representing an abstraction imposed by the logic of the market and generating its own antithetic bearers (individual values, individual subjects). This structure is directly inspired by Hegel's exposition of "abstract right," but with an addition and a subtraction. What is added is the typically Marxian correspondence between the economic form (of circulation) and the juridical form (of contract). What is subtracted is the final moment in Hegel's dialectic of abstract right, namely, the introduction of "penal law" into the system of juridical forms, which transforms a mere "legal subject" (property owner) into a *responsible*, practically *accountable subject*. This development is achieved in Hegel through the consideration of the reverse side of any lawful relation, the moment of *illegality* and *crime* (both expressed in German as *Unrecht*), which in turn calls for judiciary institutions (the courts, the penal code, the trial and the punishment). This is what Marx in his structural account of the genealogy of abstraction leaves aside or postpones, therefore relegates to a derivative function.[10] As a consequence, he also brackets (or postpones) the possibility of investigating the *moral* dimension of subjectivation as an essential element of the social structure, which goes beyond the "repressive" function of the legal apparatus and the state, subjecting the abstract individuality to a system of responsibility, recognition, accountability, and guilt.

In Althusserian terms, this would be the "interpellation of individuals as subjects," which also "interpellates" subjects *as individuals*, in order to make them *personally responsible* before the law and their own moral consciousness. From this also derives his problematic identification of bourgeois ideology with the mere domination of the values of utilitarianism or "egoism," as it is eloquently formulated in a famous passage of *Capital* (vol. 1, chap. 6), where he describes the sphere of the circulation of commodities as "the very Eden of the innate rights of man," ironically naming them "liberty, equality, property, and Bentham."[11] This does powerfully indicate the complementarity of bourgeois law and "individualistic" values with the logic of the market and its generalization (therefore it is very relevant today) but also erases other aspects of abstract individuality that are linked with the interiorization of such transindividual values as patriotism (Hegel's *Gesinnung* in the *Philosophy of Right*) or what Nietzsche and Freud described as the intimate (even unconscious) "guilt" (*Schuldgefühl*) of the bourgeois subject. The articulation of "rights" and "duties" appears more one-sided, less ambivalent and contradictory than it is in reality.

This leads us to the third moment within this first part of my discussion: the tension between antithetic "foundations" of bourgeois universalism. The genealogies of the abstract individual that I was discussing or alluding to (Weber) are not only reproducing a narrative of the construction of the bourgeois universe; they can be said to give a preference to the *constitutional* dimension of this universalism. But in history, bourgeois universalism has indeed two faces, which alternate and contradict each other: the *constitutional* and the *insurrectional* dimensions. It is important here to return to the Lockean formulation: "property in one's person" (later translated as "self-ownership," which tends to lose one of the two aspects). We know that this originally was a political motto that Locke borrowed (and appropriated) from the discourse of seventeenth-century English revolutionaries, particularly the Levellers.[12] Here we meet another aspect of the "right to have rights," which is never entirely forgotten or can always become resurrected, against a purely "statist" interpretation of "subjective rights": the emancipatory claim of rights on behalf of individuals and especially collective movements, who not only seek to emancipate themselves from what Kant later will call their "nonage" (*Unmündigkeit*) but achieve a collective subjectivation that is intrinsically political in a *noninstitutional form.* The rights that they vindicate have no precedent; they do not preexist their insurrection, in the broad sense of the term. Rousseau, of course, is an explicit supporter of this insurrectional concept of subjective rights, which make it possible for individuals to become incorporated as citizens into the "general will" of the community (people). We find the trace of his description in Hegel's understanding of the "spirit" immanent in a historical community that *collectively acts as a single subject* (*das Tun aller und jeder*).[13] Above all we find it in the Marxian definition of "class consciousness" as the *becoming conscious* of the class struggle, which is conceived as a transindividual *praxis*.

Insurrectional foundations in the broad sense amount to directly asserting (against privileges and "vertical" forms of power) the "proposition of equaliberty," with its civic implications. But the equivalence of liberty and equality is always problematic and aporetic; therefore constitutional regimes substitute the "pure" political principle with social mediations that variously combine regimes of property and regimes of community, the distribution of ownership and the conditions of membership.[14] The most recent historical example (which of course is crucial to understanding transformations of the political in Europe and the modalities of its current crisis) is provided by the institution of contemporary welfare states, incorporating the recognition of social rights into a national framework (what in other places I called the "national-social state"). What I want now to emphasize is the fact that such constructed mediations always add to the mere form of "possessive individualism" another individualistic dimension, which I will call "reflexive individualism" because it incorporates a capacity of individuals to *judge* their own behavior and the behavior of others (holding themselves and others *accountable* for their deeds, their mores) according to criteria of *normality and abnormality*. If we return for a moment to the philosophical problematic of the "empirical-transcendental subject," we see that it becomes associated with another doublet (or antithesis), which is the "pathological doublet" (the antithesis of normality and deviancy). It is of course the great achievement of Foucault to have analyzed this correspondence throughout his work (in which, for obvious reasons, I grant a special importance to the lectures at the Collège de France titled *Abnormal*).[15] The imperative that dominates the construction of abstract individuals and their "concrete" realization centrally includes *normality* (of course a fluctuating notion) as a "subjective" precondition for the articulation of ownership and self-ownership with a conscious and "responsible" incorporation in the community. We might say that, by rejecting their own abnormality (or struggling endlessly against it), individuals realize the condition for *not being excluded*, or simply *exclude themselves from exclusion*, thus anticipating their recognition by the society, the state, and first of all their fellow citizens. There is not much distance, I have to admit, between such a problematic and the old moral and political question of "voluntary servitude" (since La Boétie onward).[16] The rule of norms is inherent in the construction of social identities that grant any subject the recognition without which the society in practice denies the "right to have rights" in a community of "autonomous" citizens. This is the general target of Nietzsche's criticism and the very object of Foucault's genealogy, which essentially aims at analyzing, historicizing, and problematizing processes of identification and normalization.[17]

The question becomes now: What is Marx's position with respect to this issue of identification-normalization? Does he just ignore the problem? Or does he "resolve" it by contrasting "bourgeois" values with "proletarian" values that feature a symmetric form of identity with its own mode of normality ("class consciousness")? The latter was frequently the case in the history of revolutionary and communist organizations, but as regards Marx himself, the problem is clearly more complicated. We need to embark on a second wave of discussion.

"IMPOLITICAL" CRITIQUES OF BOURGEOIS UNIVERSALISM

In this second part of my discussion, I come to a more precise comparison of Marx and Foucault as critics of bourgeois society. But, just as Marx is impossible to understand aside from his continuous relationship to Hegel, Foucault is impossible to understand aside from his avowed relationship to

Nietzsche on "moral" matters. Both criticisms share this character: They target *social functions* (and *uses*) of a "dominant ideology"; therefore they subvert social institutions of political power (or, in the case of Foucault, "police" in the broad sense, which Rancière will oppose to emancipatory politics), but more profoundly they touch the *anthropology* that is presupposed and also reproduced by the institutions, the insurrections, the cultural changes. This is where resonances of Marx within Nietzsche and conversely may appear at a closer reading. They refer to the "transformation" of the human in history considered as a self-production of man through the mediation of powers, disciplines, structures of domination, and revolutions. As Foucault suggests in an interview from 1978 with Duccio Trombadori, one could read Marx's "production of man by man" also as a *destruction* of what man (meaning in fact "all of us") used to be and therefore the transition to communism as a *becoming other of human beings*.[18] This explains why I make use of the category of the "impolitical" in this context, to evoke an aspect of practice that exceeds both utopias and heterotopias or that is intrinsically "excessive" with regard to the *norm* representing the human as a given essence.[19] Leaving aside other uses of this category (especially those with religious connotations), it allows us to focus on the relationship between Marx and Nietzsche as critics providing alternative patterns of deconstruction of the existing institutions of individuality and community.

We can think of different ways of confronting Marx and Nietzsche, since this was in a sense the core of the development of critical theory in the twentieth century. It would seem that a good point of entry is provided by the antithesis of the categories *praxis* and *poiesis*, referring to Marx and Nietzsche respectively. A philosophy of *praxis* aims at "changing the world" (*Veränderung der Welt*, in the *Theses on Feuerbach*), where it is a question of transforming the *social world*, the ensemble or totality of social relations, through a political revolution. A philosophy (for some commentators, an antiphilosophy) of *poiesis* conversely seems to limit itself to a task of "interpretation"—but according to Nietzsche, interpretation is an *active* attitude or a way of life, since it leads to the "transmutation of values" (*Umwertung aller psychischen Werte*). As Bataille and Foucault interpreted it in turn, the main road to this transmutation is provided by "limit experiences" with an aesthetic value (not aesthetic value incorporated into separated *objects* but incorporated into individual life itself). This is a classical dilemma, but one that cannot simply appear as repetition of the "bourgeois" antithesis of individuality and community. Rather it *displaces* this antithesis onto new terms. How radical is this displacement?

We must first understand that Marx's scheme of "alienation" and the negation of the negation is not just a way of *historicizing* the naturalism of the "human essence" but (closely following the Hegelian dialectical pattern in this respect) a way to reproduce "self-ownership" in an excessive and paradoxical manner: It is not just restoring the value of community after the destruction of individualism and egoism but aiming at *another type of "human."* This is why, at the end of volume 1 of *Capital*, in the development on "The Historical Tendency of Capitalist Accumulation" (chap. 32), where Marx in fact is formulating the necessity of communism as the "end" of the history of exploitation, he would speak of the "restoration of individual property" (or appropriation of oneself and one's conditions of existence) on the basis of the "socialized mode of production," which is defined as the great achievement of capitalism. This enigmatic idea can be partly clarified through a comparison with the earlier *German Ideology* (1845), where it is explained that, when the history of the division of labor reaches the "stage of totality" (meaning in particular that every individual is now communicating with every other in the world—a utopia made less unlikely today through the use of internet networks), individuals will be connected to one another in a universal *Verkehr*, or "intercourse." However, this is not exactly the Hegelian "I that is We, and We that is I" from the *Phenomenology* or the constitution of the "ultimate" community as intersubjectivity, through the interiorization of past history.[20] Rather, it must be understood as a kind of "community of the outside" (borrowing the formula from Blanchot and Foucault), where the "integral human," or the human as "concrete totality" is made possible by the suppression of every great "division" in the social organization of activities: manual and intellectual labor but also rurality and urbanity, perhaps masculinity and femininity. In this negation of the negation or abstraction of the abstraction, it is the regime of (anthropological) differences that becomes radically transformed. I believe it important to understand that this is a critique of "abstract universalism" but *not a critique of universalism* as such: Rather, a new universalism is proposed, where the idea of "community" is also profoundly transformed. To be sure, the community (or *the common*) is vindicated against individualism and egoism, but not in the form of return to the romantic sense of "organic" community (as well observed in particular by Jean-Luc Nancy).[21] Communism in the

Marxian sense is much more the invention of a new type of individuality, a "transindividuality" materially rooted in the transformation of the mode of production and the form of life.

To read Nietzsche in comparison with this means approaching a very different form of materialism, which begins with what Benjamin called later (in one of his developments most directly inspired by Nietzsche) the "destructive character," that is, a cultural war waged against the various figures of "abstraction," which are equalization, normalization, homogenization . . . in other terms, "nihilism."[22] In the same interview with Trombadori, Foucault explains that experience in Nietzsche, Blanchot, and Bataille has a function to tear the subject apart from himself, making sure that he is no longer himself or be carried over to annihilation or dissolution.[23] This is an experience of transgressing the limits of the human as inherited from history. As opposed to a collective or social *praxis* in the Marxian sense, we have to do here with an affirmation, a self-assertion of "sovereign" masters (masters *without slaves*, it should be noted), overcoming moral values in the form of a destruction of every form of resentment or guilt—and it should be noted that this applies as well to equalitarian values, in which equality has become *an imperative*, a moral lesson to be taught. This overcoming finds its allegory in the "Overman," whose values are essentially aesthetic values. Their invention or *poiesis* requires running a personal risk of destruction (or perhaps, in Bataille's and Foucault's interpretation, a risk of *madness*). We retrieve an idea of the "impolitical" (*das Unpolitische*), albeit not in Marxian terms but rather in the legacy of Burckhardt who, exactly in the same period, defined civilization on the model of Renaissance artists and adventurers (*condottieri*) as a work of art carried on by "superior" men in shaping their own lives.[24]

We must now reflect on the new step taken by Foucault: What does Foucault "change" in Nietzsche (who clearly remains his model)? What we are interested in is a trajectory that elaborates the idea of an excessive individualism—not exactly the same as an "excessive individual"—or an individualism beyond the limits of "normality" that articulates abstract homogeneous personality with an ideal representation of the community. A permanent characteristic of Foucault's attitude is his hostility to Marxism as a political doctrine, as a theory of universal history, and as a social philosophy, but this did not prevent him from continuously using analytical instruments borrowed from Marx when studying specific institutions of power, disciplines, and forms of domination.[25] A more difficult question regards his changing attitude with respect to Nietzsche: There is clearly no question of

Foucault ever becoming *opposed* to the Nietzschean ethics or critique of the "bourgeois" moral values (which, for Nietzsche, were essentially "Christian" values secularized). Therefore, there is also no question of Foucault ever becoming exactly a "humanist" in the sense that he had sharply rejected himself. However, there is a necessity to interpret his "turn" from an *ethics of transgression* toward an *ethics of governmentality* (which is also a change in political "style"), when Foucault increasingly turns from the analysis of modernity toward the study of ancient discourses that valorize the "care of the self" and also certain forms of asceticism. As we know, this is a hotly debated issue, which revolves around the question whether there exists a "first Foucault," who would be more subversive, and a "second Foucault," who would be leaning toward liberalism or libertarianism.

I agree that there is a change, although with qualifications. Foucault I could be exemplified through the title (and content) of the 1978 lecture at a criminology congress in Toronto: "The Dangerous Individual."[26] The dangerous individual is a product of the penal and psychiatric order that "defends society" against its own degeneracy, its internal enemies whose inhumanity can be summarized in the formula: either criminal or mad (sometimes both).[27] If there is no way to escape that dilemma, arising from the implementation of the power-knowledge of the state in the form of discipline and punishment, then the only remaining "ethical" possibility, combining *truth telling* and *freedom*, is a special kind of "wrongdoing" that ultimately could mean *becoming oneself* the "dangerous individual": an individual that is morally "dangerous" for others but also—above all—dangerous for itself. I will call this the *tragic* Foucault, who tends toward an aesthetic identification with certain historical figures of the outlaw and the antisocial, especially those "bad guys" in history that (using a play on the Latin etymology) he called the "infamous men" (unknown and despised). It is a question of becoming "abnormal" intellectually, or to transgress the divide of normality and abnormality, and also of becoming "anonymous," a *nonsubject* who takes no responsibility for his or her actions.[28]

Foucault II seems to have moved miles away from this transgressive ideal (which perhaps was purely literary). This leads commentators to wonder: Is Foucault becoming more "liberal" and more "reasonable," moving from a Nietzschean an toward a Kantian criticism? I will not give a simple, final answer; rather I will try to displace the question, insisting on three points. First, there is no doubt that Foucault tries to escape the "tragic" dilemma: Apart from crime and madness, there are all sorts of *counterconducts* that form a "third" possibility, one not so much transgressive but *resistant* to the existing order. And there is a broad sense of "liberalism," in which a "liberal society" is one where there is room for counterconducts, even heterotopias, which are not immediately suppressed. Now, of course, if we ask the question "*how much room* is there for counterconducts in *our present* society," the answer will be "not so much." Hence the political and ethical objective proposed by Foucault: "*Ne pas être tellement gouverné*" (which means both: not being governed *like this* and *not so much*).[29] The implication is that our "liberal" societies are not very liberal in practice. Second, this definition of critique resonates not with liberalism in general but with a special tradition that can be traced back to Montesquieu's famous formula "*Le pouvoir arête le pouvoir*"[30] (power holds power in check), very influential on the American constitutional tradition, which contains an intrinsic element of *agonism* or struggle. The power that resists power or holds it in check is essentially described as "micropower," locally constituted and rooted in the singularities of circumstances and individuals (even if they can "collectivize" their struggles, as did the prison inmates in the 1970s). Foucault does not embark on general theories of the opposition between the state and civil society, which are dear to the liberal tradition. But he does not hesitate to express universalistic dimensions of the resistance against power.[31] Third, we may perceive this as a relatively restrictive understanding of resistance or struggle against domination (something like a generalized habeas corpus), lest we forget the unconditional element that remains valid in the transition from the ethics of transgression to the ethics of resistance, namely, the rejection or "refusal" of the *unbearable* violence or injustice. This "great refusal," which persists in Foucault, has profound affinities with Judith Butler's suggestion that what the power produces is *always in excess* with respect to its own needs or possibilities of control (a recurrent theme in her work since *The Psychic Life of Power*). Hence the power produces its own "impossibility" through the resistances of its "subjects," an idea that was central in Foucault as early as his description of the *order of discourse*, where the ontology of speaking bodies demonstrated that they are always only partially and provisionally controlled or subjected to discipline by power and institutions. This seems to indicate a way out of the vexed question of the "collectivization of resistances" in Foucault (since the resistance of bodies is not per se individualized).

In Foucault's thought (and this is true for both Foucault I and Foucault II), the self is a "nonsubject" in a double sense: It has no preexisting identity but emerges as individuals reject their imposed social identities (*se déprendre de soi-même*), including their previous history, and it resonates with others in an oblique manner, through the element of *discourse*, or, rather, *speech*. Here we must "short-circuit" Foucault's political experiences (particularly within the GIP: the militant group of intellectuals supporting rebellions of inmates in the prisons to "give their revolt a voice" against unbearable deprivations and arbitrary punishments) by using his "last" reflections and researches about *parrhesia*, or "free speech," in ancient Greece. Foucault's thesis is not that "political *parrhesia*" found its historical end after the collapse of ancient democracy; it is rather that a *new parrhesia*, or a new moment of free speech, provides an alternative to both communism ("revolution") and religion (or "political spirituality") as forms of collective mobilization against injustice, although preserving what they have in common subjectively, which is rebellion or uprising (*soulèvement*).

BEYOND INDIVIDUALISM AND COMMUNITARIANISM, THINKING IN RELATIONAL TERMS

How, then, to finally "reconcile" Foucault's hyperindividualism and Marx's postindividualism or simply bring them together in a kind of disjunctive synthesis (Deleuze)? We must admit, in the first place, that Marx is not exactly a "communitarian" thinker; more precisely, his concept of the community (incorporated in the idea of communism) also includes transformed individuality as a fundamental value not opposed but enhanced by "socialization." Second, we recognize that Foucault is a very paradoxical "liberal" and even less a "utilitarian" thinker. His idea of the "care of the self" displaces the "sovereign" image of the autonomous self as it emphasizes the idea of *becoming* more autonomous rather than *being* transcendentally free. This is tantamount to suggest that Marx and Foucault are both, although on very different premises, *relational thinkers*. In Marx, *praxis* is a transindividual relation, spatially as well as temporally (since its main realization, "communism," does not lie in the future, as a coming "stage" of world history; it exists in the present, among the solidarities of class struggle).[32] The agonistic dimension is equally important in how Foucault's ethics of the "care of the self" becomes obliquely articulated with similar rebellions or counterconducts. Empowerment is always singular—it is rooted in changing one's attitude in life—but the *power relation* whose "government" must be limited or held in check is common to many.

To map this disjunctive synthesis—which delineates a space of uncertainty, therefore of choices and pragmatic combinations that are meaningful for many of us—we need a problematic of "relations" and relationality that overcomes the dilemmas of organic fusion (or teleological unity) and dialectical mediation. I think this can be introduced through a quotation of Blanchot about "relations of the third kind," which seem to refer to an asymptotic convergence of communism and individualism that, as a concept or a representation eludes positive definition but does insist in the uneasiness of the transindividual subject, permanently looking for ethical and political orientations in antithetic directions. It will give me a provisional conclusion:

> We must try to think the Other, try to speak in referring to the Other without reference to the One and without reference to the Same . . . and in this way will we turn toward the third kind of relation, a relation about which one must simply say: it does not tend toward unity, it is not a relation from the perspective of unity or with unity in view, not a relation of unification. . . . A relation, then, not of fiction or of hypothesis, but one that, though diverted and caught up in the (real) relations between men, is always in play as soon as they speak and encounter one another. . . . A mobile-immobile relation, untold and without number, not indeterminate but indetermining, always in displacement, being without a place.[33]

NOTES

1. Thinkers whose project is explicitly *anthropological* (Tocqueville, Polanyi, Louis Dumont, Vincent Descombes) tend to adopt more complex positions, which *relativize* the opposition.

2. Hannah Arendt's "theorem" is formulated in *The Origins of Totalitarianism* (New York: Harvest/HBJ, 1973) in the following manner: Individuals (or groups) who are legally deprived of their civic rights are also deprived of their (universal) human rights because they no longer enjoy the "right to have rights" (267–302). See my commentary in Étienne Balibar, *Equaliberty: Political Essays*, trans. James Ingram (Durham, NC: Duke University Press, 2014), chap. 6: "Hannah Arendt, the Right to Have Rights, and Civil Disobedience."

3. Locke's original text doesn't use this terminology, which was introduced only in the twentieth century, possibly in Crawford B. Macpherson, *The Political Theory of Possessive Individualism: Hobbes to Locke* (Oxford: Clarendon, 1962). Locke speaks of "property in one's person," which makes it easier to grasp how the understanding of personality into "alienable" and "inalienable" parts of the self refers

politically to a radical (modern) transformation of relations between masters and servants into new forms of dependency, such as wage labor, based on a *contractual alienation* of the individual's capacity. See my commentary in *Equaliberty*, "The Reversal of Possessive Individualism."

4. The empirical-transcendental doublet is analyzed by Michel Foucault, *The Order of Things: An Archaeology of the Human Sciences* (New York: Pantheon, 1970); *Les mots et les choses* (Paris: Editions Gallimard, 1966). See esp. chap. 9, "Man and His Doubles."

5. For more developments on this question, see my essay "Bourgeois Universality and Anthropological Differences," in *Citizen Subject: Foundations for Philosophical Anthropology*, trans. Steven Miller (New York: Fordham University Press, 2017).

6. Every modern nation-state (even when it defines itself as a republic with universalistic principles) constructs a "fictitious ethnicity." See my essay "The Nation Form," in Étienne Balibar and Immanuel Wallerstein, *Race, Nation, Class: Ambiguous Identities*, trans (Chris Turner. London: Verso, 1989).

7. It is well deserved to ask the critical question here: Are such universalistic constructions themselves *universal*, in the extensive sense, or do they require historical and geographic (hence political) conditions? The second is clearly true. This can be shown in two manners. First, one cannot simply extend the forms and normative representations that are dominant in the "center" of the modern world-system to its colonial periphery, even if the separation is mobile and conflictual. It is in the periphery that the normative character of the abstract-concrete definitions of individuality and community is asserted most violently and therefore emerges as a *particularity*. Second, even in the "central," dominant region, there are "excluded populations" that appear *less than abstract* in their anthropological figure: the unruly and deviant *residues* of the political construction, which Hegel, in the *Philosophy of Right*, conceptualizes as "rabble" (*Pöbel*). A politically crucial moment, with philosophical consequences on the critique of abstraction, arises when this "marginal" category is pushed to center stage (this is what happens when, in Marx and others, the "rabble" becomes the "proletariat") but also when, conversely, the subaltern group that had become a historical protagonist becomes marginalized again, therefore reduced to "negative individualism," a category particularly discussed in the work of Castel. See Robert Castel and Claudine Haroche, *Propriété privée, propriété sociale, propriété de soi. Entretiens sur la condition de l'individu moderne* (Paris: Fayard, 2001).

8. See Robert Nisbet, *The Sociological Tradition* (1966; New York: Routledge, 2017). Nisbet is a conservative. In the introductory chapter of his magnum opus, Immanuel Wallerstein brilliantly explains how all postrevolutionary political ideologies, including liberalism, socialism, and conservatism, can be seen as varieties of the same problematic best expressed by liberalism. Immanuel Wallerstein, *The*

Modern World-System, vol. 4: *Centrist Liberalism Triumphant, 1789–1914* (Berkeley: University of California Press, 2011). This is also what Norbert Elias, *The Society of Individuals*, trans. Edmund Jephcott (Oxford: Basil Blackwell, 1991), had expressed as the "society of individuals."

9. See Catherine Colliot-Thélène, *Democracy and Subjective Rights: Democracy without Demos* (London: Rowman & Littlefield International, 2018).

10. One may wonder why Marx—in *Capital* or, more generally, in the *Critique of Political Economy*—cancels the reference to the penal law (and its conceptualization in Hegel, which he knows perfectly) whereas, in his early writings as a political essayist and journalist, he had provided important developments on the social function and the political uses of the judiciary. See in particular Karl Marx, "Debates on the Law on Thefts of Wood," Proceedings of the Sixth Rhine Province Assembly, Third Article, *Rheinische Zeitung* 298, suppl. (October 25, 1842). I can see two reasons. First, he wants to postpone the analysis of the state's "repressive function," of which the judiciary system and the penal law is an element, until he has constructed the political as the sphere of *class struggles*, which are absent from the determinations of circulation; second, he wants to incorporate a construction of "subjects" into the capitalist mode of production via the form of "exchange of equivalents," which makes it possible for the labor force to be at the same time *appropriated by* and *expropriated from* the worker, thus preparing a "subjective" critique of exploitation. In any case, the elimination is intrinsically linked to the "dialectical order of exposition" (*Darstellungsweise*) that, for Althusser and other readers, was so problematic.

11. Karl Marx, *Capital*, vol. 1, trans. Ben Fowkes (New York: Vintage, 1977), 280.

12. See Richard Ashcraft, *Revolutionary Politics and Locke's Two Treatises of Government* (Princeton, NJ: Princeton University Press, 1986), which remains controversial but gives an important hint to rectify the presentation of "possessive individualism" by Macpherson, who insists only on the political legitimation of market relations and the rise of capitalism, which therefore, although observing the vicinity of Locke's formula with the Levellers, has a tendency to see the latter as "bourgeois" ideologists.

13. See my commentary in "*Zur Sache Selbst*: The Common and the Universal in Hegel's *Phenomenology of Spirit*," chap. 7 of *Citizen Subject*.

14. This is a very quick summary of my essay "The Proposition of Equaliberty," in *Equaliberty*. On the "national-social state," see "New Reflections on Equaliberty: Two Lessons," from the same volume.

15. See Michel Foucault, *Abnormal: Lectures at the Collège de France, 1974–1975*, trans. Graham Burchell (New York: Picador, 2004). I have commented on this text in my essay "Civic-Bourgeois Universalism and Anthropological Difference," in

Citizen Subject. See also Pierre Macherey, *Le sujet des normes* (Paris: Editions Amsterdam, 2014).

16. Étienne de la Boétie, *The Politics of Obedience: The Discourse of Voluntary Servitude*, trans. Harry Kurz (Montreal: Black Rose, 1997).

17. We might say that the anarchist dimension of such a genealogy is best expressed by the poet Artaud in the form of an injunction praised by Deleuze: "*en finir avec le jugement*" (to eliminate judgment). Ever since Hobbes's seminal question—"who shall be judge?"—modern political philosophy has been associated with the institution of judgment and the judiciary (to which Foucault will try to substitute "government" of self and others).

18. Michel Foucault, *Remarks on Marx: Conversations with Duccio Trombadori*, trans. R. James Goldstein and James Cascaito (New York: Semiotext(e), 1991); Michel Foucault, *Power: Essential Works of Michel Foucault, 1954–1984*, vol. 3, trans. Robert Hurley (New York: New Press, 2000).

19. "Impolitical" comes from the German "*das Unpolitische*" (used by Marx, Burkhardt, Thomas Mann) through the mediation of Roberto Esposito, *Categorie dell'impolitico*, new ed. (Bologna: Il Mulino, 1999).

20. See my commentary in *Citizen Subject*, chap. 5: "*Ich, das Wir, und Wir, das Ich ist*: Spirit's Dictum."

21. In his contribution to the debate with Maurice Blanchot about communism: Jean-Luc Nancy, *The Inoperative Community*, trans. Peter Connor et al. (Minneapolis: University of Minnesota Press, 1991).

22. Walter Benjamin, "The Destructive Character," in *Reflections: Essays, Aphorisms, Autobiographical Writings*, ed. Peter Demetz (New York: Schocken, 1986), 301–3.

23. Michel Foucault, *Dits et ecrits* (Paris: Gallimard, 1994), 4:43. My translation.

24. For Karl Marx in *Misère de la philosophie: réponse à la Philosophie de la misère de M. Proudhon* (Paris: A. Frank, 1847), written in French, it is the "class struggle" that is essentially impolitical. For Jacob Burckhardt, in his 1860 *Die Cultur der Renaissance in Italien*, it is "poetry" and art generating a new type of individuality. Burckhardt is very much to Nietzsche what Feuerbach is to Marx: the "vanishing mediator" of the legacy of German idealism and its reversal. Jacob Burckhardt, *The Civilisation of the Period of the Renaissance in Italy*, 2 vols., trans. S. G. C. Middlemore (London: C. Kegan Paul & Co., 1878).

25. This was particularly visible in the great book *Discipline and Punish: The Birth of the Prison*, trans. Alan Sheridan (London: Penguin, 1977), and the preliminary Lectures at the Collège de France on 'punitive society,' now published as a separate volume: *The Punitive Society: Lectures at the Collège de France, 1972–1973*, trans. G. Burchell (London: Palgrave Macmillan, 2015). On the general question of

Foucault's attitude towards Marxism and its transformations, see my essay "L'anti-Marx de Michel Foucault," in *Marx and Foucault: Lectures, Usages, Confrontations*, ed. Christian Laval et al. (Paris: La Découverte, 2015), 84–102.

26. In 1977, Foucault gave a lecture in Toronto entitled "About the Concept of the 'Dangerous Individual' in Nineteenth-Century Legal Psychiatry." It was published first in English in the *International Journal of Law and Psychiatry* 1 (1978): 1–18. It was reprinted in *Politics, Philosophy, Culture: Interviews and Other Writings*, trans. Alan Sheridan et al. (New York: Routledge, 1988) and again in *Power*.

27. See my essay "Private Crime, Public Madness," in *Citizen Subject*, chap. 11.

28. A fascinating example for Foucault (as for Sartre) in this respect was certainly the convict-writer-rebel Jean Genet.

29. The formula, sometimes presented as a "manifesto," comes from the lecture "What Is Critique?" from 1978. See "What Is Critique?," in *What Is Enlightenment? Eighteenth-Century Answers and Twentieth-Century Questions*, ed. Ed. James Schmidt (Berkeley: University of California Press, 1996), 382–98; "What Is Critique?," in *Politics of Truth*, ed. Sylvère Lotringer (New York: Semiotext(e), 1997), 23–82.

30. Charles de Secondat, baron de La Brède et de Montesquieu, *De l'esprit des lois* (Paris: Gallimard, 1995), book 11, chap. 4.

31. In June 1981, participating in a demonstration in Geneva to support rescuing "boat people" from Vietnam, Foucault proposed to draft a new "Declaration of Human Rights." Michel Foucault, "Face aux gouvernements, les droits de l'homme," in *Dits et ecrits*, 4:707–8. This acquires again today a great resonance.

32. On transindividuality, see Jason Read, *The Politics of Transindividuality* (Leiden: Brill, 2016); and my essay "Philosophies of the Transindividual: Spinoza, Marx, Freud," in the special issue on "Transindividuality" of the *Australasian Philosophical Review* 2, no. 1 (2018): 5–25.

33. Maurice Blanchot, *The Infinite Conversation*, trans. Susan Hanson (Minneapolis: University of Minnesota Press, 1993), 67.

Critique, Power, and the Ethics of Affirmation

Rosi Braidotti

INTRODUCTION

Affirmative ethics is the opposite of the spurious and hypocritical optimism promoted by advanced capitalism. The latter emits internally contradictory injunctions, alternating coercive consumerism, that is to say collective indebtedness, with the moralizing tendency to hold the individuals responsible for the ravages of the system, thereby privatizing issues of health, wealth, and well-being. Affirmative ethics, on the other hand, avoids psychological simplifications and acknowledges the social and affective fractures as the effects of collective relations of power that call for specific forms of intervention. In response, it foregrounds the need to collectively develop an adequate understanding of the very—mostly negative—conditions one is attempting to resist or even overturn. In this respect, affirmation is the praxis of extracting knowledge from pain, the better to transform its negative effects.

In this essay, I want to explain briefly what affirmative ethics is all about and argue for its relevance to the challenges that confront us in the contemporary world. My argument is that affirmative ethics as a collective practice defies the manic-depressive logic of advanced capitalism, the mix of euphoria and anxiety that defines our era, caught between the Fourth Industrial Revolution[1] and the Sixth Extinction.[2] As such, affirmation constitutes a robust alternative to the state of disenchantment that so many progressive thinkers experience today, in these conflict-ridden, violent, and profoundly unjust times.

THE CASE FOR AFFIRMATION

Affirmative ethics emerges from a Continental philosophical tradition of critical Spinozism, notably the materialist but vital life philosophy of Gilles Deleuze.[3] Centered on the key concept of radical immanence,[4] this philosophical approach assumes that we are all "part of nature" and that living matter is one, intelligent, and self-organizing—or autopoietic.[5] Singular entities are constituted through a process ontology as different modulations within the same matter, or variations on a common theme. Deleuze develops this neo-Spinozist insight into a metaphysics of becoming, postulated on the notion of the univocity of Being.[6] In turn, this continuous approach redefines the relation between reason and the emotions, undoing the damages of Cartesian dualism by foregrounding the importance of political passions, affirmative affects, and a rigorous vision of the role of the imagination.

It would be a mistake to take this approach as a "flat" or holistic ontology. To ensure processes of individuation, we need a structure of *differentiation*. Deleuze solves the issue by introducing a nondialectical and nonantagonistic concept of difference, centered on the actualization of virtual, that is, unfulfilled, possibilities. They can only become effectual through a collective praxis that is primarily ethical, but its ethics are supposed to guide our politics—and this is the stance of affirmation. The aim of this anti-Hegelian framework is not to unfold affirmative differences in naïve and falsely harmonious coexistence, as some of Deleuze's detractors suggest.[7] The point is rather to extract the energy for collective action from social conditions that offer none. Dialectics is a manner of dealing with this problem, by fueling the energy for political resistance through opposition and the drive for recognition. Affirmative ethics takes a different and less violent path and borrows this energy from the future, so to speak, by counteractualizing alternatives that are both untimely and necessary. It mobilizes the collective power (*potentia*) to make a positive difference and puts it to the task of enacting alternatives. Like injecting hope in a socially depressed field, or turning exhaustion into an opportunity for radical transformation.

Affirmative ethics begins by bringing about a community—a "we" that is "a missing people," assembled around the shared desire to enact productive subversions of the status quo, that is to say, to actualize virtual possibilities. This need not be an anarchic rupture: Great ideas like freedom and democracy, for instance, belong to the category of the future past, in the sense that they have been around for a while but were never completely and successfully implemented. The function of the virtual is to actualize these real issues, interrupting the static and acquiescent replication of established norms and values. The virtual is the laboratory of the new.

The emphasis that a philosophy of immanence places on a continuum with an entity we are accustomed to call "nature" is further complicated, for us people of the third millennium, by the fact that we are now living in a technologically mediated world. We have evolved from the nature-versus-culture divide into a continuum of "naturecultures,"[8] which is progressing into millennial "medianatures,"[9] or even what I would call, in an affirmative posthumanist perspective, "medianaturecultures."[10]

The ideas that need to be combined and reassembled are the unity of human and nonhuman life (*zoe*); the grounded, situated nature of all entities (geo); and the high degrees of mediation (techno). The vital materialism I defend is *zoe*-geo-techno-mediated.[11] Subject formation takes place as transversal assemblages of multiple forces, relations, and agents, which includes nonhumans and flows across these multilayered locations.

Given that Spinoza famously defined the core or essence of the subject as the ontological positivity of the desire to persevere in one's existence (*conatus*), the emphasis falls primarily on positive visions of what subjects can do. This transversal view of subjectivity does not coincide with liberal individualism, nor does it fall within the binary strictures of the social-constructivist oppositions nature/culture, human/nonhuman, etc. What constitutes subjectivity is rather the ontological desire to express one's capacities or powers, the freedom to find out what a body can do, as an embedded and embodied, embrained, affective, and relational entity.[12]

A distributed notion of subject formation emerges from this, a transversal form of nonsynthetic interconnection of both human and nonhuman entities, reaching from Earth agents (air, water, soil, etc.) to multiple organic and inorganic others.[13] This approach produces a neo-Spinozist philosophy that is both materialist and vitalist, challenging the traditional equation of subjectivity with rational consciousness. It rejects the self/other dialectics as the alleged motor of subject formation.

The problem of the negative, which for Spinoza is the issue of evil, emerges immediately as a crucial ethicopolitical issue in this affirmative vision of subjectivity. The negative has a very important analytic function in vital neomaterialist philosophies but not a substantive one; negativity is subjected to the primacy of positive desire. Deleuze does not formally discard negation but uses it differentially, like Nietzsche.[14] And like Nietzsche, a categorical distinction is drawn between morality—as the implementation of socially agreed protocols—and ethics, which is about relations and forces. The negative, in this philosophical framework, stands for the reactive, reactionary power of the administrators of institutional *potestas*: the priest, the judge, the conformists, etc.

The subjects' ethical core is not their moral intentionality as much as the effects of power (as repressive—*potestas*—as well as positive—*potentia*) their actions are likely to have upon the world. The restrictive and the empowering modalities of power are not mutually exclusive but rather coexist as intertwined facets of the same process of subject formation.[15] This is a process that aims at balancing entrapment and empowerment, working toward engendering affirmative or ethically empowering modes of becoming through collective action.[16] This specific definition of power is central to the core concept of my nomadic, neomaterialist relational ethics of affirmation.[17]

Again, it bears repeating that this transversal subject-assemblage as a process of becoming—nomadic, rhizomic, relational—is not generated by dialectical opposition. It does not preexist the project that actualizes it and is neither born of nor exhausted by the performative gesture as a speech act. It is rather materially grounded and collectively expressed: Desire is always social. It is sustained by the shared desire to actualize, that is to say co-construct, affirmative conditions, values, and relations. The notion of desire as Spinozist plenitude (*potentia*) rather than Hegelian lack is one of the strengths of this vital, materialist philosophy.[18]

Ethics is about accounting for multiple power relations by providing criteria by which we can differentiate between negative/entrapping modes of relation and the affirmative/empowering ones. This operation is situated within advanced, information-driven capitalism, which is an axiomatic system aiming at profit by all and any means and, more specifically, by capitalizing on the codes (biogenetic, algorithmic, affective, etc.) of living matter itself. Because of this continuity, affirmative ethics as praxis requires a cartographic method of mapping different speeds of change and transformation. Some projects or relations deterritorialize and destabilize conventions, engendering new forms of knowledge, while others implement forms of blockage or reterritorialization that arrest and stratify relations and knowledge claims in order to capitalize on them.[19] Ethics and politics work in tandem to produce cognitive mappings of the present, the better to intervene upon it.

An affirmative ethics based on vital, materialist grounding, however, also exposes a genuine tension at the core of ethical thinking today: How to engage in affirmative ethics—which entails the creation of sustainable alternatives geared to the construction of social horizons of hope—while at the same time developing schemes of thought and action that imply resistance and opposition to the present? How to resist the present, more specifically the injustice, violence, and vulgarity of the times, while being worthy of our times, so as to engage with them in a productive, albeit oppositional and affirmative manner?

I have dealt with this tension by building on the complex understanding of the present as a multidirectional time continuum.[20] I propose to operationalize this distinction between the perception of the past—the present as the record of what we are ceasing to be—and the actualization of a possible future—the present as the seed of what we are in the process of becoming. This is a qualitative distinction between the present as the given or the actual and the present as the unfolding of the virtual. This complex vision offers critical and creative margins of intervention, opening the spaces for the composition of new subject-assemblages, activated by the shared desire for affirmative ethics. The virtual is a reservoir of yet unrealized possibilities that cannot be brought about by dialectical opposition to the present (that is, actual) conditions. They rather need to be called forth by a collective relational endeavor of co-creation of the conditions to actualize this potential.

The notion of the present as a creative moment adds an extra dimension to the task of ethical thinking. It challenges the association of critique with negativity, fault picking, and antagonistic opposition. It attaches the task of critique instead to the quest for new terms to describe the relationship between creation and critique. The challenge consists in balancing the creative potential of critical thought with the dose of negative criticism and oppositional consciousness that such a stance necessarily entails. To raise to this challenge, Deleuze and Guattari defend the parallelism between philosophy—defined as the creation of new concepts—and the arts as conceiving new modes of perception and the sciences as the providers of new knowledge practices.[21] This breeds an intense form of transdisciplinarity that questions the philosophers' longing for disciplinary purity.

In my work, I have developed a different approach, one infused by feminist, postcolonial, and race theories. They compose the relevant building blocks for transversal connections between different forms of subject formation and knowledge production. Of special relevance is the method of a feminist politics of locations as a way of grounding the practice of immanence and the ethics of affirmation.[22] It is a radical form of embodied and embedded empiricism that has also perfected the strategy for a positive renaming and regrounding of the subject.

A location is, first, a spatial category, a territory, a *milieu* that defines our respective ecologies of belonging. The diversity of possible geopolitical locations is not considered as a form of relativism but rather as a multilayered and multidirectional account of our materialist yet dynamic or vital modes of belonging. The word I would use is "perspectivism," that is to say, different viewpoints from materially embedded and embodied locations, expressing the degree and quality of experience of different subjects.[23] These differences are a matter of power, both as negative and as positive; philosophy is about producing adequate cartographies of these embodied and embedded differences, and ethics is the qualitative pursuit of affirmative, collaborative modes of relation, as opposed to a quantitative multiplication of identity claims.

In temporal terms, the politics of locations defines an embedded and embodied memory that is transgenerational, often unconscious, and also trans-species (genetic). A location is consequently a materialist temporal and spatial site of coproduction of subjects in their multiplicity—of differences between and within them—and across a broad range of diversity. Accounting for this complexity is therefore anything but an instance of relativism. On the contrary, locations provide the ground for political and ethical accountability. Critical theory, including feminist theory, operationalizes cartographies of the multiple locations, as strategic reconfigurations of what it means to become a subject in a relational, embedded, yet dynamic manner in a fast-changing world.

I have translated the contiguity of the relationship between critique and creativity methodologically into the practice of cartography and figurations of the present.[24] A cartography is a politically informed map of one's historical and social locations, to enable the analysis of situated formations of power and hence the elaboration of adequate forms of resistance. Michel Foucault worked extensively on the notion of genealogy or countermemories as a tool to draw the "diagrams of the present" in his analysis of the microphysics of power in postindustrial societies.[25] Foucault also extended this critical analysis to the specific forms of entrapment engendered by the modes of governmentality engineered by European modernity.[26] Gilles Deleuze and Felix Guattari pursued this line of inquiry much further and, by foregrounding the principle of radical immanence, provided relevant analyses of the singular actualizations of concrete power formations in advanced capitalism, defined as structural schizophrenia.[27]

What this mix of critique and creativity means for ethics is that we need to organize communities that reflect and enhance this ethically empowering or affirmative vision of the subject. Affirmative relations are the result of an ethical praxis that aims to cultivate and compose a new collective subject, an assemblage—a "we"—that is diverse not only within our species but also in a grounded, trans-species manner. "We" nowadays, in the age of the Sixth Extinction and the Fourth Industrial Revolution, have to encompass a mix of humans and nonhumans, *zoe*/geo/techno-bound computational networks and earthlings, linked in a vital interconnection that is smart and self-organizing. Deleuze and Guattari also refer—somewhat ironically—to this energy as Chaos or, borrowing from James Joyce, "Chaosmos" but qualify it as not being necessarily chaotic.[28] This high level of dynamic matter pertains rather to the geophilosophy of vital materialism they develop and more importantly to the affirmative ethics that supports the project.

In the quest for affirmative ethics, everything starts with the composition of a people, a community that collectively recognizes that "we are in *this* together" as an ethical drive that supports "collective imaginings" and works toward rejecting negativity along the lines of affirmative resistance.[29] I will return to this in my conclusion.

ETHICS OF AFFIRMATION AS PRAXIS

In order to help move the case forward, let me return to the insight about the nonlinearity of time, notably the multilayered structure of the present as both the record of what we are ceasing to be and the seeds of what we are in the process of becoming. At the ethical level, what this means is that the conditions for political and ethical agency are not dependent on the current state of the terrain: They are not oppositional and thus not tied to the present by negation. Instead, they are projected across time as affirmative praxis, geared to creating empowering relations aimed at possible futures. Taking a stand against the unacceptable aspects of present conditions cuts both ways: It means both "I prefer not to" and "I desire otherwise"—both motions emphasizing the possibility of pure potentiality, that is to say an opening that can be activated toward affirmative praxis. Ethical relations create possible worlds by mobilizing resources that have been left untapped in the present, including our desires and imagination—they activate the virtual in a web or rhizome of interconnections with others.

We have to learn to think differently about ourselves. This is extremely relevant for contemporary subjects, which cannot afford—in view of their specific historical condition, caught between the Fourth Industrial Revolution and the Sixth Extinction—to restrict the ethical instance within the limits of human otherness but have to open it up to interrelations with nonhuman, posthuman, and inhuman forces. We need an ethics that can take in and on the world, such as we inhabit it, from our respective perspectives.

Affirmative ethics builds on this realist approach and banks on radical relationality. It aims at empowerment, that is to say the increase of one's ability to relate to multiple others in a productive and mutually enforcing manner, and to create a community that actualizes this ethical propensity. What is positive in the ethics of affirmation is the belief that negative affects can be transformed. This implies a dynamic view of all affects, even those that freeze us in pain, horror, or mourning, in the sense that what they express is the power to affect and to be affected, which is definitional of all living entities. Every present event—being both actual and virtual—contains within it the potential for being overcome and overtaken; its negative charge *can* be transposed. This is not to disavow or dismiss the pain involved in being human and in resisting injustices; however, it is a way of reworking the pain in a dynamic gesture. Pain indicates exposure, not only suffering, and exposure expresses a relational ontology. Of course, the process cuts both ways, as Derrida astutely argues in his discussion of the *pharmakon*,[30] but the moment of the actualization of the virtual potential is also the moment of the neutralization of the toxic/poisonous effects of the pain. The ethical subject has the ability to grasp the freedom to depersonalize the event and transform its negative charge, moving beyond the paralysis. Affirmative ethics is a critical and clinical treatise about detoxifying from the poison of unfreedom, servitude, and betrayal of our inner nature as dynamic entities of desire.

What is negative about negative affects is not a normative value judgment but rather the effect of arrest, blockage, and rigidification that results from a blow, a shock, an act of violence, betrayal, a trauma, or just intense boredom. Negative passions do not merely destroy the self; they also harm the self's capacity to relate to others—both human and nonhuman others—and thus to grow in and through others. Negative affects diminish our capacity to express the high levels of interdependence, the vital reliance on others that is the key to both a nonunitary vision of the subject and to affirmative ethics.

Affirmative ethics equates the ethical evil with negative affects, and what is negative about them is neither a psychological mood nor a normative value judgment. In order to understand this we need to depsychologize this discussion about negativity and affirmation and approach it instead in more conceptual but also more pragmatic and secular terms. The normative distinction between good and evil is replaced by that between affirmation and negation, or positive and negative affects. They are not posited as dualistic oppositions or dialectical poles but rather as analytical dyads inscribed within a relational process ontology. This ethics consists not in denying negativity but in reworking it outside the dialectical oppositions, because negative passions diminish our relational competence and deny our vital interdependence on others. They negate the positive power (*potentia*) of our relational ethical essence, of Life as the desire to endure, to continue, by becoming other-than-itself.

The ethical good is accordingly equated with radical relationality aiming at affirmative empowerment. The ethical ideal is to increase one's ability to enter into modes of relation with multiple others and to create a community that actualizes this ethical propensity. This ethics consists not in denying negativity, which does play an analytic function, but in rejecting the sexualized, racialized, and naturalized hierarchies that are enforced by the dialectical system and its power-infused oppositions. Consequently, affirmative ethics is not about the avoidance of pain but rather a different way of reworking it. It is about transcending the resignation and passivity that ensue from being hurt, lost, and dispossessed, activating it beyond the dialectics of recognition and the politics of resentment. The positivity here is not supposed to indicate a facile optimism or a careless dismissal of human suffering. The emphasis on the pursuit and actualization of positive relations and the ethical value attributed to affirmation do not imply any avoidance or disavowal of conflict.

"We-are-in-*this*-together" is the ethical formula par excellence, but "we" are not One and the same in terms of the materialist and grounded perspectives that define our locations. Critical thinkers can and must access and account for the differences in the present conditions in order to analyze the multiple formations of power as a complex strategic situation that is at work in the most intimate, as well as in the macroscopic, formations of our subjectivity. Accounting for a set of conditions, however, does not mean endorsing them. Producing an adequate cartography of the present conditions aims at identifying points of resistance but also at composing a collective assemblage—transversal subjects—who labor to actualize virtual alternatives. Far from being complicit with the system, this ethical approach aims at a clearer understanding of its effects in order to rework them, collectively, within an affirmative praxis. What it does assume, however, is that capitalism also functions by flows of transformation that continue to reterritorialize and recode social relations. By extension this means that even the margins and relations of resistance and of opening up possibilities for counteractualizations are in constant flows of restratification.

Recasting subjectivity in the affirmative mode of a praxis that activates the capacity of transversal subjects—as compounds of human and nonhuman factors, including technological mediation—to detach themselves from the historically sedimented determinations of power aims at releasing transversal lines of resistance and not integral lines of power. This is why I defend also the idea of *amor fati* as a way of accepting vital processes and the expressive intensity of a Life we share with multiple others, here and now. Being worthy of what happens to us—*amor fati*—is not fatalism but the pragmatic engagement with the present (as both actual and virtual) in order to collectively construct conditions that transform and empower our capacity to act ethically and to produce social horizons of hope and sustainable futures.

This ethical subjectivity, activated by the shared desire, is designed to create new conditions, that is to say virtual or affirmative forces. We have to be worthy of what happens to us and rework it within an ethics of relation. Of course, objectionable and unbearable events do happen. Ethics consists, however, in reworking these events in the direction of positive relations, and it rests on active transformation of the negative.

In other words, the "worthiness" of an event—that which ethically compels us to engage with it—resides not in its intrinsic or explicit value according to given standards of moral or political evaluation but rather in the extent to which it contributes to conditions of becoming. It is power as a vital force to move beyond the negative. This requires a double shift: First, the affect moves from the frozen or reactive effect of pain to proactive affirmation of its generative potential. Second, subjects move from mourning to a process of elaboration of the questions that express and enhance a subject's capacity to achieve freedom through the understanding of its limits.

Deleuze and Guattari approach the Marxist project of the epistemological break, or of ideological rupture,[31] through a different route.[32] They emphasize that to actualize this rupture requires subjects who actively desire otherwise and thus break with the *doxa*, the regime of common sense, in a radical gesture of defamiliarization. The function of the virtual is to actualize the real issues, which means precisely the effort to interrupt the acquiescent application of established norms and values and to deterritorialize them by introducing alternative ethical flows.

To accomplish this ethics, we need to engender together a qualitative leap that engages but also breaks productively with the present, by understanding how this present engenders the conditions of our bondage. The virtual or affirmative force is thus also the motor of political change.

Remember that reaching an adequate understanding of the conditions of our bondage is Spinoza's definition not only of philosophy but also of the ethical life—a life lived in the pursuit of the expression of our innermost essence.[33] This essence is the joyful affirmation of our freedom, our desire to endure, to persevere, to survive—and with us, the rest of this planet.[34] This interconnectedness changes everything because the affirmative subjects of the Anthropocene simply cannot afford, in view of their specific historical condition, to restrict the ethical life to *bios* alone, let alone to an anthropomorphic/-centric one.

Posthuman ethics is about reinventing the connection to nonhuman, inhuman, faster-than-human forces. This "ecosophical" dimension resonates with the "techno-sphere" as well, in a movement that pushes the quest for an ethics of affirmation not only to terrestrial and global but also to cosmic dimensions.[35]

The affirmative ethics of the posthuman subject is based upon a *zoe*/geo/techno-centered egalitarianism, posthumanism, and postanthropocentrism. It is postidentitarian and runs against the spirit of contemporary identity-loaded, consumerist capitalism and its commodification of Life itself. It favors instead nonprofit experimentations with how many "we(s)"—collective transversal subjects—we can currently assemble on multiple planetary locations and what this/these "we(s)" are capable of becoming.

What is an adequate ethical question, then? It is one capable of sustaining the subjects in their quest for more interrelations with others, that is, more "Life," motion, change, and transformation. The adequate ethical question provides the subjects with an affirmative frame for interaction and change, growth, and movement. It affirms life as difference-at-work and as endurance. An ethical question would have to be adequate in relation to how much a body can take, that is, how much freedom of action we can endure. How much of the world can we take in and on?

Affirmative ethics assumes that humanity does not stem from intrinsic freedom but rather that freedom is extracted cognitively out of the awareness of limitations. The level of understanding of both these potentials and their limitations is affectively measured by the extent to which it contributes to increase the degrees of relational power that all entities, including but not only humans, are capable of mobilizing and activating. Affirmation is about the task of pursuing freedom as a transformative collective practice of turning negative into affirmative encounters, passions, and relations; freedom achieved through the understanding of our bondage.

Very much a realist, materialist philosophy of the outside, of open spaces and embodied enactments, affirmative ethical thought yearns for a qualitative leap out of the familiar, trusting the untapped possibilities opened up by our historical location in the technologically mediated world of today. It is a way of being worthy of our times, to increase our freedom and understanding of the complexities we inhabit in a world that is neither anthropocentric nor anthropomorphic but rather geopolitical, ecosophical, and proudly *zoe* centered.[36] One of the great advantages of a vital materialist ontology is that it allows us to sustain the strong interdependencies of human life and animal, plant, technological, and geophysical lives, breaking from the anthropocentric habit that consists in separating the human from them.

The ethical gesture is a qualitative leap toward the actualization of virtual affirmations; the subjects capable of such qualitative leaps can no longer be found in any human characteristic or power or faculty alone but rather in the transversal relational force of multiple agents brought together in new assemblages that are activated toward the actualization of the virtual (that is, the as yet unrealized) patterns of becoming outside of the dominant codes.

AGAINST A REACTIVE RECOMPOSITION OF HUMANITY

This materially grounded ethics of affirmation is generated by perspectival or differential locations and takes a firm stand against the contemporary tendency to recompose a new panhuman "we"—a new endangered humanity bonded in fear and vulnerability. This "humanity" is posited as a unitary category and as an object of intense debate, just as it emerges as a threatened or endangered category.[37] This kind of cosmopolitan interconnection is reactive or negative, in that it expresses intense anxiety about the future of our species and therefore fails to intervene affirmatively in the present, preventing the actualization of virtual possibilities.

The state of current scholarship on the Anthropocene[38] and on the advanced technologies is quite telling in this respect, as it expresses deep-seated anxiety about the future of both our species and of our humanist legacy.[39] It is difficult not to be struck by the tone of moral and cognitive panic expressed by these distinguished social scientists about the prospect of the human/nonhuman/posthuman turn. The mistrust they express about our advanced technologies is only matched by their shared defense of Western culture and civilization. They also express a state of Eurocentric panic at the emergence of an earth turned into a political agent. However, their response, which consists in a new, undifferentiated corporate humanism and proposing a hasty reformulation of a panhuman "we" that is supposed to be in *this* together, raises as many questions as it answers.

There is no question that the generic figure of the human "we" is in trouble, and *this* is a serious matter. Such a sense of urgency, however, does not justify reactive reconstructions of "Humanity." An approach based on affirmative ethics argues instead for materially situated, differential perspectives that reflect the complexity of power reactions (in both the negative and the positive sense of power) that construct our present (in the double sense of the present as both actual and virtual). We need more complexity.

An ethics of affirmation requires adequate cartographies of the multiple new formations that constitute the "human" in the damaged, endangered, globalized, technologically mediated, and ethnically diverse world "we" inhabit. The differential politics of location affect the production of knowledge and self-representation. "We"—the dwellers of *this* planet at *this* point in time—are united by economic globalization and digital networks but divided by socioeconomic fractures and polarizations in wealth and access.

The rise of populism, xenophobia, and racist violence also divides us, exacerbates our divisions, and encourages aggression.

To recreate Humanity as a reactive or negative category, held together by a shared fear of survival, is not helpful. It does not enhance our understanding of the conditions of our bondage, nor does it increase our capacity to relate to one another in generative ways. Only a materially embedded cartography of our power relations that accounts for the staggering inequalities of today can help us make sense of where we are. The methodological tools of feminist, race, and postcolonial theories are important to keep the critical perspective alive. They can assist us in the challenging task of negotiating new social practices and new forms of understanding of what it means to be "human" today.

What is needed are careful renegotiations of transversal alliances across materially grounded different perspectives and also across human and nonhuman agents, which account for the ubiquity of technological mediation and the complexity of interspecies alliances. If affirmative ethics is to be based on an adequate understanding of the conditions of our historicity, such an understanding demands cartographies of what we are ceasing to be as well as what we are in the process of becoming. Knowledge production needs to be ethics driven, which in turn requires productive and affirmative forms of defamiliarization or disidentification from century-old habits of humanistic, Eurocentric, and anthropocentric ways of thinking. It is a sobering process through which the knowing subject evolves from the vision of the self he or she has become accustomed to. Spivak calls it "unlearning one's privileges," even and especially in the practice of critical theory.[40] Instead of seeking for identity-bound recognition, the ethical emphasis falls on the expression of affirmative modes of relations to multiple others. The frame of reference therefore becomes the world, in all its open-ended, interrelational, multisexed, and trans-species flows of becoming: a native form of cosmopolitanism.[41]

I want to resist the recomposition of a panhumanity and favor instead more situated and accountable perspectives. Moreover, in keeping with the neo-Spinozist perspective of ontological positivity, I do not locate the binding common factor in shared vulnerability or anxiety about human survival and extinction. I want to plea instead for the freedom to express the innermost essence of freedom and empowerment (*potentia*) that defines humans and posit on it an affirmative politics grounded on immanent interconnections within a transnational ethics of place. What we need are embedded and embodied relational and affective cartographies of the new power relations emerging from the current geopolitical and postanthropocentric world order. However, we also need new subject assemblages that allow us to argue that, considering the problems we are facing today, in the era of the "Anthropocene," "we" are indeed in *this* together.

My point is that such awareness must not blot out the power differentials and the structural injustices that sustain the collective subject ("we") and its endeavor (*this*). "We" need to acknowledge that there may well be multiple ways of recomposing "the human" from different grounded perspectives right now. To be worthy of such diversity, in a vital materialist frame, we need a planetary, differential, and affirmative ethics.

NOTES

1. Klaus Schwab, "The Fourth Industrial Revolution," *Foreign Affairs*, December 12, 2015.

2. Elizabeth Kolbert, *The Sixth Extinction* (New York: Henry Holt, 2014).

3. Gilles Deleuze, *Spinoza: Practical Philosophy* (San Francisco: City Lights, 1988); Gilles Deleuze, *Expressionism in Philosophy: Spinoza* (New York: Zone, 1990).

4. Gilles Deleuze and Felix Guattari, *A Thousand Plateaus: Capitalism and Schizophrenia* (Minneapolis: University of Minnesota Press, 1987).

5. Genevieve Lloyd, *Part of Nature: Self-Knowledge in Spinoza's Ethics* (Ithaca, NY: Cornell University Press, 1994).

6. Gilles Deleuze, *Difference and Repetition* (New York: Columbia University Press, 1994).

7. Peter Hallward, *Out of This World: Deleuze and the Philosophy of Creation* (London: Verso, 2006).

8. Donna Haraway, *Modest_Witness@Second_Millennium: FemaleMan©_Meets_Oncomouse™* (London: Routledge, 1997); Donna Haraway, *The Companion Species Manifesto: Dogs, People and Significant Otherness* (Chicago: Prickly Paradigm, 2003).

9. Jussi Parikka, *A Geology of Media* (Minneapolis: University of Minnesota Press, 2015).

10. Rosi Braidotti and Maria Hjlavajova, *Posthuman Glossary* (London: Bloomsbury Academic, 2018).

11. Rosi Braidotti, "A Theoretical Framework for the Critical Posthumanities," *Theory, Culture & Society* 36, no. 6 (2019): 31–61.

12. Rosi Braidotti, *Transpositions: On Nomadic Ethics* (Cambridge: Polity, 2006).

13. Rosi Braidotti, *Nomadic Subjects* (New York: Columbia University Press, 2011).

14. Benjamin Noys, *The Persistence of the Negative* (Edinburgh: Edinburgh University Press, 2010).

15. Michel Foucault, *Discipline and Punish: The Birth of the Prison*, trans. Alan Sheridan (London: Penguin, 1977).

16. Gilles Deleuze, *The Logic of Sense*, trans. M. Lester and C. J. Stivale (London: Bloomsbury, 2004).

17. Rosi Braidotti, *The Posthuman* (Cambridge: Polity, 2013).

18. Pierre Macherey, *Hegel or Spinoza* (Minneapolis: University of Minnesota Press, 2011).

19. Gilles Deleuze and Felix Guattari, *What Is Philosophy?* (New York: Columbia University Press, 1994).

20. Rosi Braidotti, "Memoirs and Aspirations of a Posthumanist," Tanner Lectures, Yale University, New Haven, CT, 2017, https://rosibraidotti.com/2019/11/21/memoirs-of-a-posthumanist/; Gilles Deleuze, *Bergsonism* (New York: Zone, 1991).

21. Deleuze and Guattari, *What Is Philosophy?*

22. Adrienne Rich, *Blood, Bread, and Poetry* (London: Virago, 1987); Rosi Braidotti, *Patterns of Dissonance* (Cambridge: Polity, 1991).

23. Rosi Braidotti, *Posthuman Knowledge* (Cambridge: Polity, 2019).

24. Rosi Braidotti, *Metamorphoses: Towards a Materialist Theory of Becoming* (Cambridge: Polity, 2002); Braidotti, *Transpositions*.

25. Foucault, *Discipline and Punish*, 205.

26. Foucault, *Discipline and Punish*.

27. Deleuze and Guattari, *A Thousand Plateaus*.

28. Deleuze and Guattari, *What Is Philosophy?*, 204. The term is borrowed from James Joyce, *Finnegan's Wake* (Oxford: Oxford University Press, 2012), 118.

29. Moira Gatens and Genevieve Lloyd, *Collective Imaginings* (London: Routledge, 1999).

30. Jacques Derrida, "Plato's Pharmacy," in *Dissemination* (London: Athlone, 1981), 61–172.

31. Louis Althusser, *For Marx* (London: New Left, 1969).

32. Deleuze and Guattari, *A Thousand Plateaus*.

33. Benedict de Spinoza, *Ethics* (London: Penguin, 1996).

34. Genevieve Lloyd, *Spinoza and the Ethics* (London: Routledge, 1996).

35. Braidotti, *The Posthuman*.

36. Braidotti, *The Posthuman*.

37. Dipesh Chakrabarty, "The Climate of History: Four Theses," *Critical Enquiry* 35 (2009): 197–222.

38. Braidotti and Hjlavajova, *Posthuman Glossary*.

39. See Jürgen Habermas, *The Future of Human Nature* (Cambridge: Polity, 2003); Francis Fukuyama, *Our Posthuman Future: Consequences of the Biotechnologi-*

cal Revolution (London: Profile, 2002); Peter Sloterdijk, "Rules for the Human Zoo: A Response to the Letter on Humanism," *Environment and Planning D: Society and Space* 27 (2009): 12–28; Jacques Derrida, *Philosophy in a Time of Terror: Dialogues with Jürgen Habermas and Jacques Derrida*, ed. Giovanna Borradori (Chicago: University of Chicago Press, 2003).

40. Gayatri C. Spivak, *A Critique of Postcolonial Reason: Toward a History of the Vanishing Present* (Cambridge, MA: Harvard University Press, 1999); elaborated in Sarah Danius, Stefan Jonsson, and Gayatri Chakravorty Spivak, "An Interview with Gayatri Chakravorty Spivak," *boundary* 2 20, no. 2 (1993): 24–50.

41. Braidotti, *Transpositions*; Braidotti, *The Posthuman*.

The Promise of Practical Philosophy and Institutional Innovation

Drucilla Cornell

INTRODUCTION

My work has clearly, from the beginning, been informed by an idea from the young Marx from *Theses on Feuerbach*, which is that "the purpose of philosophy is to transform the world, and not just to understand it."[1] For some it might seem odd to think of Jacques Derrida as my ally in this understanding of the purpose of philosophy. But I have throughout my work defended the idea that Derrida can be an ally of the revolutionary left. My hope here is to present some of my key concepts within the overarching framework of what Jacques Derrida has called "*Negotiations*."[2] I will start by quoting Derrida in full because the ideas he addresses are ones I will refer to in what will follow:

> Let us begin by distinguishing affirmation and position. I am very interested in this distinction. For me it is of the utmost importance. One must not be content with affirmation. One only needs position. That is, one must create institutions. Therefore, one needs position. One needs

a stance. Thus, negotiation, at this particular moment, does not simply take place between affirmation and negation, position and negation: it takes place between affirmation and position, because the position threatens the affirmation. That is to say that in itself institutionalization in its very success threatens the movement of unconditional affirmation. And yet this needs to happen, for if the affirmation were content to—how shall I say it—to wash its hands of the institution in order to remain at a distance, in order to say, "I affirm, and then the rest is of no interest to me, the institution does not interest me . . . let the others take care of that," then this affirmation would deny itself, it would not be an affirmation. Any affirmation, any promise in its very structure requires its fulfillment. There is no promise that does not require its fulfillment. Affirmation requires a position. It requires that one move to action and that one do something, even if it is imperfect.[3]

From the *Philosophy of the Limit* and *Beyond Accommodation* onward, I argue that Derrida's notion of "deconstruction as justice" always has to be read through his understanding of "negotiations."[4] We are called to "negotiate," as he tells us, precisely because it's not enough to abstractly heed our responsibility to the other. In other words, we are not called by some faceless other. We are called to act in this situation by a particular injustice, and we are often called to act before we know the truth about the situation.

In the *Philosophy of the Limit*, I gave an example from my own life, of a *decision* in Derrida's sense of the word, which was to answer the call of the Black Panther Party and join those who were engaged in the armed self-defense of the Black Panthers.[5] The Panthers called on white people to support them in their struggle after five young men were slaughtered in their sleep in Chicago. It was believed then, and we know it now to be true, that the FBI had made a decision to systematically wipe out the Black Panthers. Then, however, we were called to act before we knew—or could know—this information, before we knew that it was true. We were called, in other words, to "negotiate" a very difficult and challenging reality, without any certainty that the danger we were undertaking was based in any knowledge of what the actual situation really was. And yet, we were called—to take action in the armed self-defense. The "we" that I am referring to here is the Marxist-Leninist group I was then a part of, Venceremos.[6]

I bring up my decision to join the armed self-defense of the Black Panthers because it shows us why Derrida writes that affirmation requires a position. It's not simply enough to affirm the horrific reality of anti-Black racism not only in the United States but throughout the world. We need to take a position. The position we take will inevitably refer back to our location in a particular time and place, and it is from these local conditions that we are called. I was an antiracist activist and, indeed, also Marxist-Leninist long before I was a feminist. However, like so many others of my generation who were committed activists, I became a feminist by experiencing and grappling with how badly women were often treated within those revolutionary movements.

My history, however, as an antiracist activist and Marxist-Leninist has been deeply informed by my notion of "ethical feminism," which I first defended in my book *Beyond Accommodation*.[7] I used the word "ethical" because my argument was that feminism was not primarily about the struggle over what women are or are not but rather how the feminine within sexual difference had to be reconfigured, and this is why the aesthetic is so important in feminism: It opens up a way for the feminine to be released from its imprisonment in what, to paraphrase Jacques Lacan, is the inevitable symbolic obliteration of the feminine within sexual difference. Ethical feminism, broadly construed, is an apotropaic gesture against the incessant fading of the diversification and differentiation of the feminine within forms of cultural representation. This gesture not only operated against simplistic notions of what women are but also sought to bring to light how reigning definitions of the feminine undergird notions of civilization, as well as a philosophically bloated conception of man. "Man" here, as will become clear when I discuss Sylvia Wynter, is not only genderized but also Europeanized and whitened.[8] This is why ethical feminism has never separated itself from a very simple idea: There is no such thing as a woman who is not always already racialized.

My resources for *Beyond Accommodation* were the writings of Jacques Derrida, Jacques Lacan, and Luce Irigaray. I worked primarily through Derrida's own writing and deconstructive reading of Lacan to show that the phallus need not be erected as a transcendental signifier to establish us neatly into either the masculine or the feminine position.[9] More radically, I claimed that these positions cannot be so rigidly signified as they are in Lacan. This is to say that the masculine and the feminine can shift in their significance.

Derrida is relentless in his deconstruction of phallogocentrism throughout all of his work, which is why I argued that the challenge presented by deconstruction is indeed ethical—ethical in that it offered a hope for new choreographies of sexual difference. And that said, and again in alliance with Derrida, I argued that we cannot neutralize sexual difference or jump over the material and symbolic reality—which can never be separated—of how the feminine is an abjected position. This affirmation of the feminine within sexual difference had to be aesthetically reconfigured to open up spaces—spaces that I later called the "imaginary domain," in which the feminine is not locked into the either/or of the "glorified mother" or the "hated witch."[10]

Of course, a number of feminists have challenged this idea by arguing that we do not need any affirmation of the feminine within sexual difference—that we can move within or toward new choreographies of sexual difference in which the feminine and masculine are always already displaced; that the idea of sexual difference, in the way I have just elaborated, is humanist in its most extreme form; and that it does not take into account the posthumanist literature or the ways that viruses and bacteria are themselves sexed.[11]

I still hold onto the argument that we need to affirm the *feminine* within sexual difference. Today, however, I would reformulate this position by drawing on the work of Deleuze and Guattari, which I discuss at length with Stephen Seely in our most recent book.[12] Let me attempt to summarize my reformulation with Stephen to see what we can gain from Deleuze and Guattari's notion of "becoming woman" read through the rhizome.[13]

However, before turning to Deleuze and Guattari, I want to emphasize that Derrida's insistence that "deconstruction is justice" is crucial to keep Deleuze and Guattari's notion of "becoming woman" from being conflated into the idea that "anything goes." As Seely and I argue, Deleuze and Guattari question whether there is a way of "becoming woman" that entails a bodily redoing of our ways of being in the world—one that releases the feminine within sexual difference from its so-called *rootedness* in the facticity of the body—the body seen here only as the weight and burden of imposed phallocentric fantasies.[14] In other words, this becoming is not a transcendence or an overcoming of sexual difference but rather a creative, material reconfiguration of it. While Deleuze and Guattari are extremely critical of certain elements of Lacanian psychoanalysis and thus would never put it this way, we can argue that the rhizomatic process of "becoming woman" is not "rooted" in a dreadfully burdensome body that can only weigh women down. Much to the contrary, in this formulation the very meaning of "woman," as well as the meaning of the "feminine," can constantly be resymbolized—an idea that takes me back to my thinking in *Beyond Accommodation*, where

I argued that the feminine can always be resymbolized through aesthetic configurations—including some of the most dreadful myths of the feminine within sexual difference. In that book I used the example of Toni Morrison's rewriting of the myth of the "killing mother" as a myth of the feminine and indeed the maternal—a myth, however, that shifts in its meaning when it is put in the horrific context of slavery.[15] To return to the language of Deleuze and Guattari, we would say that the feminine *can always be actualized otherwise*. And this is indeed a crucial aspect of any feminism that does not simply try to step over the materialization of the meaning of "woman" or of bodily sexual difference.

For Deleuze and Guattari, Virginia Woolf's experience of "becoming woman" by materially challenging and remaking her body—which she tells in *Orlando*, a story about being sexed differently—evidenced the kind of belonging that is not a prison or a simple negation of sexual difference.[16] Likewise, in Woolf's *The Waves*, Deleuze and Guattari find the drama of consciousness being *rooted* in a body that is continually being washed away and redone *in* and *through* the metaphor of the "sands of time."[17] This kind of consciousness does not consider either the simple destruction of the body or sexual difference as something akin to the self-obliteration of the death drive but rather reveals how bodies can melt together into other bodies so as to undo phallic ordering. Yet Virginia Woolf is always writing *through* the feminine within sexual difference because, if there is a beyond of the imposed meanings of "woman" and "women," then it's not simply one that is *out there somewhere*—nor is it inscribed in a feminine that can never be symbolized—such that the feminine can do nothing but break up the older orders of already prescribed meanings as a traumatic real, in the Lacanian sense. Instead, the feminine, as it is symbolized as *an other* to man, is accomplished through a revolutionary act of "becoming woman"—and for Deleuze and Guattari, this redoing is always both symbolic and embodied, just as much as it also transfigures the bodies of those who are either identified as masculine or who have taken the symbolical identity of masculinity in a racist, heterosexist, phallocentric society.[18]

Deleuze and Guattari's notion of "becoming woman" is not an instance of two men dreaming of being women but is instead the insistence that "becoming woman" needs to be actualized so that sexual difference can be lived differently from the imposed bodily and psychic boundaries, constraints, and meanings that seem to lock us into a prison from which the only escape is disavowal, self-destruction, and denial. In other words, "becoming woman," in their sense, is not about imitating or transforming oneself into a woman but is instead a project that entails deterritorializing one's desire, body, and mind from the domain of man—a project that cannot proceed if one simply tries to neutralize the feminine or step over its abjection.[19]

THE LIMIT AND JUSTICE

At a conference at the Cardozo Law School, in an essay titled "The Force of Law," Jacques Derrida made a statement that "deconstruction is justice"[20]—and that justice can never be reduced to an order of truth, a procedure of legitimation, or any stabilized set of ideals.[21] Derrida also famously called us to *justice as a debt* we owe both to those who have come before us and to those who will come after us—and to those who have tragically died in the struggle to achieve a more just world. At the time when I wrote the *Philosophy of the Limit*, many of Derrida's followers argued that this meant that we should simply and constantly deconstruct all attempts to imagine justice, to configure justice, to take a position on what justice is or is not. However, what Derrida famously demonstrates in this essay is that *law*—or at least "law" in a modern legal system—involves an inevitable aporia.[22] The aporia to which he refers again and again can be summarized as follows: A judge is called to do justice to the individual case before him or her. The judge is not simply called to calculate and apply precedent as if the law were a machine. The judge is called to *interpret*, in Dworkin's sense of the word, and these interpretations always take the judge back to what is "right" or "just" in the law.[23] Of course, Derrida did not explicitly refer to Dworkin's famous defense of "law as interpretation," but without his understanding of the "law as integrity," Derrida's critique of positivism—or his antipositivist *position*—simply would not hold.[24]

The other side of the aporia is that a judge is also called to interpret or apply law. That is, to judge from within a principle or rule that is universalizable and has become incorporated into the legal system as a principle or rule. In other words, a judge is judging and interpreting through law and not through equity—if I can sound like a lawyer for a second.

Throughout the *Philosophy of the Limit*, I disagreed that Derrida's notion of "deconstruction as justice" only led to an endless stream of deconstructive exercises—ones that got a lot of academics off the ethical and political hook. I used the example of Justice Blackmun in the famous case of *Roe v. Wade*.[25] Justice Blackmun, in the law he was interpreting, did not have the jurisprudential resources to decide *Roe v. Wade* the way he did—and he knew it. At that time, gender equality was defined narrowly through the Aristotelian principle that "like should be treated alike," which meant that when women were *really different* than men, it was legally acceptable to treat them so. Pregnancy, thus, presented a huge problem. But Blackmun, of course, could also not rely on the "due process clause" and its notions of freedom, liberty, and privacy.[26] A woman needed to consult with a doctor about her decision to have an abortion, and in her second trimester she needed institutional support in order to get an abortion. We often forget that for Justice Blackmun the "three trimester system" was about what kind of support women needed in the second trimester. It was only in the third trimester that the state had any interest that could be weighed against a woman's interest in her bodily integrity.[27]

Roe v. Wade has been trashed by almost everyone, from the right to the left, but I read this judgment differently. I read the judgment as Blackmun heeding *the call to justice* as well as the demand to *negotiate*. Blackmun read thousands of pages of testimonies from women who had suffered from illegal abortions, yet he was called to do justice, and even without the legal resources, he *negotiated* a framework that, as imperfect as it might be judged according to existing law, he felt was nonetheless still one that heeded that call to justice. Within the fields of critical legal studies, my answer at this time was precisely that those of us who are in law are also called like Justice Blackmun, that we are also called, without his power as a judge, nonetheless to do justice and to *negotiate*. To *negotiate* through what I will later defend as "aesthetic ideas," which is to say, visions of justice that can be judged to do better or worse in terms of the struggle to create a better world.

As Derrida reminds us, there has been a danger on the left—a danger that I wrote about extensively in *The Philosophy of the Limit*—to deny the importance of institutions.[28] Or, as Derrida states,

> It is always in a counter-institution—at least a virtual one or one that is being formed—always in its name that such challenges to the establishment have taken place to seek in turn some new legitimacy. Too often the discourse of wild an-institutionalism—which is itself very coded—serves, whether it likes it or not, the more or less hidden interests of the market or of private institutions. One learns to detect these appropriations and their cunning mechanisms.[29]

This need to take a position is inseparable from building institutions and indeed from fighting for ideals. Derrida, somewhat surprisingly to many, said that *negotiations* were against theory—or what he called *theoreticism*. To quote Derrida again: "The suspension of negotiation I am talking about, on the contrary, is a suspension that cannot be theoretical; theory is not possible, or rather, theoretism is not possible."[30]

This means that the call to what we on the left would hear as a *call to practice* exceeds any theorization. Indeed, later in *Negotiations* Derrida even describes his struggle as one that is between what is an "absolute call to do justice to the other" and to what he later refers to as "the dialectic":

> But the dialectic (a Hegelian would say) is precisely the dialectic of the nondialectic and the dialectic. So what is the dialectic? It is that against which I raise the value of an affirmation, that is, a conventional Hegelianism or else another Hegelianism? This is an open question for me. When I say Hegelianism, I also say Marxism. From this point of view, in any case, there is not much difference. Thus, the concept of negotiation that we discussed earlier can sometimes seem nonphilosophical, that is, non-Hegelian, non-Marxist, etc., precisely in its acute specificity, or it can carry a Hegelianism or a Marxism to its fulfillment, for with Hegel there is always plenty to say: the dialectic is not the dialectic: the dialectic is the dialectic of the nondialectic and the dialectic. So here I do not have an answer. What I am doing is perhaps still very Hegelian or very Marxist or perhaps radically non-Hegelian, non-Marxist.[31]

Why is Derrida insisting on this point? It is because the ethical, the political—and even politics—must often precede and indeed almost inevitably will precede through what he calls the *undecidable*.[32]

In 1992, my fundamental argument was that deconstruction was not a theory of the impossible. Those who told us that justice was impossible because of deconstruction had completely misread Derrida's *Negotiations*. Instead *deconstruction as justice* tells us that we are always already called to take a position, to get our hands dirty, and to fight for a better world. And that no theory of the impossible, including the theory that tells us that the overthrow of capitalism is impossible, can hold against what Derrida calls the "force of deconstruction." What Derrida, of course, also tried to emphasize here is the idea that deconstruction was not simply part of a "linguistic turn" but rather, through his readings of Nietzsche, that deconstruction served as a *material force* to undo the stagnation of institutions that hold us as prisoners in the name of sophisticated forms of pessimism.[33]

THE IMAGINARY DOMAIN

The "imaginary domain" was my first attempt to develop an aesthetic idea that could be institutionalized and therefore, yes, this was me heeding the call to get my hands dirty and not simply stay out of the fray of institutional legal battles about the meaning of gender and sexual difference within law.[34] However, as I have already suggested, there were serious problems concerning who had "standing" before the law in terms of gender equality. This is because gender identity was defined through the Aristotelian principle of "formal equality" as well as through a basic comparison between the categories of men and women.[35] Given this definition of gender equality, gays and lesbians did not have "standing" as a matter of gender discrimination, since their discrimination was understood as an interclass discrimination, which thus made it legally acceptable. Black women who braided their hair also did not have standing, since this was conceived of as just a matter of dress or hairstyle.[36] At the time, I wanted to open up the notion of standing in order to redefine and reconfigure not only the categories of sexual identity and difference but those of racial identity and difference, which I did through my formulation of the imaginary domain. I also did this in the interest of acting against a certain critique of rights that claimed that any conception of civil rights would only reinscribe "victim identity"—and of course, here I'm speaking of the rightfully famous work of Wendy Brown.[37] I grounded my notion of the aesthetic idea of the imaginary domain through Kantian philosophy, and I will return to Kant's view of the imagination in a moment.

However, for now, I want to stress that the imaginary domain returned to Virginia Woolf's call for a *room of one's own*—now not as a literal reality, although of course we might need that, too—but as a domain that allows the imagination to run freely in a field of what seems to be given identities. As a legal and moral matter, the imaginary domain is bound by our respect for others as well as by the need for a space of play and for somatic freedom. Hence, my notion of "the degradation-prohibition."[38] By this I meant to indicate that no one should fall below the register of the human and the respect for humanity because of our "sexual practices" or any other form of reidentification. This was to act against what Sylvia Wynter calls "liminal othering."[39] This gesture against liminal othering through the degradation prohibition became associated with what I called "ethical feminism"—specifically in terms of gender debates before the law.

The right to the imaginary domain was universalizable as the moral and psychical space necessary for each one of us to come to terms with who we are as a *sexuate being*. *Sexuate being*, broadly defined, means nothing more than who we are as embodied, finite creatures who also must confront sexual differentiation and pleasure. The space of the "imaginary domain" was limited—as I have argued through the degradation principle—and I did not mean "degradation" here in a flowery or imprecise way. Rather, *degradation* was meant only to forbid those social practices, whether legalized or not, which actually took away from someone their equal standing as a person because of their expressed sexuality, that is to say, their articulated or reconfigured *sexuate being*.

For Kant, as is well known, aesthetic ideas are the only ways we can portray the great ideas of Reason, including Freedom, because they can *be thought* but *not known* within the categories of the understanding. I tried to develop Kant's notion of the imagination, largely relying on *The Critique of Judgment*, for three reasons.[40]

The first was in connection to Hannah Arendt's claim that the notion of the *sensus communis*, to which Kant refers in "Judgments of the Beautiful," always turns us to a "*should-be*" of a community that would be brought into being by the judgment itself.[41] It was this future orientation in Kant that facilitated what he called an "enlarged mentality." This emphasis on the enlarged mentality was the second reason I turned to Kant and his *Critique of Judgment*, since the enlarged mentality allows us to envision new worlds as well as to make judgments about the beautiful. The third reason is that Kant brings "imagination" and "sensibility" together, and indeed, within later critiques of capitalism, including those of thinkers like Herbert Marcuse, it is precisely the corruption of the sensibility by the "one-dimensional society" that inevitably affects our capacity to imagine otherwise.[42]

I obviously cannot go over all of my attempts to rework Kant's *Critique of Judgment* in my remarks here, so I will address my most recent thoughts about these topics, which I owe to my collaboration with Stephen Seely. Today, it seems to me that a theory of the imagination is best served, at least within European philosophy, through Spinoza, precisely because Spinoza brings "sensibility," or what he would call "affect," together with the "imagination."[43] Many scholars have been reading Spinoza for much longer than I have, so I will only briefly summarize what it is that many of you might already know. This pertains to why the imagination is fundamental to Spinoza's notion of "trans-individuality." Spinoza famously posited that *the mind is an idea of the body*, which means that every encounter with another body, in any degree of complexity, prods us to constantly imagine and reimagine ourselves. Given the inherent imperfectability of our idea of our own body in its interaction with others, we are thus always *imagining and reimagining who we are*.

In Spinoza's philosophy, our imagination is integral to how we are constantly *affected* by others. However, "affect," for Spinoza, is not an emotion but rather a *relation*, or a passage of and through and between states of increased and diminished capacity caused by affective encounters. Even though some recent theorists suggest that affect is unmediated by representation—as if we were simply bumping into one another without consciousness—Spinoza tells us again and again that when bodies interact, there are corresponding ideas of affection. And thus, when we interact with others, we inevitably imagine what those interactions were or are—either according to the affects of joy or according to the diminished power of the sad affects. Put more simply, *imagination*, in Spinoza's philosophy, infuses the *entire life of a being*, which has profound implications for ethical and political practices. Furthermore, the imagination, for Spinoza, is also inherently connected to what he calls "common notions"—notions that constitute the very foundations of reason. In other words, because bodies share certain things in common, we can struggle to develop *adequate ideas*, ones in contrast to "the necessary" but *inadequate ideas of the imagination*.[44]

Spinoza, of course, worried about the dangerous force of the imagination, but, even so, I believe that he offers one of the most vibrant notions of the collective imagination that European philosophy has ever given us. I am aware that some young thinkers have argued that the "imaginary domain" could best be justified through Spinoza's notion of *hilaritas* or Deleuze and Guattari's notion of *haecceity*, and I'm happy with either one of those justifications. However, I need to emphasize again that the imaginary domain *is an aesthetic idea* and therefore, if it works as a *negotiation*, it should be justified and justifiable by a number of philosophical positions—including non-European philosophical positions.

With this, I turn to Stephen Seely's and my own grappling with Sylvia Wynter's argument that "man" is overrepresented and that the *practice of the human has yet to begin*. Seely and I look to Wynter as our attempted answer to some of the recent posthumanist literature.

WYNTER AND POSTHUMANISM

At the heart of Wynter's work is a reinterpretation of Fanon's idea of *sociobiogenesis*. In Wynter's view, Fanon's great discovery was not simply the fact that bodies are socially constructed but rather that human beings materialize themselves biologically through a genesis of symbolic forms that, in turn, become autopoetically functioning systems—ones that actually serve as biological adaptations to the world around us.[45] The notion of "sociobiogenesis" integrally ties the biological and the symbolic through *autopoiesis*, which, in turn, functions as a recursive system that—although created by human beings—is projected out beyond our agency as a set of pregiven and established meanings, indeed, also as our world of so-called fact.

In 1992 I formulated a critique of Niklas Luhmann's concept of "autopoetic recursivity" by referencing deconstruction, and I would make the same criticism through Derrida today with respect to Wynter's own notion of "autopoetic adaptation" when it is seen as functioning as a closed system.[46] For now, I simply want to put Wynter's famous concepts of "Man I" and "Man II" within the context of sociobiogenesis, to demonstrate that these are not merely ideas or ideology; rather, they are autopoetic adaptations to the world around us.[47]

"Man I" famously turned on the idea that the earth was fallen and sinful and that only the heavens were pure and uncontaminated. In other words, it would take the "Second Coming" to redeem the earth—when the only group empowered on earth was the church, which stood in for the purity of the heavens. This is encapsulated in a monotheistic universe. However, as the power of the church breaks down, Christianity conceives of a more forgiving God that must have given man—and it's always *man*—a rational, knowable universe. Crucially, it is that opening up of the idea of "God" and "Reason" that allows for the great adventures of imperialism to begin.

When the imperialists landed in the "new world," given that they lived in "Man I," they could not conceive of the human beings that they met there as "humans." What was found instead in those adventures were beings who could not be seen or conceived as human because they did not have a Christianized, monotheistic worldview. Therefore, because they could not exist as human, their lands were stolen, and they could be exterminated.[48]

"Man II" is a turn away from the wholesale obliteration of the human and those others of the so-called New World who were not Christian. It turns to a difference in kind, justified by a particular interpretation of Darwin, in which degrees of "humanness," most frequently judged by *homo oeconomicus*, become the new way of ensnaring us in a racism that is part of our autopoetic adaptation to the world.[49] Due to imperial domination, "Man I" and "Man II"—or the thinking of "Man"—is not so much a thinking or a social program, as I have already insisted, but rather a *materially recursive system* that necessarily liminalizes all those judged beyond the white European encapturement of the definition of man. The functioning of this system necessarily creates a *blackened liminal other*. Or to quote Wynter,

> Because the negative proscription of the *liminal* category is the very condition of each human order's functioning as an organizationally and cognitively closed self-regulating system or autopoetic system (Maturana and Varela, 1980), the premise of this category's proscription is central to the "ground" from which the "regimes of truth" of each epistemological order and its disciplinary paradigms are rule-governedly generated. The liminal category's empirical exclusion, like that of the exclusion of the inner city ghetto of South Central Los Angeles, *is therefore a condition of each order's "truth."*[50]

Wynter is so important for both Stephen and myself because when the liminal other moves out of its negative position, it exposes the truth of the autopoetic adaptive system. As she tells us, the damned of the earth don't have to inquire into the truth; they are the truth. It is they, and we who join them, who institute another truth—and indeed another practice of the human, and we do so in the struggle to undo the liminal others' recursively enforced status as below the human.

As I wrote in 1992, I believed that reading Derrida and Luhmann together could open the notion of *autopoesis* to the *undecidable* in such a way that gives us more space for revolutionary action, but for now, I just want to emphasize the fact that the "liminal other" is not a perspective but a struggle—a struggle that institutes another practice of *being human*—beyond "Man."[51] It is that possible practice of being together, as human, in *"the spirit of revolution beyond the dead ends of man"* that Stephen Seely and I emphasize in our new book.[52] And thus we are called, in Derrida's sense, to Ferguson, to New York City, and to Baltimore—to participate or not—in the insurrections that are disrupting the "order of man" on the streets, which is the only place that it can be disrupted. Do we heed that call or not? This is why, for Wynter, the buck stops with us.

UBUNTU

By 2003, I had joined the Caribbean Philosophical Association and began my long journey to think through and negotiate what it means to shift the geographies of reason. In 2001, I went to South Africa in a fairly regular academic capacity, and at the end of my trip I met two high school teachers in Kayamandi, who invited me to attend a lecture on uBuntu at Kayamandi High School. As I argued in my latest book, *Law and Revolution*, ethical feminism, as I understood it, not only demands that we recognize the intellectual heritages of those who have been liminalized; it also demands that we grapple with the possibility that these heritages should not only be given notational equality but that they might offer us a better understanding of key concepts such as "Freedom" and "Equality" compared to those offered by European philosophy.[53]

In Xhosa and Zulu traditions, when a baby is born, its umbilical cord is buried, and where it is buried marks the place of the beginning of one's journey to become a person. In other words, from the very beginning of our symbolic life, which starts with the burial of the umbilical cord, we are caught within an affective web of relationality that is fundamentally transindividual.[54] What I do necessarily will *affect* you. uBuntu *means that I am only a person in this web of relations that also promotes and allows your flourishing.*

As a web of affective relations in space and time, things are always changing, but one thing does not change, and that is that we are tethered to obligations from the very beginning of life. This means that this affective intertwinement, which is always ethical, does not only constitute who we are and who we are to become but recognizes that we must find a way to realize our singularity as a unique person. And as that singularity, we become someone who defines our responsibility to the world around us.[55]

If a community is committed to individuation and the achievement of a unique destiny for each person, which is often reflected in an individual's name—and yet not determined by that name—then that person, in turn, is obliged to enhance the community that supports him or her not simply as an abstract duty correlated with a "right," but in a way that allows for the form of participation that D. A. Masolo has called *participatory difference*.[56] In other words, "participatory difference" means that each one of us is different from the others but also that part of this difference is a responsibility toward the creation and sustenance of a human and ethical community. For the great African philosopher Kwasi Wiredu, participatory difference includes the principle of "sympathetic impartiality" as we seek to imagine others and ourselves as uniquely singular and different human beings.[57] The South African philosopher Mabogo P. More summarizes the different aspects of uBuntu in his own profound and succinct definition.

> In one sense, *ubuntu* is a philosophical concept forming the basis of relationships, especially ethical behavior. In another sense, it is a traditional political-ideological concept referring to socio-political action. As a moral or ethical concept, it is a point of view according to which moral practices are founded exclusively on consideration and enhancement of human well-being; a preoccupation with human welfare. It enjoins that what is morally good is what brings dignity, respect, contentment, and prosperity to others, self, and the community at large. *Ubuntu* is a demand for respect for persons no matter what their circumstance may be. In its politico-ideological sense it is a principle for all forms of social or political relationships. It enjoins and makes for peace and social harmony by encouraging the practice of sharing in all forms of communal existence.[58]

As an ethical as well as political concept, uBuntu in a profound sense encapsulates the moral obligations for human beings who must live together. The aspirational aspect of uBuntu is that we must strive together to achieve the public good, so that we can all survive and flourish—each one of us in our singularity.

It is this aspirational aspect of uBuntu that has led many of the counter-hegemonic groups of South Africa to identify uBuntu with revolutionary struggles for socialism.[59] The uBuntu project was both a research and an advocacy project, and of course, as such, it had to negotiate the complicated political situation in South Africa. One facet that has been hailed and critiqued is the project's advocacy for the reconstitutionalization of uBuntu and the development of an uBuntu jurisprudence at the level of the constitutional court. The critique of the project is that indigenous ideals should not be reincorporated within a Western and Europeanized constitution. The other side of the debate is that uBuntu is necessarily creolized and that there is no such thing as pure indigeneity.[60] The debate about whether uBuntu should be constitutionalized continues. It is once again a *negotiation*.

REFLECTIONS ON THE ETHICAL

As I wrote earlier in this essay, I was deeply influenced by both Jacques Derrida, and of course Derrida's interpretation of Emmanuel Levinas, in my thinking of ethical feminism. Of course, Levinas argues that the ethical is beyond ontology in that the Other, who calls to us in the face-to-face relationship, can never be reduced to the order of being.[61] Derrida often echoes Levinas and his understanding of the ethical, as I did. Ethical feminism as I initially defined it followed the Derridean engagement with Levinasian ethics, in that ethical feminism aspired to a nonviolent relationship to the other. Ethical feminism expands the meaning of feminism, so that it is not simply about the struggle for the rights of women—as necessary as those rights are—but much more importantly it is about challenging any form of race, gender, sexual difference, or class exploitation that throws some of us below the bar of humanity. I still hold to my defense of ethical feminism, which of course would include the struggles of gays, lesbians, and the transgendered, and through the imaginary domain would protect the legal and moral right of each one of us as a sexuate being to have the space to symbolize and materialize our own erotic life.[62]

But I was troubled that something was missing in the evocation of the face of the Other as the call to ethical responsibility. I was worried that the separation of the ethical from ontology might be too simple. Was the Other an abstraction even if it was purportedly "met" in a face-to-face relationship? I had these worries long before my introduction to the philosophy of uBuntu.

As I struggled to understand uBuntu, uBuntu offered me an entirely different way of thinking about the subject/other relationship, as well as the relationship of the ethical to ontology. As I wrote in the previous section, in uBuntu we are part of an affective chain that connects all humans and indeed all beings as rhythmic bodies whose vital forces are moving through humans, as well as what often gets called nature. In uBuntu, the Other is not an abstraction, and the self is not subjected to an ethical relationship. Instead, we are all immersed together in the motion of this affective field, which includes our actions. Everything one does or does not do will actually have consequences and affect that affective field. As a result, both ethics and ontology are rethought, and the Other is no longer a beyond but with us in this field of rhythmic bodies. Therefore, there comes to be a new meaning of the relationship between ethics and political empowerment, for when we act together to promote maximum vitality we also create new forms of solidarity. The call of the Caribbean Philosophical Association to shift the boundaries of reason became crucial to my own redefining of ethical feminism from within the philosophy of uBuntu. Within the United States there has long been a dispute among feminists over whether care is a more profound feminist ethic than justice precisely because care embraces our connection to one another as a core relational concept.[63] The criticism was that theories of justice relied on a fantasy of autonomy—understood as self-determination. But these theories could not capture the reality of our fundamental interconnectedness. In uBuntu there is not this contrast between care and justice, and indeed the struggle to end capitalist exploitation has been interpreted to be integral to uBuntu because under capitalism it is not possible to maximize and empower our vital forces, as well as those of all beings around us. The concept of uBuntu has become central to my own continual rethinking of ethical feminism. It is not just that we challenge Eurocentrism through its false postulation of one continent proclaimed the continent of reason but also that we come to realize that African philosophy and, in this case, uBuntu—this was certainly my own experience as I learned about it over many years—is a better way of thinking about transindividuality and why the ethical relationship can never be separated from the collective struggles that empower us and maximize the force and life of beings.

NOTES

1. Karl Marx and Friedrich Engels, *The German Ideology* (New York: International Publishers, 1972), 121–24.

2. Jacques Derrida, *Negotiations: Interventions and Interviews, 1971–2001* (Stanford, CA: Stanford University Press, 2002).

3. Derrida, *Negotiations*, 25–26.

4. See, generally, Drucilla Cornell, *The Philosophy of the Limit* (London: Routledge, 1992); Drucilla Cornell, *Beyond Accommodation: Ethical Feminism, Deconstruction, and the Law* (Lanham, MD: Rowman and Littlefield, 1999); Drucilla Cornell, Michel Rosenfeld, and David Gray Carlson, eds., *Deconstruction and the Possibility of Justice* (New York: Routledge, 1992).

5. Cornell, *The Philosophy of the Limit*, 167–68.

6. Peter Osborne, *A Critical Sense: Interviews with Intellectuals* (London: Routledge, 2013), 146.

7. Cornell, *Beyond Accommodation*, 21–78. See also Seyla Benhabib, Judith But-

ler, Drucilla Cornell, and Nancy Fraser, *Feminist Contentions: A Philosophical Exchange* (New York: Routledge, 1995), 75–106.

8. Sylvia Wynter, "Unsettling the Coloniality of Being/Power/Truth/Freedom: Towards the Human, After Man, Its Overrepresentation—An Argument," *New Centennial Review* 3 (2003): 257–337.

9. Jacques Derrida, *Resistances of Psychoanalysis* (Stanford, CA: Stanford University Press, 1998), 39–69.

10. Drucilla Cornell, *The Imaginary Domain: Abortion, Pornography, and Sexual Harassment* (London: Routledge, 1995), 122–40.

11. Drucilla Cornell and Stephen D. Seely, *The Spirit of Revolution: Beyond the Dead Ends of Man* (Hoboken, NJ: John Wiley & Sons, 2016), 33–47.

12. Cornell and Seely, *The Spirit of Revolution*, 34–42.

13. Cornell and Seely, *The Spirit of Revolution*, 40–42.

14. Cornell and Seely, *The Spirit of Revolution*, 40–42.

15. Cornell, *Beyond Accommodation*, 59.

16. Cornell and Seely, *The Spirit of Revolution*, 40–42.

17. Cornell and Seely, *The Spirit of Revolution*, 40–42.

18. Cornell and Seely, *The Spirit of Revolution*, 39–40.

19. Cornell and Seely, *The Spirit of Revolution*, 39–40.

20. Cornell, *Deconstruction and the Possibility of Justice*, 15.

21. Cornell, *Deconstruction and the Possibility of Justice*, 15–29.

22. Cornell, *Deconstruction and the Possibility of Justice*, 16–26.

23. See Ronald Dworkin, *Law's Empire* (Cambridge, MA: Harvard University Press, 1986), 45–86.

24. See Dworkin, *Law's Empire*, 176–224.

25. Harry A. Blackmun and US Supreme Court, *US Reports: Roe v. Wade*, 410 US 113, 1972, 147–54, http://www.loc.gov/item/usrep410113/.

26. Blackmun and US Supreme Court, *US Reports: Roe v. Wade*, 147–54.

27. Blackmun and US Supreme Court, *US Reports: Roe v. Wade*, 147–54.

28. Cornell, *The Philosophy of the Limit*, 91–115.

29. Derrida, *Negotiations*, 67.

30. Derrida, *Negotiations*, 13.

31. Derrida, *Negotiations*, 26.

32. Derrida, *Negotiations*, 31.

33. Derrida, *Negotiations*, 215–56.

34. Cornell, *The Imaginary Domain*.

35. Cornell, *The Imaginary Domain*, 22.

36. Cornell, *The Imaginary Domain*, 214–17.

37. Wendy Brown, *States of Injury: Power and Freedom in Late Modernity* (Princeton, NJ: Princeton University Press, 1995).

38. Cornell, *The Imaginary Domain*, 10.
39. Cornell and Seely, *The Spirit of Revolution*, 9.
40. Drucilla Cornell, *Moral Images of Freedom: A Future for Critical Theory* (Lanham, MD: Rowman & Littlefield, 2007).
41. Annelies Degryse, "*Sensus Communis* as a Foundation for Men as Political Beings: Arendt's Reading of Kant's *Critique of Judgement*," *Philosophy and Social Criticism* 37 (2011): 345–58.
42. Herbert Marcuse, *One-Dimensional Man: Studies in the Ideology of Advanced Industrial Society* (Boston: Beacon, 1991).
43. Cornell and Seely, *The Spirit of Revolution*, 132–42.
44. Cornell and Seely, *The Spirit of Revolution*, 132–42.
45. Sylvia Wynter, "Towards the Sociogenic Principle: Fanon, the Puzzle of Conscious Experience, of 'Identity' and What It's Like to Be 'Black,'" in *National Identities and Sociopolitical Changes in Latin America*, ed. Mercedes F. Durán Cogan and Antonio Gómez-Moriana (New York: Routledge, 2001), 30–66.
46. Cornell, *The Philosophy of the Limit*, 116–45.
47. See Wynter, "Unsettling the Coloniality of Being/Power/Truth/Freedom"; Cornell and Seely, *The Spirit of Revolution*, 122–32.
48. See Wynter, "Unsettling the Coloniality of Being/Power/Truth/Freedom"; Cornell and Seely, *The Spirit of Revolution*, 122–32.
49. See Wynter, "Unsettling the Coloniality of Being/Power/Truth/Freedom"; Cornell and Seely, *The Spirit of Revolution*, 122–32.
50. Sylvia Wynter, "No Humans Involved: An Open Letter to My Colleagues," *Forum N.H.I. Knowledge for the 21st Century* 1 (1994): 67.
51. Cornell, *Philosophy of the Limit*, 116–54.
52. Cornell and Seely, *The Spirit of Revolution*.
53. Drucilla Cornell, *Law and Revolution in South Africa: uBuntu, Dignity, and the Struggle for Constitutional Transformation* (New York: Fordham University Press, 2014), 124–48.
54. Cornell, *Law and Revolution in South Africa*, 124–48.
55. Cornell, *Law and Revolution in South Africa*, 149–68.
56. D. A. Masolo, "Western and African Communitarianism: A Comparison," in *A Companion to African Philosophy*, ed. Kwasi Wiredu (Oxford: Blackwell, 2004), 495.
57. Kwasi Wiredu, "Mortality and Religion in Akan Thought," in *Philosophy and Cultures*, ed. Henry O. Oruka and D. A. Masolo (Nairobi: Bookwise, 1983), 6–13.
58. Mabogo More, "South Africa under and after Apartheid," in *A Companion to African Philosophy*, ed. Kwasi Wiredu (Oxford: Blackwell, 2004), 156–57.
59. Cornell, *Law and Revolution in South Africa*, 7.

60. Jane Gordon, *Creolizing Political Theory: Reading Rousseau through Fanon* (New York: Fordham University Press, 2014), 1–17.

61. See, generally, Cornell, *The Philosophy of the Limit*.

62. Cornell, *The Imaginary Domain*.

63. The concept of an ethic of care is rooted in an interpretation of Carol Gilligan's important book *In a Different Voice: Psychological Theory and Women's Development* (Cambridge, MA: Harvard University Press, 2016).

Ethics of Circular Time

Slavoj Žižek

WHAT'S UP IN DIGITALIZED DREAMSPACE

The seven deadly sins are all defined in their opposition to a virtue: pride versus humility, avarice (not grabbing to spend but grabbing to *have*) versus generosity, envy versus charity, wrath/anger versus kindness, lust versus self-control, gluttony versus temperance, sloth versus zeal. The contrast between the seven sins and the Decalogue is clear: From the legalistic prohibition of precisely defined external acts (murder, theft, celebrating false gods . . .), we pass to the inner attitudes that cause external evil. This accounts for the structure of the seven sins: first, the three sins of the ego in its relationship to *itself*, as its lack of, or inability to, self-control, as its excessive, intemperate explosion (lust, gluttony, anger); then, the three sins of the ego in its relation to its *object* of desire, that is, the reflexive internalization of the first three sins (pride of *having* it, avarice to *get hold* of it, envy toward the *other* who has it—in symmetry to the lust of consuming it, the gluttony of swallowing it, the anger at the Other who has it); finally, sloth as the zero level, as the assertion of the gap toward the object of desire, which, according to Agamben, is again secretly structured into three[1]—the melancholic sadness of not *having* it, *acedia* as the despair at not being able to *get hold* of it, laziness as indifference toward those who have it ("too lazy to bother, even to be envious"), as an ethical attitude: I know what my duty is, but I cannot bring myself to do it, I don't care. . . . Should we then claim that there are deadly sins?

On the other hand, is it not possible to oppose the first six sins along the axis of self and Other? Thrift is thus the opposite of envy (the desire to have it versus envying the Other who allegedly has it), pride (in one's self) the opposite of wrath (at the Other), and lust (experienced by the self) the opposite of gluttony (the insatiable craving for the object). And the three aspects of sloth can also be deployed along this axis: *Acedia* is neither thrift nor envy with regard to the possession of the Good; melancholy proper is neither masochistic, self-indulgent lust nor unsatisfied craving; and, finally, laziness is neither lust nor gluttony but indifference. Sloth is not the simple (anti)capitalist laziness but a desperate "illness toward death," the attitude of knowing one's eternal duty but avoiding it; *acedia* is thus the *tristitia mortifera*, not simple laziness but desperate resignation—I want the object, not the way to reach it, so I resign myself to the gap between the desire and its object. In this precise sense, *acedia* is the opposite of zeal.[2] What *acedia* ultimately betrays is thus desire itself—*acedia* is unethical in Lacan's sense of a compromise on desire, of *céder sur son désir*.[3]

One is even tempted to historicize the last sin: Before modernity, it was melancholy (resisting to pursue properly the Good); with capitalism, it was reinterpreted as simple laziness (resisting the work ethic); today, in our "post-" society, it is depression (resisting to enjoy life, to be happy in consumption). *Red Angel*, a Japanese black-and-white World War II drama from 1966, tells the story of a soldier who is recuperating in a hospital after losing both his hands in combat.[4] Desperately longing for some sexual pleasure, he asks a friendly nurse to masturbate him (he cannot do it himself, being deprived of his hands). The nurse does it, and, taking mercy on him, the next day she sits on him on the bed, performing a full sexual act. When she comes to him the day after, she finds his bed empty and is told that during the night the soldier committed suicide by throwing himself out of the window—the unexpected pleasure was too much for him. . . . We confront here a simple ethical dilemma: Would it have been better for the nurse not to perform sex with the soldier, so that he would probably survive (and lead a miserable existence), or did she do the right thing, although it led to the soldier's suicide (getting a passing taste of full pleasure, which, being aware that this cannot last since he will be soon deprived of it forever, was too much for him)? Lacan's "do not compromise your desire" definitely imposes the second choice as the only ethical one.

Perhaps this type of depression is the necessary obverse of the permissiveness that suffuses our lives: More and more, the only way (not only to enhance but just) to simply set in motion our pleasures is to introduce pain—say, in the guise of guilt. The title of the report on a legal case in Mexico that appeared in the *Guardian*—"Mexican Man Cleared in Sexual Assault of Schoolgirl Because He Didn't 'Enjoy' It" says it all: A Mexican judge has freed a wealthy young man accused of abducting and sexually assaulting a schoolgirl, on the grounds that the perpetrator did not enjoy himself. Judge Anuar González found that although Diego Cruz (twenty-one years old) was accused of touching the victim's breasts and penetrating her with his fingers, he had acted without "carnal intent"—and so was not guilty of assault.[5] This logic is weird—would it not be more obvious to claim the opposite: If the man's motivation were sexual, one could (not excuse it but) at least accept this type of uncontrollable passion as an alleviating circumstance; if his motivation was not pleasure but—what? peer pressure? the need to hurt and humiliate the girl?—then his act is inexcusable. The way to explain this weird logic is to presuppose its underlying premise: Experiencing pleasure as such makes us guilty, so that without pleasure there is no guilt. Within this horizon, the obverse also holds: There is no pleasure without guilt, in the sense that every pleasure is accompanied by guilt, but it is also that, in a more radical sense, guilt provides the surplus-pleasure that transforms a simple pleasure into intense *jouissance*.[6] And is a homologous reversal of similar pain into surplus-enjoyment not at work in our experience of postapocalyptic video games and movies? Alfie Bown provides a succinct formula of their attraction as thinly disguised utopias:

> Jeffrey Tam has written that "dystopian disasters are really just a fresh chance, an opportunity to simplify our existence and leave everything behind." The problem we are faced with is not so much a lack of utopia, because this is really what dystopic dreams are: the enjoyment of a chance to re-start in a more simplified world thinly veiled by the apparent horror of dystopic collapse. In other words, it is utopia repackaged. . . . The chance to envisage changes to capitalist modernity is

eradicated, leaving only dreams of tempering its destructiveness (*Stardew Valley*) or of starting afresh after the apocalypse (*Fallout*).[7]

An early postapocalyptic megaflop from 1997, Kevin Costner's *Postman*, stages this in an obscenely open way. Set in 2013, fifteen years after an unspecified apocalyptic event has left a huge impact on human civilization and erased most technology, it follows the story of an unnamed nomadic drifter who stumbles across the uniform of an old US Postal Service mail carrier and starts to distribute mail between scattered villages, pretending to act on behalf of the "Restored United States of America." Others begin to imitate him, and, gradually, through this game, the basic institutional network of the United States emerges again—the utopia that arises after the zero point of apocalyptic destruction is the same United States we have now. It is easy to see how, although they may appear as an exemplary case of the "Hollywood Left" critically depicting the self-destructive potentials of capitalist civilization, postapocalyptic fantasies' actual political implication is that there is no way out of capitalist dynamics: Not only does the postapocalyptic restoration end up in a utopia of the same society that preceded the apocalypse, just with some minor superficial embellishments, but the very story of a new beginning after the apocalypse, as it were, clears the slate and then repeats a basic bourgeois modern myth. Bown ingeniously turns around Freud's standard thesis about the dream as the disguised fulfillment of a repressed infantile wish:

> While Freud might argue that dreams are the disguised fulfillment of a repressed, infantile wish, in the context of this discussion the diagnosis can be reformulated in the following way: dreams are disguised *as* the fulfillment of a repressed, infantile wish. Whilst the dream is the dream of the other, it is disguised as the fulfillment of the subject's internal or instinctive desire.[8]

One should recall here Marx's classic critique of Hobbes: Capitalist civilization is not just an attempt to regulate and contain the wilderness of the state of nature through the social contract; this state of nature itself is already capitalism at its zero level. And the same holds for the zero-level state in apocalyptic games and movies: It stands for capitalism, for the specific capitalist constellation disguised as a wild state of nature. . . . However, where does the claim that every formation of our desires is a historically specific product of social struggles (and in this sense is political) leave us? Bown gives to this claim a Lacanian spin, pointing out that the Lacanian theory of desire provides the best conceptual apparatus to understand how the digital universe (our "big Other"), especially that of video games, determines our desires. Recall the scene from Terry Gilliam's *Brazil* in which, in a high-class restaurant, the customers get a dazzling color photo of the meal on a stand above the plate and on the plate itself a loathsome, excremental, paste-like lump. The shocking effect of this scene resides in the fact that it enacts what Lacan called *separation*: It tears apart what in our experience appears as one and the same thing. We perceive the lump (real food) through the fantasy lenses (of the photo). Food literally tastes differently if it is viewed through different fantasy frames—and today, this frame is to a large extent constructed through digital media.

There is another absolutely crucial feature of the scene from *Brazil* that one should note: When the waiter presents to the customers around the table the menu, and the hero (Pryce) refuses to choose, just telling him to bring any of the choices, the waiter gets more and more angry and insists the hero must make a choice. The irony of this detail cannot but strike the eye: The waiter insists on the choice precisely because what each of the customers will get is (what looks like) the same excremental lump, just with a different colorful photo above it—a freely made choice is needed to sustain the appearance that, precisely, appearance (what we see on the photo) matters, that there is a substantial difference between different excremental lumps.

But, again, what does this externalization and historicization of our desires achieve? Should an emancipated subject simply fully accept this radical alienation of its desire, that is, the fact that its desire is never "its own" but regulated through external sociosymbolic mechanisms? Bown refers repeatedly to Lacan's axiom "desire is the desire of the Other,"[9] which he interprets in two ways. The first is that what we desire is never the expression of our innermost authentic intentions but is always (over)determined by sociosymbolic regulations that decide not only how we want to realize what we want but even what we want; the second is that our desire is always a desire for the other's desire, a desire to be desired and recognized by the other (another subject).[10] This reflectivity of desire is perfectly rendered by "Nosedive," the first episode of the third season of *Black Mirror*, set in an alternate reality where people can rate one another using their phones and where your ratings can affect your entire life. It tells the story of Lacie, a young woman overly obsessed with her ratings who, after being chosen by her popular childhood friend as the maid of honor for her wedding, sees it as an opportunity to improve her ratings and achieve her dreams—access to many places is allowed only with a rating above 4.5 (out of 5). She fails, everything goes wrong, and she ends up with a ranking of 0; she then has the technology to be ranked removed and is jailed for her actions. While in her cell, Lacie begins to exchange insults with another prisoner, and their mutual anger turns to mutual delight as they realize they are free to do it. . . . But is this still alternate reality? According to a report in *Business Insider*, China might use data to create a score for each citizen based on how trustworthy they are:

> The Chinese government is planning on implementing a system that connects citizens' financial, social, political, and legal credit ratings into *one big social trustability score*. The idea would be that if someone breaks trust in one area, they'd be adversely affected everywhere. The Chinese plan for a more widespread scoring system has been in the works since 2015. But in September, the government released bullet points of proposed penalties for those who "break social trust" (which could be done by defaulting on a loan, for example, or voicing a dissenting opinion against the government online). According to the policy documents, here's what could happen if you're a low scorer: You won't be considered for public office, You'll lose access to social security and welfare, You'll be frisked more thoroughly when passing through Chinese customs, You'll be shut out of senior level positions in the food and drug sector, You won't get a bed in overnight trains, You'll be shut out of higher-starred hotels and restaurants and will be rejected by travel agents, Your children won't be allowed into more expensive private schools.[11]

But, again, is this really just another story about the Chinese totalitarian horror? Are we not doing the same already, just in a more discreet way—instead of how data are gathered when we apply for a job or ask for a bank credit, let's take a look at a more subtle example:

> At a recent "Transport for London" talk, the possibility of "gamifying" commuting within London was discussed. In order to facilitate this possibility TfL have made the internet API and data streams used to monitor all London Transport vehicles (buses, Tube trains, Overground trains, ferries) Open Source and Open Access, in the hope that app developers will build London focused Apps based around the public transport system, maximizing profit. One idea is that if a particular

Tube station is becoming clogged up due to other delays, TfL could give "in-game rewards" for people willing to use alternative routes and thus smooth out the jam. Whilst traffic jam prevention may not seem like evidence of a dystopia of total corporate and state control, it actually shows the dangerous potentiality in such technologies. It shows that the UK is not as far away from the "social credit" game system planned for implementation in Beijing, to rate each citizen's trustworthiness and give them rewards for their dedication to the Chinese state. Whilst the UK mainstream media reacted with shock to these innovations in Chinese app development, a closer look at the electronic structures of mapping and controlling our movements shows that a similar framework is already in its development phase in London too. In the "smart city" to come it won't be just traffic jams that are smoothed out but any inefficient misuse or dangerous occupation of space.[12]

Furthermore, one should bear in mind that such grading is never all-encompassing: It always presupposes a double exemption. Decades ago, *Mad* magazine published a series of variations on the theme of four levels of hierarchy. Say with regard to fashion, there are those at the bottom who live outside fashion and simply don't care about it; then there are those who try to catch up with fashion but are always behind the curve; those who can afford to be fully in sync with the latest fashion; and, finally, those on the very top, who, like those at the bottom, don't care what they wear because they determine fashion—what they decide to wear *is* the fashion. . . .[13] Will it not be the same with rating social trust? At the bottom, there are the outsiders who don't care about their grade; then there are those who lag behind and try to elevate their grade; those who achieve top grades; and, finally, those who, again, like those at the bottom, don't care about their grade because everything is accessible to them directly (say, in China, top members of the state *nomenklatura* certainly will not have to worry about their grades). These two exceptions from grading, the top and the bottom, are both in some sense free; they both don't worry about it, and one can even claim that those at the bottom are more free, since those at the top have many other worries (will they stay at the top?). This external couple of the two free agents (at the top and at the bottom) is the truth of the internal hierarchy of those with higher grades and those with lower grades. Perhaps those at the bottom, excluded from grading, proudly ignoring it, are one of the new figures of today's proletarians, who are, as already Marx pointed out, free in the double sense—free as deprived of social possessions and simply free.

Today, those above grading are, of course, the great corporations linked to government agencies—they exemplify the privatization of our commons. The figure of Elon Musk is emblematic here—he belongs to the same series as Bill Gates, Jeff Bezos, Mark Zuckerberg, etc., all "socially conscious" billionaires. They stand for global capital at its most seductive and "progressive," in short, at its most dangerous. Musk likes to warn about the threats new technologies pose to human dignity and freedom—which, of course, doesn't prevent him from investing in a brain-computer–interface venture called Neuralink, a company centered on creating devices that can be implanted in the human brain, with the eventual purpose of helping human beings merge with software and keep pace with advancements in artificial intelligence. These enhancements could improve memory or allow for more direct interfacing with computing devices: "Over time I think we will probably see a closer merger of biological intelligence and digital intelligence."[14] Every technological innovation is always first presented like this, emphasizing its health or humanitarian benefits, which should blind us to their more ominous implications and consequences: Can we even imagine what new forms of control this so-called neural lace contains? This is why it is absolutely imperative to keep it out of the control of private capital and state power, that is, to render it totally accessible to public debate. Assange was right in his strangely ignored key book on Google: To understand how our lives are regulated today and how this regulation is experienced as our freedom, we have to focus on the shadowy relation between private corporations, which control our commons, and secret state agencies.[15] We shouldn't be shocked at China but at ourselves, we who accept the same regulation while believing that we retain full freedom and that media exist just to help us realize our goals (while in China people are fully aware that they are regulated).

However, we should return here to our main argument. Bown focuses on how the big Other (in the guise of digital programs) functions as the external site that determines and regulates our desires, with the obvious reference to Lacan's motto "desire is the desire of the Other." But if our desires always already were decentered, what is new in digitalization? Was desire not *always* like this? Is the digital big Other just a new case of the symbolic big Other, a case that enables us to become aware of how we are decentered and regulated (spoken and not speaking, as Lacan put it)? Lacan's answer is a resolute no: What is threatened in the digitalization of our daily lives is not our free subjectivity but the big Other itself, the agency of the symbolic order, in its "normal" functioning. Another of Lacan's axioms, above "desire is the desire of the Other," is "there is no big Other," and we should take this statement in its strongest sense, as opposed to a mere "doesn't exist": "*Le grand Autre n'existe pas*" would still imply that there is a big Other as a virtual order, a symbolic fiction that structures our activity although it exists only in its effects, as a normative reference of our symbolic acts, while "*il n'y a pas de grand Autre*" has a much stronger meaning; it implies that the big Other cannot even persist as a coherent symbolic fiction, since it is thwarted by immanent antagonisms and inconsistencies. Insofar as "the big Other" is also one of Lacan's names for the unconscious, *il n'y a pas de grand Autre* means also that the unconscious is not an alienated substance determining the subject: The Freudian unconscious is a name for the inconsistency of Reason itself (Lacan even uses the shortened formula *Ics*, which can be read as the condensation of *inconscient* and of *inconsistance*). And this brings us to the crux of the matter: For Lacan, there is something like the subject (in the strict sense of the subject of the signifier and/or the unconscious) only insofar as there is no big Other. Either at the level of its deepest desires or at the level of the social and ethical substance of its being, the subject cannot rely on any firm substantial support; it is caught in the abyss of its freedom. We can see now why "*il n'y a pas de grand Autre*" also brings us to the very core of the ethical problematic: What it excludes is the idea that somewhere—even if as a thoroughly virtual point of reference, even if we concede that we cannot ever occupy its place and pass actual judgment—there must be a standard that allows us to take a measure of our acts and pronounce their "true meaning," their true ethical status.

There is another level of how to read "desire is the desire of the Other," on the top of the imaginary (the mediation of my desire with others' desires) and the symbolic (the overdetermination of my desire by the big Other)—that of the Real: Constitutive of subjectivity is the subject's confrontation with the Real of the Other's desire in its abyssal impenetrability. It is because of this abyss in the core of the big Other that there is no big Other, and it is because of this abyss in the Other that not only is a subject irreducibly alienated, (over)determined by the Other, never directly its own, but, much more radically, that it cannot even be completely alienated in the sense of being grounded in an external substantial entity (as in "it's not me, it's the unconscious big Other that determines my desires"). One should introduce here Lacan's key distinction between (signifying) alienation and separation: The subject is not only alienated in the big Other, but this big Other is already alienated from itself, thwarted from within, separated from its real core, and it is this separation in the heart of the big Other that sustains the space for subjectivity. For Lacan, the subject is not threatened by the big Other, it is not in danger of being overwhelmed and stifled by the big Other (in short, it is not a humanist agent trying to dominate "objective structures" that determine it); rather, it is constituted, it emerges at the site of the inconsistency of the big Other. In other words, it is through its own lack/inconsistency that structure (the big Other) is always already subjectivized, and this abyss in the big Other also opens up the space for the subject to articulate its authentic desire—the ultimate lesson of Lacan is not that our desires are decentered, not our own but (over)determined by the big Other. The ultimate lesson is not that the subject is "castrated," deprived of its agency, but that the big Other itself is castrated, and this castration of the Other is excluded in paranoia.

So what has this ABC of Lacanian theory to do with the prospect of the subject's thorough digitalization? With this digitalization, with the rise of complex digital networks that "know the subject better than the subject itself" and that, as is the case with video games, directly regulate and manipulate its desires, one cannot any longer say that "there is no big Other": The big Other in a way falls into reality; it is no longer the symbolic big Other in the sense of a virtual point of reference but a really existing object out there in reality that is programmed to regulate and control us. There is a clear psychotic-paranoiac potential in this shift: In paranoia, the big Other falls into reality and becomes an actual agent that persecutes the subject. The irony is that, in global digitalization, paranoia is not just a subjective illusion but structures reality itself—we are "really" controlled by actual external machinery, so that the true madman is the one who ignores this reality of digital control. However, there is a catch here. Recall Lacan's claim that when a husband is pathologically jealous of his wife, his jealousy is pathological even if all his suspicions about her sleeping around with other men are true;[16] in the same vein, we should say that our paranoia about being digitally controlled is pathological even if we really are totally controlled— why? What a pathological paranoiac doesn't take into account is that the digital big Other, overloaded with data, is immanently stupid; it doesn't (and cannot) "get" what all these data amount to, so it cannot ever function as a true paranoiac Other who knows us better than we know ourselves. The digital big Other is by definition (not a man but) a machine that "knows too much"; it is unable (not to take into account all the complexity of the situation but) to simplify it, to reduce it to its essentials.

What digitalization threatens is not our self-experience as a free personality but the virtual/inexistent big Other itself, which gets externalized/materialized in a positively existing machine as part of reality. To put it even more pointedly, digitalization doesn't decenter the subject; it abolishes its decentering. The point of Lacan's assertion of the subject's constitutive "decenterment" is not that my subjective experience is regulated by objective unconscious mechanisms that are "decentered" with regard to my self-experience and, as such, beyond my control (a point asserted by every materialist) but rather something much more unsettling—I am deprived of even my most intimate "subjective" experience, the way things "really seem to me," that of the fundamental fantasy that constitutes and guarantees the core of my being, since I can never consciously experience it and assume it. . . . According to the standard view, the dimension that is constitutive of subjectivity is that of the phenomenal (self-)experience—I am a subject the moment I can say to myself: "No matter what unknown mechanism governs my acts, perceptions and thoughts, nobody can take from me what I see and feel now." Say, when I am passionately in love, and a biochemist informs me that all my intense sentiments are just the result of biochemical processes in my body, I can answer him by clinging to the appearance: "All that you're saying may be true, but, nonetheless, nothing can take from me the intensity of the passion that I am experiencing now." Lacan's point, however, is that the psychoanalyst is the one who, precisely, *can* take this from the subject; that is, his ultimate aim is to deprive the subject of the very fundamental fantasy that regulates the universe of his (self-)experience. The Freudian "subject of the unconscious" emerges only when a key aspect of the subject's phenomenal (self-)experience (his "fundamental fantasy") becomes inaccessible to him, that is, is "primordially repressed." At its most radical, the unconscious is the inaccessible phenomenon, not the objective mechanism that regulates my phenomenal experience. So, in contrast to the commonplace that we are dealing with a subject the moment an entity displays signs of "inner life," that is, of a fantasmatic self-experience that cannot be reduced to external behavior, one should claim that what characterizes human subjectivity proper is rather the gap that separates the two, that is, the fact that fantasy, at its most elementary, becomes inaccessible to the subject; it is this inaccessibility that makes the subject "empty." We thus obtain a relationship that totally subverts the standard notion of the subject who directly experiences himself, his "inner states": an "impossible" relationship between the empty, nonphenomenal subject and the phenomena that remain inaccessible to the subject.

The entire topic of how today's digitalization poses a threat to autonomous human subjectivity should thus be abandoned: What digitalization threatens is not human(ist) subjectivity but the decentered Freudian subject. The very alternative between autonomous/authentic human subjectivity and a posthuman(ist) machinic flux of desire (celebrated, among others, by Guattari) is false, as it obfuscates the true shift, the shift in the status of the big Other. The key question is thus: Will the digital Other (the machinery registering and regulating our lives) "swallow" the symbolic big Other, or will a gap between the two persist? Can a computer write a love letter that—through its very failures, confusions, and oscillations—encircles the Woman-Thing as the impossible object? The problem is not "can a computer do X?" but "Can it *fail* to do X in the right way, so that its failures evoke the contours of what they fail to touch?" Or, to put it another way, the ultimate difference between the digital universe and the symbolic space proper concerns the status of counterfactuals. Recall the famous joke from Lubitsch's *Ninotchka*: "'Waiter! A cup of coffee without cream, please!' 'I'm sorry, sir, we have no cream, only milk, so can it be a coffee without milk?'" At the factual level, the coffee remains the same coffee, but what we can change is to make the coffee without cream into a coffee without milk—or, more simply, to add the implied negation and to make the plain coffee into a coffee without milk. The difference between "plain coffee" and "coffee without milk" is purely virtual. There is no difference in the real cup of coffee, and exactly the same goes for the Freudian unconscious: Its status is also purely virtual; it is not a "deeper" psychic reality—in short, unconscious is like the "milk" in "coffee without milk." And therein resides the catch: Can the digital big Other, which knows us better than we know ourselves, also discern the difference between "plain coffee" and "coffee without milk?" Or is the counterfactual sphere outside the scope of the digital big Other, which is constrained to facts in our brain and social environs that we are unaware of? The difference we are dealing with here is the difference between the "unconscious" (neuronal, social . . .) facts that determine us and the Freudian "unconscious" whose status is purely counterfactual. This domain of counterfactuals can only be operative if subjectivity is here, since the basic twist of every signifying structure (the "primordial repression" of the binary signifier) implies a subject, or, as Lacan put it, a signifier is that which represents a subject for another signifier. Back to our example, in order to register the difference between "plain coffee" and "coffee without milk," a subject has to be operative.

The digital machinery that sustains video games not only directs and regulates the gamer's desire; it also, as Bown emphasizes, "interpellates" the gamer into a specific mode of subjectivity:[17] a pre-Oedipal not-yet-castrated subjectivity that floats in a kind of obscene immortality: When I am immersed into a game, I dwell in a universe of undeadness where no annihilation is definitive, since, after every destruction, I can return to the beginning and start the game again. . . . One should note here that this obscene immortality was the stuff of fantasy long before cartoons—say, in the work of de Sade. The axiom of the philosophy of finitude is that one cannot escape finitude/mortality as the unsurpassable horizon of our existence; Lacan's axiom is that, no matter how much one tries, one cannot escape immortality. But what if this choice is false? What if finitude and immortality, like lack and excess, also form a parallax couple, what if they are the same from a different point of view? What if immortality is an object that is a remainder/excess over finitude, what if finitude is an attempt to escape from the excess of immortality? What if Kierkegaard was right here, but for the wrong reason, when he also understood the claim that we humans are just mortal beings who disappear after their biological death as an easy way to escape the ethical responsibility that comes with the immortal soul? He was right for the wrong reason insofar as he equated immortality with the divine and ethical part of a human being—but there is another immortality. What Cantor did for infinity, we should do for immortality, and assert the multiplicity of immortalities: The Badiouian noble immortality/infinity of the deployment of an Event (as opposed to the finitude of a human animal) comes after a more basic form of immortality that resides in what Lacan calls the Sadean fundamental fantasy: the fantasy of another, ethereal body of the victim, which can be tortured indefinitely and nonetheless magically retain its beauty (recall the Sadean figure of the young girl sustaining endless humiliations and mutilations from her depraved torturer and somehow mysteriously surviving it all intact, in the same way Tom and Jerry and other cartoon heroes survive all their ridiculous ordeals intact). In this form, the comical and the disgustingly terrifying (recall different versions of the "undead"—zombies, vampires, etc.—in popular culture) are inextricably connected. (Therein resides the point of proper burial, from *Antigone* to *Hamlet*: to prevent the dead from returning in the guise of this obscene immortality.)

We are not describing here a mere fantasy but a fantasy that can be enacted as a real-life mode of subjectivity—say, I can act in my love life as if I am experimenting with ever new partners, and, if the relationship doesn't work, I can erase it and start again. . . . Instead of celebrating such an immersion into the gaming dreamworld as a liberating stance of playful repetitions, we should discern in it the denial of "castration," of a gap constitutive of subjectivity. And we should not confuse the denial of this gap with the loss of contact with hard external reality: Our point is not that when we float in the gaming dreamspace we lose contact with hard reality but, on the contrary, that we ignore the gap of the Real that is hollow external reality itself—the idea of being fully immersed into gaming dreamspace is structurally the same as the idea of being fully immersed into external reality as one of the objects in it. In short, our "free" floating in the digital dreamspace and the dreaded possibility that we are totally controlled and regulated by digital machinery are two sides of the same coin; that is, our immersion into the digital space can be experienced in the two opposed ways of free floating and of total control.

CIRCULAR TIME IN CINEMA . . . AND IN REALITY

At a conceptual level, the main result of our immersion into the "undead" dreamspace of video games is that it breaks with linear time and throws us into a circular time with no end and where we can always return to the same point and begin again. The opposition of these two times gives birth to many paradoxes with important implications and consequences. *The Discovery* deploys an interesting version of circular time. Here is the film's story:[18] It opens with a TV interview with Thomas Harbor, the man who has scientifically proved the existence of an afterlife, which has led to an extremely high suicide rate. The interviewer asks Harbor if he feels responsible, to which he says no. Directly after this statement, a member of the crew kills himself on air. We then jump two years ahead: Harbor's son Will travels on a ferry where he meets Isla, a strange young woman; they engage in a conversation, and Will notes that Isla looks very familiar. He says he is upset that people keep killing themselves; Isla agrees it is an easy way out. Will also shares a memory he had while being dead for a minute, where he saw a young boy at a beach. When they arrive at their destination, Will is picked up by his brother Toby, who drives him to an isolated mansion where their father has constructed his new station. Will notes people working for him, and Toby says they have all attempted suicide. They enter a room where Will meets Lacey and Cooper, two scientists who are working on his father, who is connected to a machine, Lacey and Cooper repeatedly killing and reviving him. Will blames his father for the high suicide rate.

Later, Will sees Isla on the beach walking into the water with a backpack full of stones. He runs after, barely saving her. He brings her to the mansion, where she is taken in. Will also reveals to Isla that his mother killed herself when he was younger. At a later meeting, Thomas reveals he has invented a machine that can record what dead people see in the afterlife; this requires a dead person, so they steal the corpse of Pat Phillips from the morgue. The next day, they try to record the afterlife, but nothing happens. After the failed attempt, Will enters the room alone and replaces a piece of wiring he had removed from the machine, which then shows a sequence of a man driving to a hospital, visiting someone, and fighting with a woman there. Will finds the hospital from the recording online and visits it but finds that the hallway from the video is gone: The hospital had been remodeled a decade ago. Will drives Isla to the hospital, shows her the recording, and tells her that he thinks the device records memories rather than the afterlife. After breaking into the hospital, they find a file from Pat Phillips's father, who died in that hospital. Isla finds out that the man in the recording has a different tattoo from the one she saw on Pat earlier. Will drives her to the beach, where she reveals to him that she had a son and that he died while she was asleep. Later they seek out the woman from the video, who is revealed to be Pat's sister. She tells them that Pat left her alone with their dying father and that he never visited him in the hospital.

Isla and Will grow closer together and share a kiss, which is interrupted by Toby. Together they rush to Thomas, who is hooked up to the machine and dead. They observe that he is seeing the night their mother killed herself, except that Thomas stops her. When others succeed in reviving Thomas, he realizes that the "afterlife" is an alternate version of their existing life: It takes you to a moment you regret from your life and lets you change the outcome. "I always said the afterlife was a different plane of existence," he says. "But what if it's a different plane of *this* existence?" The group agrees to destroy the machine, and Thomas prepares to give a speech, which is interrupted by Lacey shooting Isla (who claims Lacey has just "relocated" her). Isla dies in Will's arms. Later, a devastated Will hooks himself up to the machine.

He arrives back on the ferry, where he meets Isla again, who states that this is a memory. It is revealed that Will is living in a memory loop trying to prevent Isla's death and that he restarts on the ferry every time. Isla says that he has now saved her and that now they both will move on. Back to reality, although Toby and Thomas try to revive Will, he dies, promising Isla to remember her. In the final scene, Will stands on the beach, where he sees a little boy and pulls him out of the water. His mother, Isla, arrives and thanks Will. They don't recognize each other. After she leaves, he looks back, first confused and then with a knowing look.

Many critics claim that, after a good beginning, the film gets confused, aiming at some kind of metaphysical depth but not able to decide which direction to develop its speculations in—a reproach that rather betrays the laziness of the critics themselves to think. Yes, there are inconsistencies in the film, but its basic line of reflection is clear.

How does the passage from one to another dimension (state of the soul) take place? It is not full actual death that is needed for our mind to pass into another level: A near-death state between life and death is enough, a state when we become "flatliners," when we are in a total coma but can still be resuscitated.

It is easy to see the attraction of the first twist in the film's plot: Will travels to his father and finds that he is repeatedly "killed" (put into a flatline state, neither living nor dead) by his assistants in order to record his soul's postmortem activities . . . Is the undead father who returns to haunt us not one of the ultimate nightmares? If we accept this premise, there is no need for some supernatural spiritual magic, and we can also easily accept that these travels back into alternate realities can become self-aware: "Will knows he's been sent back and Isla is equally self-aware. 'This is just your memory,' Isla tells him. 'You were never able to stop me from killing myself until this life.'"[19] Yes, but she tells him this as an appearance in his dying mind: "It becomes apparent that Will has been returning to this moment over and over, each time hoping to save the mysterious woman on the boat who killed herself. Only now it's different: He knows he's in a loop and he's looking for a way out."[20] And precisely through this self-awareness he finds a way out, but a tragic one: He knows that Isla wants to kill herself because of the death of her son, so he understands that it is not enough to save her from drowning—the only way to do it is to travel further back, to the beach where her son drowned, to save him. But this means that he will never meet her again, not even in his alternate-reality dreams. In short, the only way to save her is to lose her, to erase even the past of meeting her—or, to quote the director, who says, when discussing the final beach scene: "[Will] realizes that he may never see [Isla] again, so in his mind this ultimate act of love is connected to her son because the only reason she ever wanted to take her own life was because she lost her son. So he finds a way in his mind to get to the beach."[21]

Repetition (repeatedly returning to the same point in the past in order to act in it differently) is thus not a process of playfully reenacting the past but the activity set in motion by an ethical failure. The need to repeat disappears once the past failure is corrected: When Will goes back to the beach and saves the child he can die totally. His mind will no longer postpone death and travel to alternate realities, and, through his act, Isla too will find peace in death. As such, *The Discovery* should be compared with *Arrival*, another film about temporal paradoxes in which the heroine makes the wrong choice (she chooses to marry and have a child although she is aware of the catastrophic outcome). *The Discovery* inverts the situation of *Arrival*: In *The Discovery*, the future (life of the soul after death) is revealed to be composed of its past's dreams, while in *Arrival*, the past (flashback) is revealed to be the future.

Arrival subtly subverts the standard Hollywood formula of the production of a couple as the frame of a catastrophic encounter—subtly, since it appears to follow this formula: The final outcome of the arrival of aliens is that Louise and Ian decide to form a couple and produce a child. Here is a brief outline of the plot:[22] The film opens with what appears to be a flashback scene. We see the heroine, the linguist Louise Banks, taking care of her adolescent daughter, who is dying of cancer. Then we jump to the present time: While Louise is lecturing at a university, twelve extraterrestrial spaceships appear above various parts of Earth, and the US Army colonel Weber visits Louise and asks her to join Ian Donnelly, a Los Alamos physicist, to decipher the language of the alien creatures on the ships and find out why they have arrived. They are brought to a military camp in Montana near one of the spacecraft and make contact with two of the seven-limbed aliens on board. Ian nicknames them Abbott and Costello. Louise discovers that they have a written language of complicated circular symbols, and she begins to learn the symbols that correspond to a basic vocabulary. As she becomes more proficient, she starts to see and dream vivid images of herself with her daughter and of their relationship with the father. When Louise asks what the aliens want, they answer: "Offer weapon." A similar translation of "use weapon" is made by scientists at another of the landing sites. Fear of a potential threat from the aliens leads other nations to close down communication on the project, and some prepare for an attack. However, Louise argues that the symbol interpreted as "weapon" might have an alternative translation, such as "tool" or "technology."

Rogue US soldiers plant explosives in the spacecraft. Unaware, Louise and Ian reenter. The aliens give them a much larger and more complex message. Abbott ejects Ian and Louise from the craft as the explosion occurs, which leaves them unconscious. When Louise and Ian come round, the military prepares to evacuate, and the spacecraft moves higher above the ground. Ian works out that the symbols relate to the notion of time, and they conclude that the aliens must want the nations of Earth to cooperate. Meanwhile, China notifies the world that its military is planning to attack the spacecraft located off its coast. Louise rushes back to the spacecraft in Montana, which dispatches a shuttle to take her inside. She meets Costello, who communicates that Abbott is dying or dead. Louise asks about her visions of a daughter, and Costello explains that she is seeing the future (her "visions" were not flashbacks but flashforwards). Costello also communicates that they have come to help humanity by sharing their language, which is the "weapon" or "tool" because it changes the perception of time. The aliens know that three thousand years in the future they will need humanity's help in return.

Louise returns as the camp is being evacuated. She has a vision of herself at a future UN reception, being thanked by General Shang for convincing him to suspend China's military attack. He explains that she had called his private mobile telephone; he shows her its number, which he says he knows he must do without understanding why. In the present, Louise steals a satellite phone and calls Shang but realizes she does not know what to say. Her vision continues with Shang explaining that she had convinced him by repeating his wife's last words in Mandarin, which he tells Louise. This convinces Shang in present time, the Chinese attack is called off, and the twelve spacecraft then disappear from Earth.

When packing to leave the camp, Ian admits his love for Louise. They discuss life choices and whether they would change them if they knew the future. Louise foresees that Ian will father her daughter Hannah but will leave her after discovering that she knew their daughter would die before adulthood. Nevertheless, when Ian asks Louise if she wants to have a baby, she agrees.

Hannah, the daughter's name, which can be read forward and backward, is an obvious code for the film itself. If we read it from the first scene forward, aliens arrive on Earth to justify her sad life (death of her child and loss of her husband) as the result of a meaningful decision made knowing the outcome. (At the film's end, when the couple embraces, Louise turns into an alien—but if we read it this way, an enigma remains: She says to Ian, "Nice to embrace you again"—so when did they embrace before? Only in Louise's flash-forward visions of them as a couple?) And, of course, we can read it in the way directly suggested by the film: Everything begins with the arrival of the first flashback/forward that opens the film—*when*, in what present, does it take place *as flashback/forward*? Does she not experience flashbacks only when in contact with the heptapods who teach her to do it? Or is the true present the beginning (the present in which she talks in a voiceover) and all the main story a flashback that includes flashforwards? All these paradoxes arise when our human, sequential mode of awareness is suddenly confronted with a holistic circular one, or, as Ted Chiang, who wrote the story on which the film is based, said:

> Humans had developed a sequential mode of awareness, while heptapods had developed a simultaneous mode of awareness. We experienced events in an order, and perceived their relationship as cause and effect. They experienced all events at once, and perceived a purpose underlying them all.[23]

Living in such a circular time radically transforms the notion of acting: Our common idea of the opposition between free choice and determinism is left behind:

> "The heptapods are neither free nor bound as we understand those concepts; they don't act according to their will, nor are they helpless automatons," Louise says in Chiang's story. "What distinguishes the heptapods' mode of awareness is not just that their actions coincide with history's events; it is also that their motives coincide with history's purposes. They act to create the future, to enact chronology."[24]

We should especially not directly link this opposition of circular and linear to the duality of feminine and masculine: It is Louise, the woman, who (based on her grasp of the language of the heptapods) does the act, makes the decision, and thereby undermines the circular continuity from within, while Ian (the man) ignores the heptapod Other and in this way continues to rely on it. (We should note that heptapods have the form of a squid, a kraken, even, the ultimate form of animal horror. The signs of their language are formed with their ink, gushing out like squid's ink. As such, heptapods are not feminine but asexual monsters.) When Louise gets in contact with this different universe through her visions, her entire process of making key decisions concerning her life changes:

> "If you could see your whole life laid out in front of you, would you change things?" she asks her future husband Ian Donnelly. "Put another way, would you rob someone of their existence, and yourself of the time shared with them on Earth, if you knew they would one day would feel pain, and you would feel their loss?" . . . "What if the experience of knowing the future changed a person?" Louise ponders. "What if it evoked a sense of urgency, a sense of obligation to act precisely as she knew she would?" And it is precisely because Louise understands what it will be like to lose her daughter that she chooses to bring her into the world nonetheless.[25]

In this circular view, not only the past but also the future is fixed; however, although a subject doesn't have the choice of directly selecting its future, there is a more subtle possibility of the subject breaking out of the entire circle of future and past. This is why willing the inevitable (choosing the future we know will happen) is not just an empty gesture that changes nothing. The paradox is that it changes nothing, it just registers a fact, if we do it, but it is necessary in its very superfluity—if we don't do it, if we don't choose the inevitable, the entire frame that made it inevitable falls apart, and a kind of ontological catastrophe occurs:

> There is likely a reading of *Arrival* which might argue that this means time is circular, and all things are predestined to occur in a certain way. That there is no free will. It is the old "time is a circle" adage of science fiction. . . . Rather, Villeneuve's film (and the Chiang story it is based on) suggests free will and choice exists if one chooses to do nothing. Time is not immutable, hence why the aliens' presence on Earth is still high stakes for them.[26]

What is a true choice? When, in a difficult ethical predicament where the right decision would have cost me a lot, I doubt, oscillate, search for excuses, and then I realize that I *don't really have a choice*—a true choice is the choice of no-choice. But an obvious question arises here: Why will the heptapods need our—human—help? What if it is because time is *not* just a self-enclosed circle? What if they need to break out of their circular notion of time, what if they need our cuts, shifts, onesidedness? It is a decision (like the one Louise faces) that breaks the circle of time. So we should not perceive the relationship between us (humans) and the heptapods as a relationship between those who think fragmentarily, in a linear way, breaking the Whole, and those who think holistically, overcoming the linear flow of time, replacing it with a circular contemporaneity. Heptapods need us, and this need is proof that their holistic approach is also flawed: The circle as the basic form of their "language" is really an ellipse; it circulates around a disavowed cut that always already ruins its perfection. What this means with regard to temporality is that there is predestination: We cannot change the future, but we can change the past. This is the only consistent answer to the key question: What do they want from us? Why do *they* need us? They got stuck in their circularity and they (will) need our ability to intervene into a circle with a cut (decision). This is why the claim that "the alien race [of heptapods] attempts to display to mankind they are their own worst enemy, *not* some outside force from the beyond"[27] is deeply misleading: If we humans are our own worst enemies, why, then, would they need us? What can we offer them except our blindness? Is it not that we should rather turn this claim around: While we, humans, have external enemies, the real worst enemy of a holistic race that sees it all can only be that race itself. This is why the heptapods' universe, although it may appear more stable than ours, is effectively much more fragile and prone to dangers:

> In researching the heptapod language, it is explained that those who "speak" it can see the entirety of their own personal timeline, from start to finish, and their version of "free will" means that they CHOOSE not to change anything that is destined to happen. . . . In *Arrival*'s deterministic universe, free will exists in the form of following through on a choice you already know you'll make. In effect, by choosing not to alter the future, you're creating it, and actively affirming it.[28]

OK, but what happens if they choose change, if they choose *not* to assert the inevitable? (Note how the situation is here the opposite of the one in Protestantism where the future is predestined but you don't know what your predetermined fate is—here you know it.) When Louise explains to her daughter why she got divorced from her father, she says: "He said I made the wrong choice."

Or, with regard to religion, while heptapods are immersed in a holistic spirituality that transcends divisions and encompasses all linear deployment in a circular unity, we humans are marked by Christianity, in which the Event of Christ stands for a radical gap, a cut between Before and After that breaks the Circle. One should therefore resist the temptation to see in Louise's choice some kind of ethical grandeur (in the sense that she heroically chose the future although she was aware of its terrible outcome): What she does is an extremely selfish act of neglecting others' suffering. This is why she gets caught in a circle: not because of her spiritual contact with the heptapods but because of her guilt. The irony is that, while Louise literally saves the world (by phoning the Red Army commander and thereby preventing the Chinese attack on the heptapods), with her final choice she ruins her world.

NOTES

1. Giorgio Agamben, *Stanzas: Word and Phantasm in Western Culture*, trans. Ronald L. Martinez (Minneapolis: University of Minnesota Press, 1993).

2. How are we to relate the couple of zeal and sloth to the "oriental" Buddhist couple of desire and nirvana (liberation from desire)? Is Nirvana sloth raised to the absolute? Is zeal desire raised to the ethical level?

3. Jacques Lacan, *The Seminar of Jacques Lacan Book VII: The Ethics of Psychoanalysis 1959–1960*, ed. Jacques-Alain Miller, trans. Dennis Porter (London: Routledge, 2008).

4. *Red Angel*, dir. Yasuzô Masumura (Daiei Studios, 1966).

5. David Agren, "Mexican Man Cleared in Sexual Assault of Schoolgirl Because He Didn't 'Enjoy' It," *Guardian*, March 27, 2017, http://www.theguardian.com/world/2017/mar/28/mexican-man-cleared-sexual-assault-schoolgirl-because-he-didnt-enjoy-it.

6. Nowhere is this clearer than in the direct "critical" depiction of the oppressive atmosphere of an imagined conservative-fundamentalist rule. The new TV version of *The Handmaid's Tale* confronts us with the weird pleasure of fantasizing a world of brutal patriarchal domination—of course, nobody would openly admit the desire to live in such nightmarish world, but this assurance that we really don't want it makes fantasizing about it, imagining all the details of this world, all the more pleasurable . . .

7. Alfie Bown, *The Playstation Dreamworld* (Cambridge: Polity, 2017), 48–49.

8. Bown, *The Playstation Dreamworld*, 75.

9. Jacques Lacan, *The Seminar of Jacques Lacan Book XI: The Four Fundamental Concepts of Psycho-Analysis*, ed. Jacques-Alain Miller, trans. Alan Sheridan (New York: Norton, 1981).

10. Lacan, *The Four Fundamental Concepts of Psycho-Analysis*, 91.

11. Clinton Nguyen, "China Might Use Data to Create a Score for Each Citizen Based on How Trustworthy They Are," *Business Insider*, October 26, 2016, http://www.businessinsider.com/china-social-credit-score-like-black-mirror-2016-10.

12. Bown, *The Playstation Dreamworld*, 15–17.

13. The example is drawn from Slavoj Žižek, *Less Than Nothing: Hegel and the Shadow of Dialectical Materialism* (London: Verso, 2012), 314.

14. Nick Statt, "Elon Musk Launches Neuralink, a Venture to Merge the Human Brain with AI," *The Verge* (blog), March 27, 2017, http://www.theverge.com/2017/3/27/15077864/elon-musk-neuralink-brain-computer-interface-ai-cyborgs.

15. Julian Assange, *When Google Met WikiLeaks* (New York: OR, 2014).

16. Jacques Lacan, *The Seminar of Jacques Lacan Book III: The Psychoses 1955–1956*, ed. Jacques-Alain Miller, trans. Russell Grigg (New York: Norton, 1997), 76.

17. Bown, *The Playstation Dreamworld*, 34.

18. *The Discovery*, dir. Charlie McDowell (Endgame Entertainment, Netflix, and Protagonist Pictures, 2017); "*The Discovery* (film)," Wikipedia, https://en.wikipedia.org/wiki/The_Discovery_(film).

19. Dan Jackson, "The Guy behind Netflix's *The Discovery* Explains the Mind-Bender Ending," *Thrillist* (blog), April 2, 2017, http://www.thrillist.com/entertainment/nation/netflix-discovery-ending-explained-theories.

20. Jackson, "The Guy behind Netflix's *The Discovery* Explains the Mind-Bender Ending."

21. Jackson, "The Guy behind Netflix's *The Discovery* Explains the Mind-Bender Ending."

22. *Arrival*, dir. Denis Villeneuve (Lava Bear Films et al., 2016). Based on Ted Chiang, "Story of Your Life," in *Starlight 2*, ed. Patrick Nielson Hayden (New York: Tor, 1998); "*Arrival* (film)," Wikipedia, https://en.wikipedia.org/wiki/Arrival_(film).

23. Dan Jackson, "That Twist Ending of *Arrival* Makes You Rethink the Whole Movie," *Thrillist* (blog), November 18, 2016, http://www.thrillist.com/entertainment/nation/arrival-movie-ending-big-time-twist.

24. Nick Statt, "How the Short Story That Inspired *Arrival* Helps Us Interpret the Film's Major Twist," *The Verge* (blog), November 16, 2016, http://www.theverge.com/2016/11/16/13642396/arrival-ted-chiang-story-of-your-life-film-twist-ending.

25. Statt, "How the Short Story That Inspired *Arrival* Helps Us Interpret the Film's Major Twist."

26. David Crow, "Explaining the *Arrival* Ending," *Den of Geek* (blog), February 22, 2017, http://www.denofgeek.com/us/movies/arrival/259944/explaining-the-arrival-ending.

27. Jay Dyer, "*Arrival* (2016)—The Film's Secret Meaning Explained," *21st Century Wire*, November 15, 2016, http://www.21stcenturywire.com/2016/11/15/arrival-2016-the-films-secret-meaning-explained/.

28. Statt, "How the Short Story That Inspired *Arrival* Helps Us Interpret the Film's Major Twist."

The Road Not Taken
Environmental Ethics, Reciprocity, and Non-Negative Nonagency

Thomas Claviez

SUBJECT VERSUS OBJECT, MEANS VERSUS ENDS—AGENCY VERSUS?

Two roads diverged in a yellow wood,
And sorry I could not travel both

I think it is safe to say that almost all contributions that are tagged "post-humanistic" have one goal in common: to reduce, if not to abolish, the difference between the subject and the object.[1] The objective behind that goal—a goal as old as Romanticism itself—refers to one of the basic presuppositions of poststructuralism: that all binary oppositions have both a logical and an axiological—that is, normative—aspect to them, or, to be more precise, that any logical opposition is always also inhabited by a normative opposition that tends to favor one of the poles, while the other pole always carries mainly negative connotations. This pertains to almost all of the binaries that have been at the focus of the debates ensuing from poststructuralism and that we are all too familiar with: male and female, black and white, North and South, same and other, means and ends, center and periphery—the list could go on indefinitely. The question that, in my view, has never been sufficiently addressed is just *why* this is the case: whether, that is, the indissoluble combination of a logical opposition with an axiological hierarchy constitutes something like an anthropological constant, grows out of a historical contingency or an ideological predisposition, or is simply a regrettable accident.[2] One of the instances in which the problem becomes specifically visible is when we put the following question: Is the opposition between good and bad—the ethical question per se—in itself a logical or an axiological opposition, that is, a descriptive or a prescriptive one? If it were both, how could we even claim that there is a difference between the two? If it were either one or the other, the question remains as to where to draw the line. There seems to be a problem here.

Now, if this diagnosis about poststructuralism is right—that is, that it poses the problem of binary oppositions in both axiological and logical terms—then there are actually two possible ways to proceed. In both, however, the problem just laid out will still be there to haunt us: We could either start from the ethical end and argue that our task is to *acknowledge* the other (or otherness), negotiate the axiological denigration of the second pole, while leaving the logical opposition intact; or we could try to dissolve the logical opposition between the two, hoping that, in the process, the axiological hierarchies will be deconstructed as a kind of "collateral" effect. The latter version, I think it is safe to say, is the road that about 90 percent of the disciplinary heirs of poststructuralism have taken, be they gender studies, postcolonial varieties, or, as mentioned, posthumanism.

What is, however, rather paradoxical about this latter strategy, if you take a closer look, is that difference—whose hardnosed existence constituted the problem in the first place—actually vanishes: What we get instead of black and white are fifty shades of gray that do not allow for any clear delineations to be drawn. Difference seems to be nowhere because it is everywhere. Instead, that is, of acknowledging the other or otherness as *the axiological, or ethical, problem*—in fact, the very problem of *any ethics as such*—difference or alterity is logically deconstructed out of existence, presuming, as I mentioned, that the normative quarrels associated with them will magically disappear as a result of solving—or rather, dissolving—the logical one. The problem is that they don't, and a glance at the actual debates within posthumanism might indicate why. My argument is that, of all the oppositions addressed by poststructuralism and its offspring, one has suffered a pitiful disregard, and that is the one of agency and its opposite. But what exactly *is* this opposite?

Behind the attempts of almost all recent contributions to ecocriticism, especially of the posthumanism variety, from the work of Bruno Latour, via Jane Bennett's *Vibrant Matter* and Timothy Morton's *Realist Magic* to Rosi Braidotti's *The Posthuman*, of deconstructing the subject/object divide lurks, I will argue, the goal (if unacknowledged) of tackling just this opposition between agency and its opposite.[3] That is, their purpose is to grant *agency* to that part which, up to now, has been consigned to the losing side of the subject/object divide: the object. Actor-Network Theory—the name gives it away—sets out to make us aware that we are always part in and of a network where what we formerly deemed things—or, in Kantian terms, means—are also actors or agents that are acting with, against, or upon us. In so doing, what posthumanism tries to achieve is to grant an *ethical* status to parts of our environment that, up to now, have been excluded from our moral considerations because they haven't been granted agency. The questions that consequently arise are the following: (1) What connection is there between agency and being granted the status of ethical or moral subjecthood? And (2) are we to assume that objecthood is then by default connected to agency's contrary, passivity? But there is an even more pressing question: (3) Presuming that agency *is* what provides moral subjecthood, does the fact that objects, or means, allegedly do *not* act (or—and this will become important—at least *cannot be held responsible for their acts*) imply that they cannot claim the tag of "moral" objecthood? And is "moral objecthood" not in fact a contradiction in terms? If it is, is granting objects agency a possible way to ensure a moral status for them? Or do we have, as I have argued, to rethink agency's opposite, passivity? But, in light of what I said about poststructuralism's tendency to deconstruct binary oppositions, what would be contrary to agency or, rather, of "acting"?[4] Could we, axiologically speaking, even *think* of the opposite of "acting" in non-negative terms? And how does the fact that we, as I will argue, seem not able (or willing) to do so relate to the posthumanists' efforts to achieve just that: granting objects agency?

IRRECIPROCITY AND PASSIVITY: EMMANUEL LEVINAS

And be one traveler, long I stood
And looked down one as far as I could
To where it bent in the undergrowth;

Before I address the question of agency—and the neglect, if not dismissal, of its unidentified other not only by environmental ethics or posthumanism but in almost all areas affected by moral philosophy—let me clarify *why* I contend that the problem of agency (and its other) has not been sufficiently addressed.

The one scandalon in Levinas's ethics—which theorists such as Jean-François Lyotard, Paul Ricoeur, and even Jacques Derrida have, at one point or another, and with different amounts of success, tried to write out of Levinas's philosophy[5]—is the very passivity (or, as he calls it, a "passivity more passive than any passivity," a passivity that *precedes* the distinction between passivity and activity) that forms the core of his ethics. Michael Newman puts this rather succinctly:

> Levinas' approach to responsibility moves from the active, through the passivity of activity . . . to a passivity more passive that is the opposite or deprived form of activity, in other words, a passivity that can no longer be synthesized, and which therefore is no longer subordinate to activity. The passivity more passive than the passivity of activity will neither be a passive activity (passive synthesis) nor a reactive passivity, one that would relate to activity. The paradox that is difficult to grasp here is that Levinasian "passivity" is related to the normal sense of passivity and at the same time incommensurable with it, as if at the point at which passivity becomes hyperbolic a rupture takes place.[6]

It is important to note here that Levinas's notion of "a passivity more passive than any passivity" is closely related to the hyperbolic assumption, formulated in *Otherwise Than Being*, that I become "hostage" to the other.[7] While this latter formulation has been the subject of heated debates, no one has, in my view, exhaustively addressed the concept that lies at the root of the debate: that of passivity and its complicated relation to its other, agency. And it is this passivity that is intricately related to the second backbone of his ethics: irreciprocity.

Needless to say, with the activity/passivity binary, we find ourselves in the presence of another of those notorious oppositions that presumably would constitute easy prey for a deconstructive attack; strangely enough, I do not know of any prominent attempt to take on this pair activity/passivity, let alone a "passivity more passive than any passivity." One of the reasons—and here again, we enter the logical/axiological problem outlined earlier—may be that there hardly exists, in any language known to me, a verb that could formulate the contrary of "to act" in a non-negative way.[8]

One of the reasons why Levinas evokes a passivity *beyond* the activity/

passivity divide, one that escapes the logical-cum-axiological problems outlined earlier, might be that what he wants to get at is a *non-negative concept of passivity*. Let me add that I, when I talk about the "contrary of 'to act,'" emphatically do not mean simply "not to act" here: What I am trying to get at is a verb that would denote "being acted upon," that is, *being at the receiving end of an other's action*. One problem that poses itself is that, when we are talking about verbs, we are talking by definition about actions, and thus the contrary of "to act" might not even fall into the purview of the class called verbs. But this is not really the case: There *are* verbs that try to capture it. However, the only verb that does in English is "to suffer"; in German, it would be the closely connected word *erleiden*—both of which clearly do not evoke positive connotations. Not acting thus means—to suffer. This becomes visible in the following quotation from Ricoeur in *Oneself as Another*, a passage that makes sufficiently clear why the "hyperbole" of passivity does not sit well with his own approach: "Suffering is not defined solely by physical pain, nor even by mental pain, but by the reduction, even the destruction, of the capacity for acting, of being-able-to-act, experienced as a violation of self-integrity."[9]

As for nouns, things do not look much better: The contrary to an actor is either a patient or a sufferer, both of which still retain a pathological air to them. That is, while "not-acting," that is, abstaining from action, can be considered a rational choice—as a consequence of a deliberate decision not to act—being acted upon is not only irrational but *escapes the realm of the rational altogether*. Why? Because the rationality of somebody can only be measured according to the degree his actions—or intentional nonaction— fit a presumed goal. However, there can emphatically be no goal if we are suffering, or can there?[10] What this excursus affords us, however, is a first inkling as to what Levinas means when he invokes a passivity that precedes the distinction between active and passive: This distinction is in itself a rational one, and thus we can think the activity/passivity divide as encompassing deliberate action on the one hand and/or the deliberate and intentional decision *not to act* on the other. That is why distinguishing between "not-acting" and suffering someone else's acts is of immense importance: The latter cannot possibly be subjected to this rational distinction. It escapes reason; whether it might, in Levinas's words, precede it is an open question. It certainly puts reason into question; it *is* its other. And the question it raises might be none other than *the* ethical question.

This might also explain why Levinas, when he tries to give a "face" to the

Other (writ large) that otherwise would have to remain unrepresentable, he chooses the widow, the orphan, and the stranger. A lot has been written about whether these have been appropriate choices, whether he should have chosen a signifier at all for something that, according to his own views, cannot be represented, and why he chose the figures that he did. Let me just point out that, from the perspective of agency, and in light of what has been and will be said, these choices make sense: What unites all three figures is that, while they doubtlessly can be considered "moral subjects" (or can they?), what they share is an alleged lack of agency or, presumably, the lack of a person *to act on their behalf*.[11] We might want to keep this in mind for what follows.

Now, while these remarks might give the impression of a self-indulgent, semantic sophistry, their implications extend further than that, in as far as agency in itself plays a central role in almost all known moral philosophies of Western provenance. Only insofar as someone acts can he or she actually become a moral subject, a subject, that is, that qua his or her actions acquires the responsibility for these acts and consequently can be held accountable for them. (I will leave out the distinction between intentionalist and consequentialist varieties of this assumption.) This, needless to say, entails also the opposite conclusion: that I cannot be made responsible for what I have suffered at the hands of others, while I certainly can be made responsible for acts that I intentionally *abstained from doing*. What hardly ever is taken seriously into account, however, is the fact that any action on my or anyone else's part requires someone who "suffers" it—and, for that matter, *any action*, not only criminal ones. Needless to say, the person at the receiving end of my action can by default not be made responsible for my action; nor, as I have pointed out, can she or he be made responsible for suffering mine. The victim usually is not held—cannot be held—accountable. This seems all but commonsensical—but it isn't. We have arrived at a rather unique constellation: Suffering constitutes a *logical* contrary to acting but is itself not a "rational" category.

If agency constitutes one of the main moral categories—indeed, is what *makes* me a moral subject—then what happens to the ones that "suffer" my actions? It might well be that the physical law "action equals reaction" might have blinded us to the fact that, in the case of an act, the presumed *re*action might not come from he or she who suffers it, and if so, the reaction would still only come once my action *has* been suffered and accordingly would have to be distinguished from it. Even Michel Foucault's assumption that power—usually conceived as the power to act—always creates a counter-power seems to be based on this physical law.¹² Such a mechanistic understanding of action, however, is not what I am talking about and is not what is taking place when I act upon another.

MORAL SUBJECTHOOD AND/AS AGENCY, PART I

> Then took the other, as just as fair,
> And having perhaps the better claim,
> Because it was grassy and wanted wear;

How important action is in many contexts—and at the expense of its contrary, suffering—I will pursue further in what follows. Suffice it here to say that one of the most puzzling, unsolved contradictions in the work of Immanuel Kant's moral philosophy has its roots here: the fact that he felt forced to make humans' "will" the very law that is imposed upon them from above.¹³ In light of what I have said so far, the reason is rather simple, almost banal: When we assume that such an unconditional law as Kant's moral law exists, our sheer passive acceptance of it would actually prevent us from becoming moral subjects ourselves, ones who are, or can be made, responsible only for their *acts*—in this case, the act of willingly and actively embracing something imposed upon me from the outside that I passively receive. If we were to sheepishly follow a law that we would not actively will and endorse, we could not become moral subjects according to Kant's criteria. The entire debate surrounding Nazi crimes and the Eichmann trial, for example, might serve to illustrate this conundrum.

This brings me back to one of the questions asked earlier: whether, and at what point, animals can be considered moral subjects and where, if any, a line could be drawn as to what distinguishes a moral subject from a presumably amoral object. A moral object cannot exist, if we presume the capability to act rationally and to take responsibility for an action to be a requisite for a moral subject. That is at least how Kant's famous Golden Rule defines it: an end in itself and not just a means.¹⁴ A means by definition is "used"—that is, is acted upon—in order to achieve an end exterior to it. An "end in itself" is where my action ends because there the ends of the other's action start. One should, however, keep in mind that Kant explicitly says that we should treat a human being *also* as an end and *not only* as a means, leaving open the possibility of both. But can both be the case simultaneously?

The caveat that Kant includes—the one that provides the possibility of being treated as *both* means *and* ends (just not *exclusively* as a means)—seems to indicate a certain awareness and possibility that we sometimes *do* treat others as means and not exclusively as ends but that the former attitude should not prevail. And, as we have seen, this awareness is quite relevant, since acting is what constitutes a moral subject. However, this opens two pressing questions: (1) Would there not have to be somebody/something at the receiving end of any action done? (2) Would not that, however, imply that, as someone "being acted upon" or becoming a subject of—or rather, an object of, by being subjected to—someone else's action, I would, by temporarily becoming a means, lose my status as a moral subject? The small word "also" consequently gains an enormous significance: Can I actually be—in view of the fact that I am either acting or being acted upon—simultaneously means *and* end?

If we return, then, to the question as to where the dividing line could be drawn as far as moral subjecthood is concerned, what has been said so far acquires relevance. The question, to be more precise, is offered by the following example: On what basis can we grant moral subjecthood through rational agency and then allow primates to be killed but, on the other hand, babies or demented people to stay alive? Now, the problem at first sight seems to be one of rationality and of who is accorded such a status and who isn't. However, that is only half of the truth—and here, both agency and reciprocity acquire relevance, if at a certain angle: The question is what happens when we accord the status of moral subject to what formerly was—or would, according to the definition, have to be—considered an amoral *object* (which others might deem worthy of our protection). Or again, can, in view of the Kantian problem outlined in what follows, something like a moral "object" exist? This is where the second concept—that of reciprocity—comes in. And it might be illustrated by an example that is very much to the point, though it does pertain to environmental ethics only indirectly: that of "chattel slavery."

THE PROBLEM WITH THE SOUTHERN SLAVE LAW

> Though as for that the passing there
> Had worn them really about the same,

I do not need to develop at this point just why chattel slavery was thus called: Slaves were, according to the slaveholders, not fully human—that is, rational—beings and thus could be treated like animals: like chattel, that is, or, in Kantian categories, as pure means. Here we detect a regrettable lacuna in Kant's edifice: As long as I can convincingly (or not so convincingly) maintain that someone is *not* rational, or not reasonable enough, this suffices for him or her to be treated legitimately as a means—that is, a sufferer. This does not only open Kant's universal, categorical imperative to historical contingency; it indeed opens up an entire keg of worms, in that all of this went well enough in the US South, until the Southern slaveholders—or, more specifically, the Southern courts of law—stumbled across a mighty problem, and that problem was *not one of rationality but of agency*.[15] What if the slave considered a means suddenly turns into an end and starts to act? Concretely, what if a slave acts and runs away or, worse still, acts upon his master, attacks him, and thus, for a change, makes *him* suffer? Or, to formulate the question more poignantly: Can you hold what you conceive to be an amoral object—a means, a sufferer—accountable for an action that, by default, turns him *into* an acting moral subject/ends/actor, no matter whether rational or not? While, that is, rationality can be categorically denied, action cannot.

As the potential animals the slaves were considered to be, they couldn't possibly be considered to act rationally; an object by default suffers, by definition cannot act, and consequently cannot be held responsible for an action—at least not as a rational agent aware of his or her responsibility for the act. The problem becomes clear when we take into account the linkage Kant establishes between rationality and being an end, and thus an actor, and not a sufferer: Action is necessarily linked to rationality because only as a rationally acting being can anyone be held accountable for an action. A nonrational being might be able to act, but it cannot effectively be made responsible in this way; that is why the principle of reciprocity does not work in this case.[16]

As I have written extensively on the ludicrous juridico-rhetorical gymnastics that the Southern slave-law givers were forced into to solve this unsolvable conundrum elsewhere,[17] suffice it to say that at this point agency meets up with reciprocity in the notion of the moral subject: Once I leave the irreciprocal status of being a sufferer/means/object behind, what I am granted is the reciprocity of responsibility: As I act, so I am made reciprocally responsible for the acts I commit. But wait a second: Is it that easy? Is it true that action equals reaction and thus that an almost physical reciprocity is ensured? The answer is: No.

The problem that the argument referred to earlier faces and that is also reflected in the slave-law puzzle is as follows: Do not some nonrational agents—some animals, all infants, and, for example, demented people and (historically) slaves—deserve our protection? Now, being protected is certainly not an activity; being protected means that *you retain your objecthood while still asserting a moral relevance that, however, cannot claim moral subjecthood*, as such a being is not able to fulfill the conditions of reciprocity, namely, being prepared and considered able to be held responsible for its actions. But the problem I want to get at is even more severe: a rather perverse logic at the heart of a moral philosophy based upon the distinction between moral subjects and amoral objects—upon which, after all, also much of the posthumanism debate depends. The problem appears at the transition between objecthood and moral subjecthood, and it is poised upon the connection between agency and reciprocity—and upon what falls out of the equation.

If we assume that the attempt to grant moral subjecthood to what was formerly considered an object is the attempt to give us the means to protect that object, the paradox that we are facing is the following: We start out from the assumption that, in order to offer protection to an object normally treated as a means/sufferer, *we have to accord it the status of active subjecthood*. We do this, in turn, on the assumption that it suffers because it hasn't been granted moral subjecthood (yet), that is, the status of an active agent. What, however, does it take to be or become a moral subject? Or, for that matter, that impossible thing: a "moral object"? One would have to become an agent, an agent, however, who cannot be held reciprocally responsible for his actions, because he needs protection, since he is *not* able to act in order to protect oneself. In the case of the slaves, this created a puzzle: Indeed—and almost unavoidably—the Southern lawgivers staged themselves as the "guardians" of the slaves—not unlike what some ecologists today urge us to do. If nature, or slaves, or children are accorded the status of moral subjects, this would entail that they are to be held reciprocally responsible for what they are doing. Now, we can obviously turn nature into an agent in many ways: as what feeds us or what is able to destroy us, as in tsunamis, for example. Consequently, the question as to which responsibilities we acknowledge and which we don't is, needless to say, immensely important. But can we grant "*non*rational" agency, which also entails *non*reciprocal responsibility? And what implications would this have for the linkage between agency (which is, as we have seen, by default *irreciprocal*) and the responsibility for this agency, which is irrevocably *reciprocal*?

MORAL SUBJECTHOOD AND/AS AGENCY, PART 2

> And both that morning equally lay
> In leaves no step had trodden black.
> Oh, I kept the first for another day!
> Yet knowing how way leads on to way,
> I doubted if I should ever come back.

The problem that we have identified thus is rooted in the fact that the moment something actually aspires to (which an object cannot do, since it lacks intentionality and thus responsibility) and is accorded (that is, passively receives) moral subjecthood, something absurd happens: *We admit it into moral subjecthood by granting it a power to act, the very absence of which makes our protection necessary in the first place.* The moment, that is, it is granted active subjecthood, we are denying the very origin of its claim to subjecthood, which was its need of protection because it could not act or react and thus not assume reciprocal responsibility. This, in the final analysis, opens an abyss of absurdity in our moral philosophies—and just because so much depends upon one unclarified term: agency.

I would argue that we can escape this dilemma only if we disentangle moral subjecthood from the ability to (and the responsibility for) agency, both of which are intricately connected. And I guess this is why Levinas—though he never formulated it this way—distinguished between an ethics of irreciprocity and a justice based upon reciprocity, and Kant and the problems his moral philosophy entails are a perfect illustration of the problems encountered by the latter. The problem of ethics concerns us when we are in fact dealing with things or people who, before all, *cannot act* themselves, and that is why passivity and irreciprocity are so indissolubly connected in Levinas. The problem of our traditional moral philosophies—and of justice in general—is that neither can accord moral subjecthood without presuming that the subject is active. If we take into account, however, that any active subject presupposes "suffering" objects (or means, or means who are also ends)—since, as Kant was obviously aware, subjects *do* treat other subjects sometimes as means, as they require sufferers who receive their actions in order *to constitute their subjectivity*—then we have to rethink the concept of agency. Otherwise, we have to admit to the perverse logic that I, morally speaking, *achieve my subjectivity only at the cost of others who suffer my actions and thus lose their moral subjecthood in turn.* Agency itself thus constitutes, at its heart, and by definition, an instance of irreciprocity, an irreciprocity that Levinas has identified as the ethical moment as such and that forms the core of any ethical (and not juridical) consideration whatsoever. Otherwise, moral subjectivity conceived in traditional terms of agency is a zero-sum game, as one achieved means one lost. This is not exactly the metaphor we usually connote with justice.[18]

What is more: This logic also entails another, rather troubling implication, namely, that in a juridical court the victim is implicitly but necessarily turned into a moral object—one who is turned into a sufferer by both the perpetrator and by a law that is designed to actively protect him or her. This might actually help explain the uneasiness or at least the ambivalence often experienced by the victims in court: that the actor/perpetrator is always at the center of a trial and that he or she receives much more attention—and necessarily so—than the ones upon whom the deed was inflicted.

Maybe the ability and the nonability to act is exactly where the gap between ethics and justice can be located: Ethics addresses our obligations toward the sufferer, while justice holds responsible the actor. The question is: Can that gap be bridged?

THE "REVOLT OF THE MEANS": BRUNO LATOUR AND ACTOR-NETWORK THEORY

> I shall be telling this with a sigh
> Somewhere ages and ages hence:
> Two roads diverged in a wood, and I—

In light of what has been said so far, let me return to posthumanism, and the situation now presents itself in a slightly different way. This becomes clear when we turn to an approach that has gained quite some traction among the proponents of posthumanism and also beyond: Bruno Latour's Actor-Network Theory (ANT). This theory takes into account two things: First, it is based on the assumptions of his early work—most significantly the theses put forward in the book with the programmatic title *We Have Never Been Modern*. There he argues what the title already indicates, namely, that the subject-object divide, one of the basic assumptions that both modernism and the Enlightenment pride themselves on having established, has never really been achieved. This, in turn, has repercussions on the means-end divide, since that one is, consequently, an illusion, too, as would be the divide between agency and passivity. Or does it?

Latour claims that we are entangled or enmeshed in a network of relationships, that is, that "Being," along the lines of Martin Heidegger, is always also and already "being-with," a "being-with," however, that emphatically encompasses also the being-with other *objects* as well, thus opening up ethical considerations that can be traced back to Spinoza. "No one has ever heard of a collective that did not mobilize heaven and earth in its composition, along with bodies and souls, property and law, gods and ancestors, powers and beliefs, beasts and fictional beings. . . . Such is the anthropological matrix, the one we have never abandoned." To which he later adds: "It is this exploration of a transcendence without a contrary that makes our world so unmodern, with all those nuncios, mediators, delegates, fetishes, machines, figurines, instruments, representatives, angels, lieutenants, spokespersons and cherubims."[19]

One part of ANT, however, should give us reason to pause in light of what has been said so far: that of the actor. As we have seen, any agent both requires and creates a patient at the receiving end of his/her/its action. What, on the other hand, makes ANT so interesting from a posthumanist perspective is that it grants agency to actors that have formerly not been considered as such, namely, objects, which suddenly find themselves part and parcel of the "parliament of things," as Latour so memorably puts it.[20]

The driving force and leading assumption behind the work of Latour is exactly that: to undermine, to blur, or at least to question the clear-cut distinction between subject and object and, consequently, actor and sufferer, or agent and patient. However, what are we, in the light of what has been said, to make of an "*Actor*-Network Theory"? Does not (a) an *Actor* Network always by necessity imply another *Sufferer* Network? Or even: *Is* not an *Actor* Network always also a *Sufferer* Network, if any action by default presupposes someone/something that suffers the action? And (b) are we then to assume that all the actors in the Actor-Network Theory attain (or should be granted) moral subjecthood simply *because* they act? Assuming that a stone, although it may be part of an Actor Network, is not a moral subject that we can hold responsible for its acts (like, say, a rock hitting me during a landslide), would this not, in turn, entail that we reconsider or at least problematize the connection between agency and moral subjecthood in a new way? Since Latour allegedly chose the name because he liked the acronym "ANT," "SNT" or "PNT" (for Sufferers or Patients, respectively) admittedly would not have sounded too sexy. Rather surprisingly, however, what Bruno Latour resorts to when he addresses the question of morality in ANT is Kant's moral philosophy—in light of what has been said so far, a rather surprising choice!

First of all, we have to be aware of the fact that, in Latour's *The Politics of Nature*, morality plays a subordinate role in a quartet that also involves science, politics, and economy. Moreover, there is a striking absence in this fourfold system: jurisprudence. Although he talks about a separation of powers, Latour never addresses legislation, execution, and jurisdiction in his scenario separately. Moreover, the tasks of what he calls the "Moralists" are only taken into account rather late in *The Politics of Nature*. His starting point is an "is-state" (defined by the other three discourses, science, politics, and economy) that then is complemented, at a rather late stage in his argument, by an ethical stance. What he thus circumvents is the question of what ethical stance it is that informs his "is-state" and what should be done about it.

That said, let us have a closer look at the role that morality or "the Moralists" are designed to play in his parliamentary houses. Here is how Latour defines his project:

> The Constitution that we seek to draw up affirms . . . that the only way to compose a common world, and thus to escape later from a multiplicity of interests and a plurality of beliefs, consists precisely in not dividing up at the outset and *without due process* what is common and what is private, what is objective and what is subjective. Whereas the moral question of the common good was separated from the physical and epistemological question of the common world, we maintain, on the contrary, that these questions must be brought together so that the question of the *good* common world can be raised from scratch.[21]

These lines seem to confirm what has been said earlier; however, a closer look at this paragraph shows that the distinction between "is" and "ought" becomes considerably more complex: Not only is there a division between an "is" ("common world") and an "ought" ("common good"), but this state of division is, in turn, in itself an "is" that *should* be overcome by another "ought" that should help us overcome the division and combine the two. The conclusion thus entails *two* different "oughts": (1) The two *must be brought together* in order to (2) then *raise the question of the good* common world from scratch. As I mentioned earlier, there is thus not only a (later) moral task (to raise the question of the good common world); it is preceded by a former (and maybe primary) prescription: The questions "must be brought together," and this with "due process." Where that primary "ought" comes from or who raises it remains, as far as I can tell, unanswered by Latour.

This enables him to postpone the question of morality, to be later taken up in a chapter entitled "The Contribution of Moralists" (and honestly: Who of us would want to be called a "moralist?"). Be that as it may: In this chapter, he resorts to Kant and defines the moral problem in a very Kantian manner (which, however, has spectrally un-Kantian implications) as

> *uncertainty* about the proper relation between means and ends, extending Kant's famous definition of the obligation "not to treat human beings as means but always also as ends"—provided that we *extend it to non-humans as well*, something that Kantianism, in a typically modernist move, specifically wanted to avoid.[22]

Granting such an extension, however—or actually demanding it in the sense of a moral requirement—is no easy feat, since we are uttering a moral prescriptive toward a moral philosophy that actually lays out the very foundation as to how, as well as the terms with which, moral prescriptions can be uttered in the first place. That is, if we extend Kant's axiom—not to treat human beings as means but always also as ends—to comprise nonhumans also, then the distinction between means and ends, at least in the way Kant conceived it, collapses; in fact, it becomes nonsensical, since *there are no means left to be distinguished from ends*. But if that is the case, why keep the distinction? It looks as if the double bind that we identified earlier has, at least for the moment, come back to roost.

However, maybe Kant's famous dictum might finally offer us a way out of this dilemma, since he, as mentioned earlier, already blurs the distinction when talking about means being "also" ends. This seems to open up an opportunity for Latour's attempt to close the gap between the two. Kant's moral axiom to treat humans "always also" as ends implies, even presupposes, that humans are, in fact, also sometimes treated as means; that is, they simply shouldn't be treated exclusively so, which, in turn, means that *they are not exclusively ends, either*. What Latour wants to achieve is for nonhumans, which have up to now been considered exclusively as means, also to be considered as ends:

> Ecological crises, as we have interpreted them, present themselves as *generalized revolts of the means*: no entity—whale, river, climate, earthworm, tree, calf, cow, pig, brood—agrees any longer to be treated "simply as a means" but insists on being treated "always also as an end." This in no way entails extending human morality to the natural world, or projecting the law extravagantly onto "mere brute beings," or to take into account the rights of objects "for themselves"; it is rather the simple consequence of the disappearance of the notion of external nature.[23]

This, in fact, sounds like a seductively easy solution. Just let go of the notion of external nature, and our troubles will be solved! But wait a minute: *Can means revolt?*[24] That is, can they, for example, be held accountable for what happens during such a revolution, for their act of revolt? Do they automatically become "ends" *because* they revolt?

First of all, the "disappearance of the notion of external nature" indeed does all that Latour claims it does not: It *does* in fact "extend human morality to the natural world," it *does* "project the law extravagantly onto 'mere brute beings,'" and it *does* "take into account the rights of objects for themselves." Let me explain why.

If we start with said "generalized revolt of the means," this entails an action (the revolt) being ascribed to an object (which, consequently, cedes its being just that). To consequently declare it a subject—and a moral subject in the Kantian manner at that—*it would have to be made responsible for its actions*: This is what the case of the Southern slave laws that I elaborated upon earlier has made sufficiently clear, and this is what Latour's take on the means/ends problematic does not take into account. It is, however, a problem that also Kant, and the Kantians after him, have conspicuously ignored, and it haunts our human moral philosophies even without us trying to extend them to the realm of the nonhuman. That is, if we simply make external nature disappear, and do in fact "extend human morality to the natural world," and do "project the law," that means that we expect moral subjecthood thus achieved to comprise not only the *ability* to act but also the *"response-ability"* for said acts; here is where the concept of reciprocity that Levinas challenges becomes most visible. The acts of an object that cannot be held reciprocally responsible would have to be endured irreciprocally. If we, however, were to project the law onto "mere brute beings," we would also have to project onto them the very paradox that Kant was unable

222   Thomas Claviez

to get rid of: that the brute beings should "will" the very law that subjects them, in order to retain the ability to will an act and consequently to be held accountable for it. The main problem, then, is the definition of moral subjecthood through an agency that the former can be made (reciprocally) responsible for. That is, simply to extend a blurred means-and-ends status to nonhumans does not solve anything as long as the question of agency itself—as a moral category—has not been properly addressed.[25]

It is the problem of agency not properly addressed that also undermines Karen Barad's argument when she tries to mobilize an ecological Levinasian ethics. While she is right in pointing out that for Levinas the "primordial relation of man with the material world is not negativity, but enjoyment and agreeableness of life," the fact that human life might be embedded in material agency and that matter "itself is always already open to, or rather entangled with, the 'Other'"[26] means that what she does is, like her predecessors, take the sting out of Levinas's ethics of the "hyperbolic" passivity, which constitutes its main pillar, in commingling agency with responsibility.[27]

Can this problem be solved? And if so, how? I am not sure it can, but we might want to try to take some first tentative steps in this direction. Let us return to the "also" in Kant's second Categorical Imperative. If we agree that Kant leaves open the possibility of being treated *as both a means and an end*, what does that actually mean?

NON-NEGATIVE NONAGENCY

> I took the one less traveled by,
> And that has made all the difference.

As I indicated at the beginning, there lurks a certain paradox in the assumption that only agency grants someone moral subjecthood, in that those who are in need of our ethical support are by definition those who are not able to act for themselves—are, indeed, victims of the deeds of others. However, as we have seen, we are all by default always also at the receiving end—and thus not ends ourselves—of others' deeds. But I am afraid we cannot have the cake and eat it, too: One cannot be means and ends at the same time, because *one cannot be agent and patient simultaneously, if agency is what provides moral subjecthood*. Being at the receiving end of someone else's agency by default turns me into a means; this, in turn, by necessity implies that I lose my moral subjecthood once I am being acted upon. And

I lose this status because otherwise the principle of reciprocity, embedded and based upon agency, and the responsibility that comes with it cannot be upheld.

The only way to solve this puzzle is, in my view, to try to disentangle moral subjecthood and agency, or, to be more precise, to come up with a non-negative concept of the contrary to agency that still would allow a patient to retain his/her/its status as a moral subject. I am aware that the implications—political, juridical, and more—of such a project are enormous: For one, and on the political side, it would entail a conundrum because it could seem to create a moral legitimation for passivity, which could be easily abused. Juridically or legally speaking, granting moral subjecthood to someone who has been passive might entail that responsibility is being projected upon a person that *was* in fact passive and thus nonaccountable. However, if what I have said so far is true, then similar problems are already in place and need to be addressed.

Part of the problem of even thinking along those lines is that we, as I pointed out, simply (as yet) do not have a vocabulary that would allow us to do so, since we do not have a term to denote the contrary of agency in a non-negative manner. Patients, sufferers, objects, means: These are the words at our disposal, all of which negatively connoted and none of which allowing us to overcome the problems laid out here. That is the challenge that we are facing. We might have to learn to think the impossible: a moral objecthood that includes agency (though none that can be made reciprocally responsible) or/and a moral subjecthood that includes its non-negative opposite. No small feat indeed. I think that the entire work of Latour is geared toward such a concept, but Kant's philosophy will emphatically not help us get there. If, that is, deconstruction "means to overturn this hierarchy" (in our case, that between agency and its non-negative opposite) at a certain moment *and* if neglecting this phase of change is "to forget the conflictual and subordinating structure of opposition," *but* if enacting "a *neutralization* that *in practice* would leave the previous field untouched" means "giving away any opportunity to intervene in fact," and would thus prevent "any means of *intervening* in the field effectively,"[28] then we have to admit that we are far from even having reached the first stage—let alone any means to actually "intervene in fact." However, Levinas's concept of a "passivity more passive than any passivity" might provide us with a clue about where to start. As far as the practical import or valence of such an endeavor is concerned, let me simply remind you: If reason goes somewhere imagination cannot go, we call that sublime, but if reason goes somewhere practice cannot go, we strangely enough often call that either irrelevant or noncommonsensical. . . .

NOTES

1. All epigraphs are from Robert Frost's poem "The Road Not Taken."
2. The *locus classicus* is doubtlessly Jacques Derrida's following excerpt from his *Positions* (Chicago: University of Chicago Press, 1981): "On the one hand, we must traverse a phase of *overturning*. To do justice to this necessity is to recognize that in a classical philosophical opposition we are not dealing with the peaceful coexistence of a *vis-à-vis*, but rather with a violent hierarchy. One of the two terms governs the other (axiologically, logically, etc.), or has the upper hand. To deconstruct the opposition, first of all, is to overturn the hierarchy at a given moment. To overlook this phase of overturning is to forget the conflictual and subordinating structure of opposition. Therefore one might proceed too quickly to a *neutralization* that *in practice* would leave the previous field untouched, leaving one no hold on the previous opposition, thereby preventing any means of *intervening* in the field effectively" (41).
3. As regards the concept of agency, Jane Bennett is the one who most openly tackles this problem: Right at the beginning of her *Vibrant Matter: A Political Ecology of Things* (Durham, NC: Duke University Press, 2010), she urges us to consider matter itself as "agents and forces" that are part and parcel of human agency (viii).
4. That is why Latour's "actant," which also Bennett refers to repeatedly, is only of little significance in the question I'd like to pursue here. While Bennett even speaks of "legal actants" (*Vibrant Matter*, 8–10), Latour's definition explicitly excludes "motivation"—and thus responsibility—from the picture when he defines an actant as "something that acts or to which activity is granted by others. *It implies no special motivation of human individual actors*, or of humans in general." Bruno Latour, *Pandora's Hope: Essays on the Reality of Science Studies* (Cambridge, MA: Harvard University Press, 1999), 281, emphasis mine. I will address this conundrum further in the section "The Problem with the Southern Slave Law." It partly also refers to what William Pietz—whom Bennett quotes right after her reference to Latour—refers to as the "law of deodand": The fact that "any culture must establish some procedure of compensation, expiation, or punishment to settle the debt created by unintended human deaths whose direct cause is not a morally accountable person, but a nonhuman material object"—or, in the light of the Southern Slave Law, one that counts as such. William Pietz, "Death of the Deodand: Accursed Objects and the Money Value of Human Life," *RES: Anthropology and Aesthetics* 31 (1997): 97. The main problem that is, in my view, evaded is how a "debt" can even be incurred by a nonintending object.

5. Paul Ricoeur, Jean-François Lyotard, and Jacques Derrida have tried, if in different ways, to incorporate a Levinasian ethics into their philosophies—an effort at each instance paid for by taking the sting (or the "hyperbole") out of Levinas's ethics. Paul Ricoeur, *Oneself as Another* (Chicago: University of Chicago Press, 1992), 189–90, 336–41; Jean-François Lyotard and Jean-Loup Thébaud, *Just Gaming* (Manchester: Manchester University Press, 1985), 60ff.; Jacques Derrida, "Violence and Metaphysics," in *Writing and Difference*, trans. Alan Bass (Chicago: University of Chicago Press, 1978), 100–4. See also Thomas Claviez, *Aesthetics and Ethics: Otherness and Moral Imagination from Aristotle to Levinas and from "Uncle Tom's Cabin" to "House Made of Dawn"* (Heidelberg: Winter, 2008), 35–41, 204–18. Let me add that it cannot be the purpose of this paper to address the huge impact of Levinas's philosophical approach to Western moral philosophy; that is why I am addressing this possible impact only for the limited realm of environmental ethics. Beside the work of John Llewelyn, *The Middle Voice of Ecological Conscience* (London: Macmillan, 1991), one of the more recent attempts to do so is William Edelglass, James Hatley, and Christian Diehm, eds., *Facing Nature: Levinas and Environmental Thought* (Pittsburgh, PA: Duquesne University Press, 2012).

6. Michael Newman, "Sensibility, Trauma, and the Face: Levinas from Phenomenology to the Immemorial," in *The Face of the Other and the Trace of God*, ed. Jeffrey Bloechi (New York: Fordham University Press, 2000), 98.

7. "Under accusation by everyone, the responsibility for everyone goes to the point of substitution. A subject is hostage." Emmanuel Levinas, *Otherwise Than Being or Beyond Essence* (The Hague: Nijhoff, 1981), 112. A lot has been written about this "hyperbolic" element in Levinas's ethics in philosophic circles. What seems so strange about all this excitement is that this scandalon is actually only the result of what constitutes the really "scandalous" implication of Levinas's ethics: that ethics—as "first philosophy"—should be "outsourced" from philosophy proper.

8. Two English verbs that do are to "receive" and to "sustain." I am not sure that, while being at the "receiving end" of someone's action, I really do willfully receive this action. To "sustain"—like in "sustaining a wound"—might in fact be the only example that is non-negative.

9. Ricoeur, *Oneself as Another*, 190.

10. On various occasions, Levinas qualifies suffering as "intrinsically . . . useless, 'for nothing,'" "absurd," and basic senselessness ("Useless Suffering," in *Entre-Nous: Thinking-of-the-Other* [London: Continuum, 2006], 157, 158); as "monstrosity" and "foreign of itself" ("Transcendence and Evil," in *Collected Philosophical Papers*, trans. A. Lingis [Dordrecht: Martinus Nijhoff, 1986], 180, 181); and as "non-sense par excellence" ("Le Scandale du mal," *Les Nouveaux Cahiers* 85 [1986]: 15–17, 15). What seems a bit problematic with such definitions—and the concept of "useless suffering"—is, in my view, that they by necessity also imply the existence of the

contrary, "useful suffering." And if, as Forti remarks correctly, "evil for Levinas thus resides in the break that it causes . . . with order and synthesis," then this implies that such a "useful suffering" designates a suffering that is still synthesizable and thus rationalizable. Simona Forti, *New Demons: Rethinking Power and Evil Today*, trans. Zakiya Hanafi (Stanford, CA: Stanford University Press, 2015), 112. In this regard, Levinas is still too Hegelian for my taste.

11. In fact, in all three of the main monotheistic religions, these (or comparable) figures appear. And the fact that they "have no one to act on their behalf" refers, in the last instance, to the fact that they have fallen outside the patriarchic order that informs all three religions.

12. Foucault's almost physical notion of *actio* = *reactio* is reflected in the following quotation: "The exercise of power can produce as much acceptance as may be wished for: it can pile up the dead and shelter itself behind whatever threats it can imagine. In itself, the exercise of power is not violence; nor is it a consent which, implicitly, is renewable. It is a total structure of actions brought to bear upon possible actions; it incites, it induces, it seduces, it makes easier or more difficult; in the extreme it constrains or forbids absolutely; it is nevertheless always a way of acting upon an acting subject or acting subjects by virtue of their acting or being capable of action. A set of actions upon other actions." Michel Foucault, "The Subject and Power," *Critical Inquiry* 8, no. 4 (1982): 789. While it becomes clear that power can work with rather subtle means ("inciting," "inducing," "seducing"), the fact that any reaction has to be "received" or "suffered"—"it can pile up the dead"—is on the one hand acknowledged but on the other hand simply ignored ("A set of actions upon other actions"). The dead usually can neither act nor react. While I am thus sympathetic to his caveat that "in order to understand what power relations are about, perhaps we should investigate the forms of resistance and attempts made to dissociate these relations" (780), he conceives of resistance as—agency. On the contrary, violence is what eliminates agency: "A relationship of violence acts on the body or on things; it forces, subdues, tortures, destroys, or bars all possibilities. Its opposite pole can only be passivity; and if it comes up against any resistance, it has no other option but to try to minimize it. On the other hand, for it to be really a power relationship, it can only be articulated on the basis of two elements that are indispensable to it: that . . . (the one over whom power is exercised) be thoroughly recognized and maintained to the very end as a person who acts; and that, faced with a relationship of power, a whole field of responses, reactions, results, and possible inventions may open up" (789). In short, power has to presume and uphold agency (which echoes Kant); only once it is not recognized as itself does it turn to violence, which negates agency. That is why for power to resort to violence necessarily amounts to a failure of the former.

13. Immanuel Kant, *Grounding for the Metaphysics of Morals with "On a Sup-*

posed Right to Lie because of Philanthropic Concerns," trans. James W. Ellington (Indianapolis, IN: Hackett, 1981), AA 4:421; on the problem of this contradiction, see Pauline Kleingeld, "Contradiction and Kant's Formula of Universal Law," *Kant-Studien* 108, no. 1 (2017): 89–115.

14. Kant, *Grounding for the Metaphysics of Morals,* 4:431.

15. See Mark Tushnet, *The American Law of Slavery, 1810–1860* (Princeton, NJ: Princeton University Press, 1981), 20–28; Marjorie Spiegel, *The Dreaded Comparison* (New York: Mirror, 1996), 35–42.

16. On an innovative assessment of African American culture as an "expression of quiet"—which, however, presumes a form of agency—see Kevin Quashie, *The Sovereignty of Quiet: Beyond Resistance in Black Culture* (New Brunswick, NJ: Rutgers University Press, 2012). However, Quashie never addresses the concept of agency in a detailed or critical manner. On a critical assessment of both female and black agency, see Hortense Spiller, "Mama's Baby, Papa's Maybe: An American Grammar Book," *Diacritics* 17, no. 2 (1987): 64–81.

17. See Claviez, *Aesthetics and Ethics,* 255–63.

18. That is why I agree with Forti's diagnosis that "the truth about evil lies much more in the suffering from it than in the perpetrating of it" (*New Demons,* 142). This is, however, an insight that contemporary jurisdiction would be hard put to take on board.

19. Bruno Latour, *We Have Never Been Modern,* trans. Catherine Porter (Cambridge, MA: Harvard University Press, 1993), 107, 129.

20. Latour, *We Have Never Been Modern,* 142.

21. Bruno Latour, *The Politics of Nature,* trans. Catherine Porter (Cambridge, MA: Harvard University Press, 2004), 93.

22. Latour, *The Politics of Nature,* 155.

23. Latour, *The Politics of Nature,* 155–56.

24. Although Latour is keen to replace the term "object" by the Heideggerian concept of "thing," he explicitly resorts to the Kantian term "means" in this quotation.

25. That is why, for example, Braidotti's critique of "Kantian moral responsibility" is, in my view, well taken but not thought through to its roots in agency. To simply try to declare matter "intelligent," is, for her purposes, understandable but not convincing. See Rosi Braidotti, *The Posthuman* (Cambridge: Polity, 2013), 41, 60. There is, actually, one instance in which Bruno Latour explicitly raises the question of agency: his 2014 essay "Agency at the Time of the Anthropocene," *New Literary History* 45 (2014). There, too, he tries to dissolve the subject/object distinction, arguing that "the very notion of objectivity has been totally subverted by the presence of humans in the phenomena to be described—and in the politics of tackling them" (2). While this might be true, isn't this subversion the result of the subject's

very agency? He even admits to this fact when he concedes that "the traces of our action are visible everywhere!" (5). That is, while the earth now might have become a "full-fledged actor" (3)—or is it still a "reactor"?—the problem still remains whether and on what basis we accord it the status of a moral subject. Latour is even going as far as to grant natural agents a "goal." In view of the river Atchafalaya being the deeper, compared to the Mississippi, thus threatening to empty it, Latour interprets an article that uses active verbs to describe the process as follows: "The connection between a smaller but deeper river and a much wider but higher one is what provides the *goals* of the two protagonists, what gives them a *vector*, what justifies the word "kill" and "capture" for the "steeper" and thus more dangerous actor. To have goals is one essential part of what it is to be an agent" (10). But even if the acting river has a goal—would we be prepared to hold it responsible for its action? That would be like holding an apple responsible for the fact that it falls from a tree!

26. Karen Barad, *Meeting the Universe Halfway: Quantum Physics and the Entanglement of Matter and Meaning* (Durham, NC: Duke University Press, 2007), 391, 393.

27. There have been numerous critical engagements with, and commentaries upon, the central role that agency plays in the New Materialism that has been developing in recent years. See Simon Choat, "Science, Agency, and Ontology: A Historical-Materialist Response to New Materialism," *Political Studies* 66, no. 4 (2011): 1027–42; David Keil, "The Ontological Prison: New Materialisms and Their Dead Ends," *Contradictions: A Journal for Critical Thought* 1, no. 2 (2017): 41–59; Lenny Moss, "Detachment Theory: Agency, Nature, and the Normative Nihilism of New Materialism," in *The New Politics of Materialism: History, Philosophy, Science*, ed. Sarah Ellenzweig and John H. Zammito (London: Routledge, 2017), 227–49; Christopher Gamble, Joshua S. Hanan, and Thomas Nail, "What Is New Materialism?," *Angelaki* 24, no. 6 (2019): 111–34. None of these interventions, however, addresses the ramifications of the concept of agency for a moral-philosophical context. The main realms they address are epistemology and ontology.

28. Derrida, *Positions*, 41.

"There Is No World"
Living Life in Deconstruction and Theoretical Biology

Cary Wolfe

In 1942, Wallace Stevens wrote something in "The Noble Rider and the Sound of Words" that is bound to strike many readers as strange—particularly those intimately acquainted with his famously difficult and elliptical poetry. (As Harold Bloom once wrote about Stevens's late masterpiece *An Ordinary Evening in New Haven*, "Critics can diverge absolutely on this poem because the text is almost impossible to read.")[1] Addressing the function of the poet, Stevens writes—in a statement striking for its baldness—"his role, in short, is to help people to live their lives."[2] Immediately, then, we are in the domain of ethics and the specific role of poetry within that domain. What is not yet clear is the relationship of this question to the problem of contingency, and that is not the direction in which Stevens takes the question, as it happens, in the essay. When he circles back to the question a page later, he asserts, "I repeat that his role is to help people to live their lives. He has had immensely to do with giving life whatever savor it possesses. He has had to do with whatever the imagination and the senses have made of the world."[3]

I want to take Stevens's assertion in a quite different direction, what we might call a more explicitly "ecological" one, as a larger context for his own phenomenological orientation in "The Noble Rider and the Sound of Words"—something I will attempt to do by means of articulating multiple lines of relation between contemporary theoretical biology and Jacques Derrida's meditations on the relationship between art and "world" in the second set of seminars on *The Beast and the Sovereign*. In doing so, I will insist on just how radical, robust, and material this sense of contingency is in a way that Derrida himself never fully explored, though he certainly invited us to walk through that door in his repeated forays, via Heidegger, into the question of nonhuman forms of life in relation to the problem of "world." In fact, Derrida returns explicitly to the role and function of art at the very end of the seminars, and by the time we get there, we will have, I hope, an entirely new and perhaps unexpected frame within which to contextualize and fully ramify Stevens's surprisingly pragmatist assertion about the role of the poet.

Part of my motivation here is that deconstruction has been considered less relevant than other approaches to the kinds of questions around "life" and ecology that I will be pursuing here. Vicki Kirby, for example, notes that "there is no doubt that deconstruction is out of favour in critical theory circles" today, and she wonders whether deconstruction can "reinvent itself as 'new,' as 'creative,' as different from its former manifestations."[4] I think the answer is "yes," not in spite of but *because of* the fact that in Derrida's work, as Kirby puts it, "a model, or representation, is not a third term in-between the biologist and biology or the writer and the world" but rather "the one who knows, the measuring apparatus and the object to be interpreted are strangely involved."[5]

What Kirby characterizes as the reinvention of deconstruction is part of what I have been trying to do over the past twenty years by bringing deconstruction into conversation with work in both biological and social systems theory. Take, for example, this passage from Humberto Maturana and Francisco Varela that I quoted in my book *Animal Rites* from 2003, where they offer their own version of what Kirby calls "strange involvement." The nervous system, they argue,

> does not operate according to either of the two extremes: it is neither representational nor solipsistic. It is not solipsistic, because as part of the nervous system's organism, it participates in the interactions of

the nervous system with its environment. These interactions continuously trigger in it the structural changes that modulate its dynamics of states. . . . Nor it is representational, for in each interaction it is the nervous system's structural state that specifies what perturbations are possible and what changes trigger them.[6]

But this leads to "a formidable snag," as they put it, because "it seems that the only alternative to a view of the nervous system as operating with representations is to deny the surrounding reality."[7] However, what all this indicates is the need (to use Niklas Luhmann's language) to pay attention to not just first-order but second-order observation, to shift to the observation of observations. Thus, "as observers," they explain,

> we can see a unity in different domains, depending on the distinctions we make. Thus, on the one hand, we can consider a system in that domain where its components operate, in the domain of its internal states and structural changes. . . . On the other hand, we can consider a unity that also interacts with . . . it. . . . Neither of these two possible descriptions is a problem per se: both are necessary to complete our understanding of a unity. It is the observer who correlates them from his outside perspective. . . . The problem begins when we unknowingly go from one realm to another and demand that the correspondences we establish between them (because we see these two realms simultaneously) be in fact a part of the operation of the unity.[8]

Methodologically speaking, this leads to the conclusion that

> contrary to a common implicit or explicit belief, scientific explanations . . . constitutively do not and cannot operate as phenomenic reductions or give rise to them. This nonreductionist relation between the phenomenon to be explained and the mechanism that generates it is operationally the case because the actual result of a process, and the operations in the process that give rise to it in a generative relation, *intrinsically take place in independent and nonintersecting phenomenal domains*. The situation is the reverse of reductionism. . . . This permits us to see, particularly in the domain of biology, that there are phenomena like language, mind, or consciousness that require an interplay of bodies as a generative structure but do not take place in any of them. In this sense, science and the understanding of science lead us away from transcendental dualism.[9]

—and away, it should be emphasized, from *representationalism*, whether of the idealist or realist side of the dualism, as Richard Rorty has so lucidly noted in his book *Objectivity, Relativism, and Truth*. As Rorty puts it:

> For representationalists, "making true" and "representing" are reciprocal relations: the nonlinguistic item which makes *S* true is the one represented by *S*. But antirepresentationalists see both notions as equally unfortunate and dispensable. . . . More precisely, it is no truer that "atoms are what they are because we use 'atom' as we do" than that "we use 'atom' as we do because atoms are as they are." *Both* of these claims, the antirepresentationalist says, are entirely empty. Both are pseudo-explanations.[10]

All of the foregoing will help us begin to make sense of this remarkable passage in Derrida's discussion of Defoe's *Robinson Crusoe* in the second set of seminars on *The Beast and the Sovereign*, which walks us through three possible theses and finishes off with a meditation on the last one. And note that as we read this passage, we have to hear the immediate Heideggerian resonance of the term "world" that Derrida is invoking—a resonance that for Heidegger was informed deeply, of course, by the work of Jakob von Uexküll on human and animal *Umwelten* (or life-worlds):

> 1. Incontestably, animals and humans inhabit the same world, the same objective world even if they do not have the same experience of the objectivity of the object. 2. Incontestably, animals and humans do not inhabit the same world, for the human world will never be purely and simply identical to the world of animals. 3. In spite of this identity and this difference, neither animals of different species, nor humans of different cultures, nor any animal or human individual inhabit the same world as another . . . and the difference between one world and another will remain always unbridgeable, because the community of the world is always constructed, simulated by a set of stabilizing apparatuses . . . nowhere and never given in nature. Between my world . . . and any other world there is first the space and time of an infinite difference, an interruption that is incommensurable with all attempts to make a passage, a bridge, an isthmus, all attempts at communication, translation, trope, and transfer that the desire for a world . . . will try to pose, impose, propose, stabilize. There is no world, there are only islands.[11]

Now it is the first thesis that is usually taken to be "ecological," but my point here is that by the second-order logic of deconstruction and systems theory that we will be developing in this essay, it is actually the *third* thesis that is the most radically ecological, somewhat along the lines suggested by my colleague Timothy Morton, who argues in a suite of books that ecological thinking begins precisely where "nature" ends, precisely after "the end of the world."[12]

To show why, we must track Derrida as he moves rapidly in the next moment of the seminar to a line taken from Paul Celan's poetry that echoes throughout the second seminar, the line "the world is gone, I must carry you."[13] The world is gone for precisely the reasons marshaled in Derrida's third thesis, which we will explore in more detail in a moment in the domain of theoretical biology. Contrary to Heidegger's assertion that humans are worlding and worldly, while the stone is "without world" and the animal "has a world in the mode of not having,"[14] humans in fact *do not*, Derrida suggests, have a world in Heidegger's sense. Rather, as I have argued elsewhere, "having a world in the mode of not having" is as good a definition of Dasein as we are, in fact, likely to get.[15] Why? Because, for *all* creatures, including human beings, the very thing that makes the world available to them is also and at the same time what makes the world *unavailable* to them. And this is true whether we are talking about the "map that is not the territory" (to paraphrase Gregory Bateson's borrowing of Korzybski's phrase), the *grille* and *gramme* of semiotic code or program in deconstruction, or the "blind spot" of the contingent self-reference of autopoiesis and observation in the systems theory of both Luhmann and Maturana and Varela. And this is why, as Luhmann puts it, "reality is what one does not perceive when one perceives it."[16] And this fact—that "the world is gone," and not just for nonhuman life but also humans, thus linking human and nonhuman life in their shared finitude—is precisely where ethics and ecological responsibility begin. It is not just a matter of our shared finitude as mortal beings who live and die but more radically the *finitude of our finitude*, its nonappropriability. As Derrida puts it in a later session that year, picking up the thread:

> We could move for a long time, in thought and reading, between *Fort und Da, Da und Fort*, between these two undistancing distancings . . . these two *theres*, between Heidegger and Celan, between on the one hand the *Da* of *Dasein* . . . and on the other hand Celan's *fort* in "Die Welt is fort, ich muss dich tragen": the world is far, the world has gone, in the absence or distance of the world, I must, I owe it to you, I owe it to myself to carry you, without world, without the foundation

or grounding of anything in the world, without any foundational or fundamental mediation, one on one, like wearing mourning or bearing a child, basically where ethics begins.[17]

I will return to this ethical fallout of "the world is gone," and art's place in it, later in the essay, but for now I want to continue fleshing out the broader theoretical context here a moment longer, focusing not on the antirepresentationalist "strange involvement" we have been discussing but on the fact that what Derrida calls the *machinalité* of iterability and all the forms of "writing," "script," and "code" subtended by it is (as we shall see in a moment) perfectly compatible with a robust materialist and naturalistic account of how life evolves from nonliving matter, how even the most self-reflexive forms of intentionality, awareness, and so on arise from the inorganic systematicity of repetition and recursivity that structures the "protention" and "retention," the movement and "spacing," of the infrastructure of iterability.[18]

The relationship between deconstruction and the life sciences has been taken up in the critical literature in the past, of course, by figures such as Anthony Wilden and, more recently, Christopher Johnson, in his book *System and Writing in the Philosophy of Jacques Derrida*. Johnson provides a useful overview of the interdisciplinary matrix out of which the crosstalk between deconstruction and the life sciences emerged, including the Nobel Prize–winning work in France of the theoretical biologists François Jacob, Jacques Monot, and André Lwoff on the role played by RNA in the transmission of genetic information. That work in part opened the door for the reconceptualization of "writing" in terms of code and program that Derrida famously explored in *Of Grammatology*, whose first chapter, "The End of the Book and the Beginning of Writing," opens with a section called "The Program."[19] In fact, the first chapter of Jacob's influential book *The Logic of Life* of 1965 is also called "The Programme," where he argues that "heredity is described today in terms of information, messages, and code."[20] It is in this sense that *Of Grammatology* announces that a "primary writing" therefore "*comprehends* language"[21] as we usually think of it in the same way that the "contemporary biologist speaks of writing and *pro-gram* in relation to the most elementary processes of information within the living cell. And finally,"[22] he continues,

> whether it has essential limits or not, the entire field covered by the cybernetic *program* will be the field of writing. . . . Even before being determined as human (with all the distinctive characteristics that have

always been attributed to man and the entire system of significations that they imply) or nonhuman, the *grammè*—or the *grapheme*—would thus name the element. An element without simplicity.[23]

As we know, this claim leads directly, and quite systematically, I might add, to Derrida's assertion years later—one that makes clear the theoretical underpinnings of his later, well-known work on "the question of the animal"—that "the elaboration of a new concept of the *trace* had to be extended to the entire field of the living, *or rather to the life/death relation*, beyond the anthropological limits of 'spoken' language."[24] Or, as he put it in the interview "Eating Well": "These possibilities or necessities, without which there would be no language, *are themselves not only human*. . . . And what I am proposing should allow us to take into account scientific knowledge about the complexity of 'animal languages,' genetic coding, all forms of marking."[25]

However, I would make an even stronger claim here: What we can see now is that Derrida gives us a theory of something like the relationship of the genetic (or systemic, formally code bound) and the epigenetic factors (the environmental or contextual setting in which the code is deployed) that we will see developed on the biological side by figures such as Conrad Waddington and Stuart Kauffman, among others, from the late 1950s through the 1980s and into the present day. In the 1960s, Derrida is formalizing and ramifying a theory of the relationship between the genetic and the epigenetic, which was being pioneered at the same time (1957) by Waddington but only now being formalized, after fifty years of hegemonic rule by neo-Darwinian reductionism, with its overemphasis on the genetic level of "code" or "script" alone.

Waddington, who was a mentor to Kauffman, did pioneering work on the relationship between the genetic and the epigenetic and the effects of the environment on the organism and its morphogenesis, in his theory of the "chreode," or "developmental landscape." As the biologist Denis Noble explains in an article in the *Journal of Experimental Biology*, Waddington was able to demonstrate, in a classic experiment, "the inheritance of a characteristic acquired in a population in response to an environmental stimulus"[26]—which August Weismann had attempted to do, unsuccessfully, in 1890, a failure that, along with his assumption that genetic mutation was random, laid the foundations for the neo-Darwinian "Modern Synthesis," which was counterposed to what is still, to this day, labeled as "Lamarckism."

Waddington realized that the developmental plasticity of organisms (in

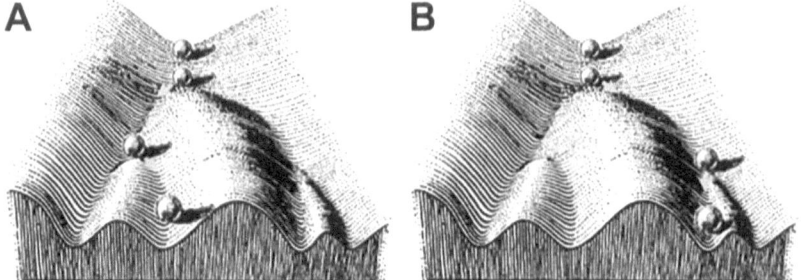

Figure 1

his case, fruit flies) could be affected by environmental factors that interceded at different points along the developmental timeline. He used the term "canalized" for this type of environmental influence, and he viewed the developmental process "as a series of 'decisions' that could be represented as a series of 'valleys' and 'forks' in a developmental landscape," pictured in Figure 1.[27]

As Noble explains,

> He knew from his developmental studies that embryo fruit flies could be persuaded to show different thorax and wing structures, simply by changing the environmental temperature or by a chemical stimulus. In his landscape diagram, this could be represented as a small manipulation in slope that would lead to one channel in the landscape being favoured over another, so that the adult could show a different phenotype starting from the same genotype. The next step in his experiment was to select for and breed from the animals that displayed the new characteristic. Exposed to the same environmental stimulus, these gave rise to progeny with an even higher proportion of adults displaying the new character. After a relatively small number of generations, he found that he could then breed from the animals and obtain robust inheritance of the new character even without applying the environmental stimulus. The characteristic had therefore become locked into the genetics of the animal. He called this process genetic assimilation. What he had succeeded in showing was that an acquired characteristic could first be inherited as what we would now call "soft" inheritance, and that it could then be assimilated into becoming standard "hard" genetic inheritance. Today, we call "soft" inheritance epigenetic inheritance, and of course, we know

many more mechanisms by which the same genome can be controlled to produce different epigenetic effects.[28]

As Noble points out, a standard neo-Darwinian explanation would be that random mutations in the population accounted for the change, but that is extremely unlikely, given the short timescale of the experiment (only a few generations), and in any event, random mutations would manifest in individuals, not in the whole group at once. A much simpler explanation, Nobel explains, is that Waddington's experiment "exploited plasticity that is already present in the population."[29]

We thus end up with the fundamental evolutionary and developmental unit being—as Gregory Bateson would put it thirteen years after the publication of Waddington's book *The Strategy of the Genes* in 1957—not organism-as-printout of a genetic code, or *even* organism-as-printout varied in its successive copies by random genetic mutations, but rather "flexible organism-in-its-environment" (with "flexible" here denoting not just behavioral flexibility but the very plasticity that Waddington had exploited in his experiment)—all versus the neo-Darwinian identification of the "unit of survival" as "the breeding individual or the family line."[30] This reconceptualization is captured quite well in Noble's modification of Waddington's chreode (Figure 2), because it emphasizes an aspect that will become crucial to Kauffman's own work on complex systems and evolution, namely, the "functional *networks*"—that is, the real-time dynamic interactions—that interact with environmental influences in specific ways to produce the developmental landscape, which can be varied by altering either the organism in question or the environmental factors that influence it.

As we shall see in a moment, this is precisely where Kauffman's work on emergence, self-organization, and complexity picks up the story—and picks it up in a way that is consonant with Bateson's insistence that the redefinition of the fundamental unit of evolution has ethical, not just scientific, consequences. In his 2015 book *Humanity in a Creative Universe*, Kauffman assumes, almost exclusively, classical chemistry and physics, and "the point is not to show that Newton's laws do not often work (they do) . . . but to begin to demolish the hegemony of reductive materialism and its grip on our scientific minds."[31] The central thrust of this section of the book, which forces us to rethink not just the evolution of the biosphere but the entire concept of ecology, is that "at least part of why the universe has become complex is due to an easy-to-understand, but not well-recognized,

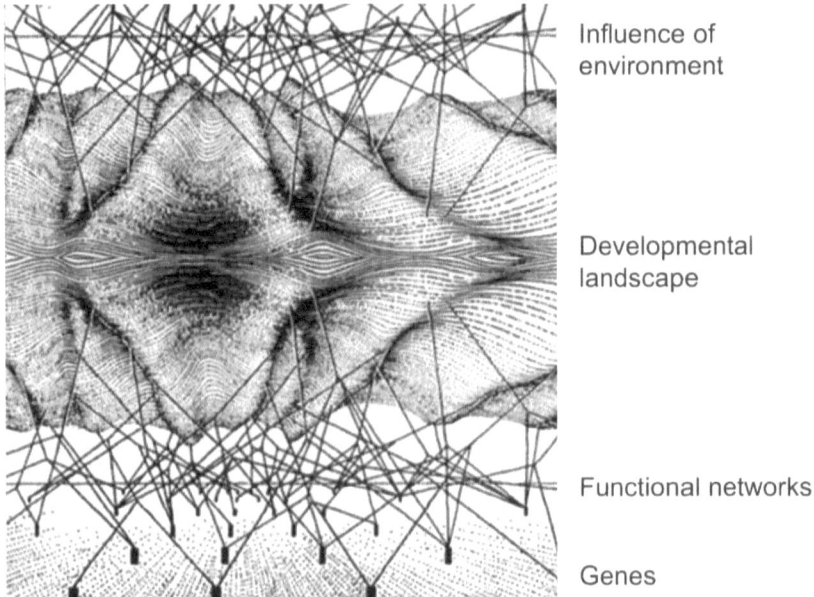

Figure 2

'antientropic' process that does not vitiate the second law [of thermodynamics]. Briefly,"[32] he continues,

> as more complex things and linked processes are created, and can combine with one another in ever more new ways to make yet more complex amalgams of things and processes, the space of possible things and linked processes becomes vastly larger and the universe has not had time to make all the possibilities. The universe will not make all possible complex molecules, organisms, organs, dust grains, mineral deposits, volcanoes, rivers, geologies, hydrogen clouds, stars, or galaxies, automobiles, or skyscrapers that are possible given the 10^{80} particles in the universe. There is an indefinitely expanding, ever more open space of possibilities ever more sparsely sampled, as the complexity of things and linked processes increases. . . . There is a deep sense in which the universe becomes complex in its exploration of these ever more sparsely sampled spaces of what is possible because "*it can*."[33]

One of the more compelling examples Kauffman gives of this principle obtains even at the level of organic chemistry, before we even arrive at the domain of autopoietic organisms, or what he calls "Kantian wholes," where we would more likely expect to find such forms of complexity. In a key passage in the book, he writes: "Proteins are linear strings of amino acids bound together by peptide bonds. There are twenty types of amino acids in evolved biology. A typical protein is perhaps 300 amino acids long, and some are several thousand amino acids long. Now,"[34] he continues,

> how many possible proteins are there with 200 amino acids? Well, there are 20 choices for each of the 200 positions, so 20^{200} or 10^{260} possible proteins with the length of 200 amino acids. This is a tiny subset of the molecular species of CHNOPS [Carbon, Hydrogen, Nitrogen, Oxygen, Phosphorus, Sulfur] with 100,000 atoms per molecule. Now the universe is 13.7 billion years old and has about 10^{80} particles. The fastest time scale in the universe is the Planck time scale of 10^{-43} seconds. If the universe were doing nothing but using all 10^{80} particles in parallel to make proteins the length of 200 amino acids, each in a single Planck moment, it would take 10^{39} repetitions of the history of the universe to make all the possible proteins the length of 200 amino acids just *once*! . . . As we consider proteins the length of 200 amino acids and all possible CHNOPS molecules with 100,000 atoms or less per molecule, it is obvious that the universe *will never make them all. History* enters when the space of what is possible is vastly larger than what can actually happen. . . . A next point simple and clear: Consider all the CHNOPS molecules that can be made with 1, with 2, with 3, with 4, with *n*, with 100,000 atoms per molecule. Call the space of possible molecules with *n* atoms of CHNOPS the phase space for CHNOPS molecules of *n* atoms. That phase space increases enormously as *n* increases. Consequently, in the lifetime of the universe, as *n* increases, that phase space will be sampled ever more sparsely.[35]

As Kauffman shows, this "non-ergodic" principle obtains even more radically and obviously at the level of the biosphere, whose "becoming cannot be prestated, is not 'governed' by entailing laws, in which what becomes constitutes ever-new Actuals that are 'enabling constraints' that do not cause, but enable ever-new, typically unprestatable, Adjacent Possible opportunities into which the evolving biosphere becomes."[36] And when we reach the level of what he calls "Kantian wholes," or autopoietic organisms, this process is even more striking.[37] If we think about the concept of biological function, for example, it is clear that while "in classical physics there are only 'happenings.' The ball rolls down the hill, bumps a rock, veers," and so on, in biology we have to distinguish function from mere physical causation. "The function of the heart is to pump blood," Kauffman notes, but the heart "causally also makes heart sounds, jiggles water in the pericardial sac," and so on.[38] Classical physics will not help us here, because "the *function* of the part is its causal consequences that help sustain the whole";[39] "function" is causal, in other words, but causal in a qualitatively different way from classical physics. As Kauffman notes, another nail in the coffin for the reductionist approach is the fact that "this capacity to define a function as a subset of causal consequences that can be improved in evolution further separates biology from physics, which cannot make the distinction among all causal consequences into a subset which are functions."[40] As Kauffman baldly puts it,

> Dawkins wrote *The Selfish Gene* (1976) as if DNA replicators were the heart of biology, and the organism merely a "vehicle" for the selfish gene in evolution. I completely disagree. Organisms are autopoietic self-creating wholes that achieve functional sufficiency, often improvable, as the biosphere becomes. . . . It is the functional closure/sufficiencies of organisms as Kantian wholes, not the genes they carry along, which is the heart of life and its evolution."[41]

Having established the importance of the concept of function, Kauffman hypothesizes that

> we cannot prestate the evolution of new functions in the biosphere, hence cannot prestate the ever-changing phase space of biological evolution. . . . If we cannot know ahead of time what new functions will arise, we cannot write differential equations of motion for the evolving biosphere: we have no idea what new entities or processes may arise and become relevant to that evolution. . . . Thus, we can have *no entailing laws* at all for biological evolution. Furthermore, as I will show [and this is a resolutely deconstructive assertion, in my view], we cannot noncircularly prestate the niche of an organism in its world.[42]

Kauffman offers a nice, compact example of this nonentailed and nonergodic process in his discussion of what are called Darwinian "pre-adaptations" or "exaptations," where we see the emergence of new, possibly useful, traits through random genetic mutation. His discussion of the evolution of the swim bladder in fish provides a neat example of how a side effect generated by random genetic mutation can become a functional asset under different environmental conditions, as Darwin surmised. The Darwinian preadaptation whereby some early versions of fish had lungs, enabling them to bounce from puddle to puddle, led in time to the biological *function* of a ratio of air and water in fish who now live wholly in water that allows neutral buoyancy in the water column. Did this change the future evolution of the biosphere, Kauffman asks.

> Yes, and in two vastly different ways. First, new daughter species of fish with swim bladders and new proteins evolved. But second, *once* the swim bladder exists, it constitutes a new Actual condition in the evolving biosphere. The swim bladder now constitutes a new, empty but Adjacent Possible niche, or opportunity for evolution. For example, a species of worm or bacteria could evolve to live, say exclusively, in the swim bladder. The Adjacent-Possible opportunities for evolution, given the new swim bladder, do not include all possibilities. For example, a *T. Rex* or giraffe could not evolve to live in the swim bladder.[43]

One of the key theoretical points here—and it is one that articulates *directly* with deconstruction as I read it—arises when Kauffman asks, "Do we think that selection, in any way at all, 'acted' to achieve the swim bladder as *constituting a new adjacent-possible empty niche* in which a worm or a bacterial species might evolve to live? No." What this means is that "evolution literally creates its own future adjacent-possible opportunities for further evolution without selection in any way 'achieving' this."[44] Further, Kauffman adds,

> Does the swim bladder, once it has come to exist, *cause* the worm or bacterial species to evolve to live in it? *No.* The swim bladder *enables, but does not cause, the bacterial or worm species to evolve to live in it.* Instead, quantum random mutations to the DNA of the bacterium or worm yield variations . . . that may be selected at the level of the whole organism by which the worm or bacterial species evolves to live in the swim bladder.[45]

Compare this with Johnson's characterization of "code" as it is theorized by Derrida's grammatology in the late 1960s: "The code, as Derrida understands it, is therefore constituted *in process* rather than in anticipation. Despite the suggestion of precedence implied . . . in Derrida's articulation of the word programme (*pro-gramme*), the gram, the trace, the inscription are never absolutely primary. There is instead a kind of *precipitation* towards sense that is ignorant of its future," so that "the system is not pulled into the future by a mysterious first (and last) principle, but is pushed *a tergo* by what is handed down, selected and recombined, from its ancestral past. This philosophy is, in essence, a philosophy of *evolution*."[46]

To return to Kauffman, then, he concludes, by way of summary, that

> the organism lives *in its world*. Causal consequences (in classical physics) pass from organism to world and back to the organism, and the functional closure or sufficiency of the organism in its world is what succeeds or fails at the level of that organism in its world. There is, therefore, no noncircular way to define the "niche" of the organism separately from the organism. But that niche is the boundary condition on selection. The "niche" is only revealed *after* the *fact*, by what succeeds in evolution.[47]

It is hard to imagine a clearer articulation, in robust naturalistic, biological terms, of what Derrida calls "the becoming-space of time and the becoming-time of space," the "will have been" of that which is "to come," with Kauffman's unprestatable and unanticipatible "what succeeds in evolution," in which Darwinian "exaptations" are precisely the material substrate, the trace, in and through which retentions of the past and protentions of the future are inscribed. Here, what Martin Hägglund calls the fundamental "negativity" of time is crucial, and it helps underscore and indeed clarify an aspect of Kauffman's argument that is often only implicit or tacit. The negativity of time "undermines *both* the idea of a discrete moment *and* the idea of an absolute continuity. Only if something is *no longer*—that is, only if there is negativity—can there be a difference between before and after. This negativity must be at work in presence itself for there to be succession. If the moment is not negated in being succeeded by another moment, their relation is not one of temporal succession but of spatial co-existence."[48] It is precisely the combination of this negativity of time with the materiality of the trace as its site of inscription—figured on a larger biological canvas as the dynamic complexity of the organism/environment relationship—that makes Kauffman's nonentailed, nonergodic evolution of the biosphere thinkable. No negativity of time, no evolution, but also: no materiality of inscription in the trace, no evolution. Indeed, we find here the site of a *double* inscription, not just on the material substrate of the living being (whether we think of Waddington's "soft" and "hard" inheritance or the exaptation of the swim bladder) but also in the dynamic contingency of the organism/environment relation in which that ontogenetic inscription happens, which can make the "same" inscription function differently at different points in time, under different circumstances.

In my view, everything I have been saying makes a thoroughgoing deconstruction of the ontology/epistemology divide not so much desirable as *unavoidable*. Epistemology is often understood, these days, as a branch of what Graham Harman and other object-oriented ontologists call "correlationism," but this charge misunderstands a couple of quite fundamental postulates of the position I have developed here and over the years. First of all, the question here is not epistemological but *pragmatic*. As both Luhmann and Maturana make clear, the veracity of the systems-theoretical analysis is not about epistemological adequation to some pregiven state of ontological affairs (whether realist *or* idealist) but is rather based on its *functional* specificity in the contingent and dynamic unfolding of real time. Contrary to the understanding of autopoietic systems as solipsistic, the operational closure of systems and the self-reference based upon it arise as a practical and adaptive necessity precisely because systems are *not* closed—that is, precisely because they find themselves in an environment of overwhelmingly and exponentially greater complexity than is possible for any single system. What this means is that systems are characterized by a kind of *finitude* that can be formalized as a complexity differential; they maintain themselves and achieve their autopoiesis, in a sense, against all odds—in the very expanding universe of increasing and evolving complexity that Kauffman describes. To put it another way, systems have to operate selectively and "blindly" (as Luhmann puts it) not because they are closed but precisely because they *are not*, and the asymmetrical distribution of complexity across the system/environment threshold is in fact what *forces* the strategy of self-referential closure.[49]

To finish off this first point, then, there is nothing to stop you on *epistemological* grounds from thinking that humors or ethers exist; indeed, the history of philosophy and of science makes that abundantly clear. But there is plenty to stop you on *pragmatic* grounds, even if, as Bruno Latour reminds us, bad ideas can work well enough under the right constraints for long periods of time. Or, as Richard Rorty quite elegantly puts it, the pragmatist "believes, as strongly as does any realist, that there are objects which are *causally* independent of human beliefs and desires."[50] She "recognizes relations of *justification* holding between beliefs and desires, and relations of *causation* holding between those beliefs and desires and other items in the universe, but no relations of *representation*."[51]

"There is no world," then—to recall Derrida's phrase once more—not in the sense of the world not being "real" but in the sense of a philosophically *realist* account of the world not being real. (And it is the utter confusion of these two claims, an ontological claim and an epistemological claim, the question of materialism and the question of realism, that has caused so much confusion in the contemporary theoretical landscape, as if disagreeing with the position called "philosophical realism" automatically means believing that the material world isn't real.) As Raoni Padui explains in an exacting and careful essay that traces this problem through the history of philosophy since Kant, "One can maintain a materialist standpoint, namely, that the entity and the real are ontologically prior to thought, while denying the direct and immediate access of thought to such an entity. In other words, one can be a materialist and an anti-realist at the same time." He continues:

> Materialism is an ontological thesis that posits that being can be independent of thinking, while realism posits the thinkability of this being independent of thinking. . . . Claiming that the existence of something prior to or independent of thought (materialism) can only be maintained if we can think or access being prior to thought (realism) . . . is clearly illegitimate, insofar as it involves the claim that there can be matter prior to thought if and only if one can think the being of matter prior to thought.[52]

However, even if we dispense with *that* problem, we need to remember that everything I have said about Derrida in particular is complicated by other strands in his work. There is a deep divide among hardcore Derrida scholars about whether his work is best read in the systematizing terms I am offering here. I am not especially interested in those debates, but I *am* interested in an aspect of his work that the system resistors would emphasize: that we need to take seriously the question that animates Derrida's engagement of Heidegger, namely, "What is philosophy," and what are its differences from scientific discourse?—a question that is only pressed upon us all the more by the poor quality of philosophizing that we find in Kauffman, Maturana and Varela, and others of similar ilk. The site where this most comes to a head in Derrida's work is in his critique of what he calls Heidegger's "dogma" regarding the differences between humans and animals. I think we should take seriously Derrida's assertion that we need to heed Heidegger's ultraphilosophical suggestion that part of what defines the specificity of philosophical (versus scientific) statements is the understanding that

Dasein is not existentially a living, empirical being: that the being of beings is not a being.[53] I've discussed this in some detail in my last book, *Before the Law*, but part of what is at stake here for Derrida is the danger of indexing philosophical questions to biological—and more pointedly (to put it in biopolitical terms) racial—taxonomies. This "constant gesture of Heidegger's," Derrida writes, "whose political implications are to be taken seriously," is not just political and pragmatic; it is also, "from the very beginning . . . a case of nothing less than determining philosophy on its own basis."[54] For Heidegger, in other words, science cannot ask the kinds of questions that philosophy asks—questions, for example, about the phenomenological domain, about mentation and consciousness, and so on, which are the product of a concatenation of material forces but cannot be reduced to them. And this brings us back to the question of "world" with which we opened and to Heidegger's famous assertion that the stone "has no world" while the animal is "poor in world" and man is "world-building." And here Derrida makes a fascinating assertion in his engagement of Heidegger when he writes that

> these three theses are theses on world. They are not theses on the stone, on the animal, or on man, but theses on the world. . . . And the moments I find the most interesting, and at the same time the most discreet, along this path are the moments when Heidegger more or less says: We don't finally know what world is! At bottom it is a very obscure concept![55]

I think this assertion—that what drives Heidegger's ultraphilosophical project is that "we don't know what world is"—opens a space to redescribe the origins of this problem (if one wants to put it that way) in terms of what Kauffman calls the nonergodic, nonentailed, and creative evolution of the biosphere, in which scientific statements (as Maturana and Varela remind us) can no longer be said to cleave neatly along the lines of "empirical" versus "speculative," because they entail the "strange involvement," as we saw earlier, of observer and observed, organism and environment. But this assertion also opens for Derrida, at the very end of the seminars on *The Beast and the Sovereign*, a domain for art and poetry, which can provide a kind of ethical uptake on this fact that "the world is gone" in a way that philosophy proper can't. As he puts it in the tenth and last session, "if *Die Welt ist fort*, if we think we must carry the other . . . this can only be one of two things." Either we "carry the other out of the world" and "share at least this knowledge without phantasm that there is no longer a world," or else the "second hypothesis," that "what I must do, with you and carrying you, is make it that there be precisely a world . . . do things so as to make *as if* there were just a world, and to make the world come into the world," to "make the gift or present of this *as if* come up poetically."[56] Unlike Kant's version of the "as if" (the *als ob*) in the form of a "regulative idea" of the world that considers phenomena "as if they were the arrangements made by a supreme reason of which our reason is a faint copy,"[57] this "poetic" "as if" does not deny or repress its fictive nature but acknowledges and embraces the fact that "the community of world," as Derrida puts it in the opening pages of the first session, "is always constructed, simulated by a set of stabilizing apparatuses."[58] If there is to be a "world," a "shared world," in other words, *we* must make it, without any taking for granted of who or what this "we" might be.[59] The ethical point—for Derrida and for Kauffman—is that the world is not given; it is *made*, and it therefore matters how we make it.

Or as Wallace Stevens put it in his own version of Derrida's permutation of the Kantian *als ob*, to return to the point with which we began: "The final belief is to believe in a fiction, which you know to be a fiction, there being nothing else. The exquisite truth is to know that it is a fiction and that you believe in it willingly."[60] For Stevens as for Derrida, however, the point is not so much epistemological as it is pragmatic and ethical, and it is driven by—made unavoidable by—a contingency that is radical precisely because it is not the privileged domain of the human alone. In fact, it is what makes the domain of life and the living (to use Kauffman's term) "creative."

NOTES

This chapter draws on ideas and reprints material, in different form, first published in *Ecological Poetics; or, Wallace Stevens's Birds* (Chicago: University of Chicago Press, 2020). Copyright © 2020 by The University of Chicago. All rights reserved.

1. Harold Bloom, *Wallace Stevens: The Poems of Our Climate* (Ithaca, NY: Cornell University Press, 1980), 306.
2. Wallace Stevens, *The Necessary Angel: Essays on Reality and the Imagination* (New York: Random House, 1942), 29.
3. Stevens, *The Necessary Angel*, 30.
4. Vicki Kirby, "Grammatology: A Vital Science," *Derrida Today* 9, no. 1 (2016): 48.
5. Kirby, "Grammatology: A Vital Science," 47.
6. Humberto Maturana and Francisco Varela, *The Tree of Knowledge: The Biological Roots of Human Understanding* (Boston: Shambhala, 1992), 169.

7. Maturana and Varela, *The Tree of Knowledge*, 133.

8. Maturana and Varela, *The Tree of Knowledge*, 135–36.

9. Qtd. in Cary Wolfe, *Animal Rites: American Culture, the Discourse of Species, and Posthumanist Theory* (Chicago: University of Chicago Press, 2003), 91. Humberto R. Maturana, "Science and Daily Life: The Ontology of Scientific Explanations," in *Selforganization: Portrait of a Scientific Revolution*, ed. Wolfgang Krohn, Gunter Kuppers, and Helga Nowotny (Dordrecht: Springer, 1990), 20.

10. Richard Rorty, *Objectivity, Relativism, and Truth: Philosophical Papers*, Volume 1 (Cambridge: Cambridge University Press, 1991), 4–5; see also 47–49, 54–55, 116–17.

11. Jacques Derrida, *The Beast and the Sovereign, Volume II*, trans. Geoffrey Bennington, ed. Michel Lisse, Marie-Louise Mallet, and Ginette Michaud (Chicago: University of Chicago Press, 2011), 8–9.

12. See, e.g., Timothy Morton, *The Ecological Thought* (Cambridge, MA: Harvard University Press, 2012); Timothy Morton, *Hyperobjects: Philosophy and Ecology after the End of the World* (Minneapolis: University of Minnesota Press, 2013).

13. Derrida, *The Beast and the Sovereign*, 9.

14. Jacques Derrida, *Of Spirit: Heidegger and the Question*, trans. Geoffrey Bennington and Rachel Bowlby (Chicago: University of Chicago Press, 1989), 50.

15. See Cary Wolfe, *Before the Law: Humans and Other Animals in a Biopolitical Frame* (Chicago: University of Chicago Press, 2013), 63–86.

16. Niklas Luhmann, *Social Systems*, trans. John Bednarz Jr. and Dirk Baecker, intro. Eva M. Knodt (Stanford, CA: Stanford University Press, 1995). For an expanded discussion of what falls between the dashes here—and in relation to Stevens's poetry specifically—see Cary Wolfe, *What Is Posthumanism?* (Minneapolis: University of Minnesota Press, 2010), chap. 10.

17. Derrida, *The Beast and the Sovereign*, 105.

18. Wolfe, *Before the Law*, 57.

19. Christopher Johnson, *System and Writing in the Philosophy of Jacques Derrida* (Cambridge: Cambridge University Press, 1993), 165.

20. François Jacob, *The Logic of Life: A History of Heredity* (Princeton, NJ: Princeton University Press, 1973), 1.

21. Jacques Derrida, *Of Grammatology*, trans. Gayatri Chakravorty Spivak (Baltimore, MD: Johns Hopkins University Press, 1976), 7.

22. Derrida, *Of Grammatology*, 9.

23. Derrida, *Of Grammatology*, 9.

24. Jacques Derrida and Elisabeth Roudinesco, "Violence against Animals," in *For What Tomorrow . . . : A Dialogue*, trans. Jeff Fort (Stanford, CA: Stanford University Press, 2004), 63, italics added.

25. Jacques Derrida, "'Eating Well,' or, The Calculation of the Subject: An

Interview with Jacques Derrida," in *Who Comes after the Subject?*, ed. Eduardo Cadava, Peter Connor, and Jean-Luc Nancy (New York: Routledge, 1991), 116–17.

26. Denis Noble, "Conrad Waddington and the Origin of Epigenetics," *Journal of Experimental Biology* 218 (2015): 816.

27. Noble, "Conrad Waddington and the Origin of Epigenetics," 816.

28. Noble, "Conrad Waddington and the Origin of Epigenetics," 816.

29. Noble, "Conrad Waddington and the Origin of Epigenetics," 816.

30. Gregory Bateson, "Form, Substance, and Difference," in *Steps to an Ecology of Mind* (New York: Ballantine, 1972), 451.

31. Stuart Kauffman, *Humanity in a Creative Universe* (Oxford: Oxford University Press, 2015), 40.

32. Kauffman, *Humanity in a Creative Universe*, 41.

33. Kauffman, *Humanity in a Creative Universe*, 41–42.

34. Kauffman, *Humanity in a Creative Universe*, 42–43.

35. Kauffman, *Humanity in a Creative Universe*, 43.

36. Kauffman, *Humanity in a Creative Universe*, 64.

37. Kauffman, *Humanity in a Creative Universe*, 67.

38. Kauffman, *Humanity in a Creative Universe*, 65.

39. Kauffman, *Humanity in a Creative Universe*, 66.

40. Kauffman, *Humanity in a Creative Universe*, 67.

41. Kauffman, *Humanity in a Creative Universe*, 69.

42. Kauffman, *Humanity in a Creative Universe*, 70.

43. Kauffman, *Humanity in a Creative Universe*, 72.

44. Kauffman, *Humanity in a Creative Universe*, 73.

45. Kauffman, *Humanity in a Creative Universe*, 73.

46. Johnson, *System and Writing in the Philosophy of Jacques Derrida*, 169, 63.

47. Kauffman, *Humanity in a Creative Universe*, 75.

48. Martin Hägglund, "The Trace of Time: A Critique of Vitalism," *Derrida Today* 9, no. 1 (2016): 43.

49. See Luhmann, *Social Systems*, 12–58.

50. Rorty, *Objectivity, Relativism, and Truth*, 101.

51. Rorty, *Objectivity, Relativism, and Truth*, 97.

52. Raoni Padui, "Realism, Anti-Realism, and Materialism," *Angelaki: Journal of the Theoretical Humanities* 16, no. 2 (2011): 92.

53. Jacques Derrida, *The Animal That Therefore I Am*, ed. Marie-Louise Mallet, trans. David Wills (New York: Fordham University Press, 2008), 155.

54. Derrida, *The Animal That Therefore I Am*, 144–45.

55. Derrida, *The Animal That Therefore I Am*, 151–52.

56. Derrida, *The Beast and the Sovereign*, 268.

57. Derrida, *The Beast and the Sovereign*, 270.

58. Derrida, *The Beast and the Sovereign*, 8.

59. Cf. Kelly Oliver's foregrounding of this aspect of the seminars, which is somewhat different in emphasis from my own, in "The Poetic Axis of Ethics," *Derrida Today* 7, no. 2 (2014): esp. 125, 129.

60. Wallace Stevens, *Opus Posthumous*, rev. ed., ed. Milton J. Bates (New York: Vintage, 1990), 189.

Works Cited

Agamben, Giorgio. "The Silhouette of Jean-Luc Nancy." In *Nancy Now*, ed. Verena Andermatt Conley and Irving Goh, x–xii. Cambridge: Polity, 2014.
———. *Stanzas: Word and Phantasm in Western Culture*. Trans. Ronald L. Martinez. Minneapolis: University of Minnesota Press, 1993.
Agren, David. "Mexican Man Cleared in Sexual Assault of Schoolgirl Because He Didn't 'Enjoy' It." *Guardian*, March 27, 2017. http://www.theguardian.com/world/2017/mar/28/mexican-man-cleared-sexual-assault-schoolgirl-because-he-didnt-enjoy-it.
Althusser, Louis. *For Marx*. London: New Left, 1969.
———. "Ideology and Ideological State Apparatuses: Notes towards an Investigation." In *Lenin and Philosophy and Other Essays*, 85–126. New York: New York University Press, 2001.
Arendt, Hannah. *The Origins of Totalitarianism*. New York: Harvest/HBJ, 1973.
Aristotle. *Nicomachean Ethics*. Trans. Harris Rackham. Cambridge, MA: Harvard University Press, 1982.
———. *Physics Book 5–8*. Trans. Philip H. Wicksteed and Francis M. Cornford. Cambridge, MA: Harvard University Press, 1934.
———. *Politics*. Trans. Benjamin Jowett. Mineola, NY: Dover, 2000.
Arrival. Dir. Denis Villeneuve. Lava Bear Films et al., 2016.
Ashcraft, Richard. *Revolutionary Politics and Locke's Two Treatises of Government*. Princeton, NJ: Princeton University Press, 1986.
Assange, Julian. *When Google Met WikiLeaks*. New York: OR, 2014.
Badiou, Alain. *Deleuze: The Clamor of Being*. Trans. L. Burchill. Minneapolis: University of Minnesota Press, 2000.
———. *Ethics: An Essay on the Understanding of Evil*. Trans. Peter Hallward. London: Verso, 2012.

———. "The Event in Deleuze." *Parrhesia* 2 (2007): 37–44.

———. *Number and Numbers*. Trans. Robin MacKay. London: Polity, 2008.

———. "Ontology Is Mathematics." In *Theoretical Writings*, ed. and trans. Ray Brassier and Alberto Toscano, 3–93. London: Continuum, 2004.

Bailly, Jean-Christophe, et al., eds. "La communauté, le nombre." *Aléa* 4 (1983), special issue.

Baldick, Chris. *Oxford Dictionary of Literary Terms*. 3rd ed. Oxford: Oxford University Press, 2008.

Balibar, Étienne. "L'anti-Marx de Michel Foucault." In *Marx and Foucault: Lectures, Usages, Confrontations*, ed. Christian Laval et al., 84–102. Paris: La Découverte, 2015.

———. *Citizen Subject: Foundations for Philosophical Anthropology*. Trans. Steven Miller. New York: Fordham University Press, 2017.

———. *Equaliberty: Political Essays*. Trans. James Ingram. Durham, NC: Duke University Press, 2014.

———. "Philosophies of the Transindividual: Spinoza, Marx, Freud." Trans. Mark Kelly. *Australasian Philosophical Review* 2, no. 1 (2018): 5–25.

Balibar, Étienne, and Immanuel Wallerstein. *Race, Nation, Class: Ambiguous Identities*. Trans. Chris Turner. London: Verso, 1989.

Barad, Karen. *Meeting the Universe Halfway: Quantum Physics and the Entanglement of Matter and Meaning*. Durham, NC: Duke University Press, 2007.

Barthes, Roland. *Mythologies*. Trans. Annette Lavers. London: Paladin, 1972.

Bataille, Georges. *The Accursed Share: An Essay on General Economy*. Vol. I. Trans. Robert Hurley. New York: Zone, 1988.

———. *The Accursed Share: An Essay on General Economy*. Vol. II–III. Trans. Robert Hurley. New York: Zone, 1989.

———. *Eroticism*. Trans. Mary Dalwood. London: Penguin, 2012.

———. *Guilty*. Trans. Bruce Boone. Venice: Lapis, 1988.

———. "Hegel, Death, and Sacrifice." *Yale French Studies* 78 (1990): 9–28.

———. *Inner Experience*. Trans. Stuart Kendall. New York: SUNY Press, 2014.

———. "The Labyrinth." In *Visions of Excess: Selected Writings, 1927–1939*, trans. Allan Stoekl with Carl R. Lovitt and Donald M. Leslie Jr. Minneapolis: University of Minnesota Press, 1985.

———. *On Nietzsche*. Trans. Stuart Kendall. New York: SUNY Press, 2015.

———. "The Notion of Expenditure." In *Visions of Excess: Selected Writings, 1927–1939*, trans. Allan Stoekl with Carl R. Lovitt and Donald M. Leslie Jr. Minneapolis: University of Minnesota Press, 1985.

———. "The Sacred Conspiracy." In *Visions of Excess: Selected Writings, 1927–1939*, trans. Allan Stoekl with Carl R. Lovitt and Donald M. Leslie Jr. Minneapolis: University of Minnesota Press, 1985.

———. *The Unfinished System of Non-knowledge*. Ed. Stuart Kendall. Trans. Michelle and Stuart Kendall. Minneapolis: University of Minnesota Press, 2007.

Bateson, Gregory. "Form, Substance, and Difference." In *Steps to an Ecology of Mind*, 448–65. New York: Ballantine, 1972.

Bauman, Zygmunt. *Community: Seeking Safety in an Insecure World*. Oxford: Polity, 2001.

Benhabib, Seyla, Judith Butler, Drucilla Cornell, and Nancy Fraser. *Feminist Contentions: A Philosophical Exchange*. New York: Routledge, 1995.

Benjamin, Walter. *Reflections: Essays, Aphorisms, Autobiographical Writings*. Ed. Peter Demetz. New York: Schocken, 1986.

Bennett, Jane. *Vibrant Matter: A Political Ecology of Things*. Durham, NC: Duke University Press, 2010.

Bernstein, Richard J. *The New Constellation*. New York: Polity, 1991.

———. *Radical Evil: A Philosophical Interrogation*. New York: Polity, 2002.

Biles, Jeremy, and Kent L. Brintnall, eds. *Negative Ecstasies: Georges Bataille and the Study of Religion*. New York: Fordham University Press, 2015.

Blackmun, Harry A., and US Supreme Court. *US Reports: Roe v. Wade*. 410 US 113. 1972. http://www.loc.gov/item/usrep410113/.

Blanchot, Maurice. *The Infinite Conversation*. Trans. Susan Hanson. Minneapolis: University of Minnesota Press, 1993.

———. *The Unavowable Community*. Trans. Pierre Joris. Barrytown, NY: Station Hill, 1988.

———. *Vicious Circles: Two Fictions and "After the Fact."* Trans. Paul Auster. Barrytown, NY: Station Hill, 1985.

———. *The Writing of the Disaster*. Trans. Ann Smock. Lincoln: University of Nebraska Press, 1995.

Bloom, Harold. *Wallace Stevens: The Poems of Our Climate*. Ithaca, NY: Cornell University Press, 1980.

Bosteels, Bruno. "Can Change Be Thought? A Dialogue with Alain Badiou." In *Alain Badiou: Philosophy and Its Conditions*, ed. Gabriel Riera, 237–61. Albany: SUNY Press, 2005.

Bourdieu, Pierre. "La précarité est aujourd'hui partout." In *Contre-feux. Propos pour servir à la résistance contre l'invasion néo-libérale*, 95–101. Paris: Liber-Raisons d'Agir, 1998.

Bown, Alfie. *The Playstation Dreamworld*. Cambridge: Polity, 2017.

Bracken, William F. "Is There a Puzzle about How Authentic Dasein Can Act?

A Critique of Dreyfus and Rubin on *Being and Time*, Division II." *Inquiry* 48 (2005): 533–52.
Braidotti, Rosi. "Memoirs and Aspirations of a Posthumanist." The 2017 Tanner Lectures, Yale University, New Haven, CT. https://rosibraidotti.com/2019/11/21/memoirs-of-a-posthumanist/.
———. *Metamorphoses: Towards a Materialist Theory of Becoming*. Cambridge: Polity, 2002.
———. *Nomadic Subjects*. New York: Columbia University Press, 2011.
———. *Patterns of Dissonance*. Cambridge: Polity, 1991.
———. *The Posthuman*. Cambridge: Polity, 2013.
———. *Posthuman Knowledge*. Cambridge: Polity, 2019.
———. "A Theoretical Framework for the Critical Posthumanities." *Theory, Culture & Society* 36, no. 6 (2019): 31–61.
———. *Transpositions: On Nomadic Ethics*. Cambridge: Polity, 2006.
Braidotti, Rosi, and Maria Hjlavajova. *Posthuman Glossary*. London: Bloomsbury Academic, 2018.
Brazil. Dir. Terry Gilliam. Embassy International Pictures, 1985.
Brown, Wendy. *States of Injury: Power and Freedom in Late Modernity*. Princeton, NJ: Princeton University Press, 1995.
Bruns, Gerald L. "Blanchot/Levinas: Interruption (On the Conflict of Alterities)." *Research in Phenomenology* 26 (1996): 132–54.
Burckhardt, Jacob. *The Civilisation of the Period of the Renaissance in Italy*. 2 vols. Trans. S. G. C. Middlemore. London: C. Kegan Paul & Co., 1878.
Butler, Judith. *Precarious Life: The Powers of Mourning and Violence*. London: Verso, 2016.
———. *The Psychic Life of Power: Theories in Subjection*. Stanford, CA: Stanford University Press, 1997.
Bykova, Marina F., ed. *The German Idealism Reader: Ideas, Responses, and Legacy*. London: Bloomsbury Academic, 2019.
Campe, Rüdiger. *The Game of Probability*. Trans. Ellwood H. Wiggins Jr. Stanford, CA: Stanford University Press, 2012.
Carman, Taylor. "On Being Social: A Reply to Olafson." *Inquiry* 37 (1994): 203–23.
Castel, Robert, and Claudine Haroche. *Propriété privée, propriété sociale, propriété de soi. Entretiens sur la condition de l'individu moderne*. Paris: Fayard, 2001.
Cavarero, Adriana. *Horrorism: Naming Contemporary Violence*. New York: Columbia University Press, 2011.
Chakrabarty, Dipesh. "The Climate of History: Four Theses." *Critical Enquiry* 35 (2009): 197–222.

Chiang, Ted. "Story of Your Life." In *Starlight 2*, ed. Patrick Nielson Hayden. New York: Tor, 1998.
Choat, Simon. "Science, Agency, and Ontology: A Historical-Materialist Response to New Materialism." *Political Studies* 66, no. 4 (2011): 1027–42.
Claviez, Thomas. *Aesthetics and Ethics: Otherness and Moral Imagination from Aristotle to Levinas and from "Uncle Tom's Cabin" to "House Made of Dawn."* Heidelberg: Winter, 2008.
———. "A Metonymic Community? Toward a Poetics of Contingency." In *The Common Growl*, ed. Thomas Claviez. New York: Fordham University Press, 2016.
———. "Neorealism, Contingency, and the Linguistic Turn." *Humanities* 8, no. 4 (2019): 176–92.
———. "Traces of a Metonymic Society in American Literary History." In *American Studies Today: New Research Agendas*, ed. Winfried Fluck et al., 299–322. Heidelberg: Winter, 2014.
Colliot-Thélène, Catherine. *Democracy and Subjective Rights: Democracy without Demos*. London: Rowman & Littlefield International, 2018.
Condorcet, Antoine-Nicolas de. *Sketch for a Historical Picture of the Progress of the Human Mind*. Trans. June Barraclough. 1795; London: Weidenfeld and Nicholson, 1955.
Cornell, Drucilla. *Beyond Accommodation: Ethical Feminism, Deconstruction, and the Law*. Lanham, MD: Rowman and Littlefield, 1999.
———. *The Imaginary Domain: Abortion, Pornography, and Sexual Harassment*. London: Routledge, 1995.
———. *Law and Revolution in South Africa: uBuntu, Dignity, and the Struggle for Constitutional Transformation*. New York: Fordham University Press, 2014.
———. *Moral Images of Freedom: A Future for Critical Theory*. Lanham, MD: Rowman & Littlefield, 2007.
———. *The Philosophy of the Limit*. London: Routledge, 1992.
Cornell, Drucilla, Michel Rosenfeld, and David Gray Carlson. *Deconstruction and the Possibility of Justice*. New York: Routledge, 1992.
Cornell, Drucilla, and Stephen D. Seely. *The Spirit of Revolution: Beyond the Dead Ends of Man*. Hoboken, NJ: John Wiley & Sons, 2016.
Critchley, Simon. "Demanding Approval: On the Ethics of Alain Badiou." *Radical Philosophy* 100 (2000): 16–27.
———. *Ethics-Politics-Subjectivity: Essays on Derrida, Levinas, and Contemporary French Thought*. London: Verso, 1999.
———. *Very Little . . . Almost Nothing*. London: Routledge, 1997.
Crow, David. "Explaining the *Arrival* Ending." *Den of Geek* (blog). Feb-

ruary 22, 2017. http://www.denofgeek.com/us/movies/arrival/259944/explaining-the-arrival-ending.

Danius, Sarah, Stefan Jonsson, and Gayatri Chakravorty Spivak. "An Interview with Gayatri Chakravorty Spivak." *boundary 2* 20, no. 2 (1993): 24–50.

De la Boétie, Etienne. *The Politics of Obedience: The Discourse of Voluntary Servitude*. Trans. Harry Kurz. Montreal: Black Rose, 1997.

Degryse, Annelies. "*Sensus Communis* as a Foundation for Men as Political Beings: Arendt's Reading of Kant's *Critique of Judgement*." *Philosophy and Social Criticism* 37 (2011): 345–58.

DeLanda, Manuel. *A New Philosophy of Society: Assemblage Theory and Social Complexity*. London: Bloomsbury Academic, 2006.

Deleuze, Gilles. *Bergsonism*. New York: Zone, 1991.

———. *Difference and Repetition*. New York: Columbia University Press, 1994.

———. *Expressionism in Philosophy: Spinoza*. New York: Zone, 1990.

———. *The Logic of Sense*. Trans. M. Lester and C. J. Stivale. London: Bloomsbury, 2004.

———. *Nietzsche and Philosophy*. New York: Columbia University Press, 1983.

———. *Pure Immanence: Essays on a Life*. New York: Zone, 2003.

———. *Spinoza: Practical Philosophy*. San Francisco: City Lights, 1988.

Deleuze, Gilles, and Claire Parnet. *Dialogues II*. New York: Columbia University Press, 2007.

Deleuze, Gilles, and Felix Guattari. *A Thousand Plateaus: Capitalism and Schizophrenia*. Minneapolis: University of Minnesota Press, 1987.

———. *What Is Philosophy?* New York: Columbia University Press, 1994.

DeLillo, Don. *Libra*. New York: Viking, 1988.

———. *The Names*. New York: Vintage, 1989.

Derrida, Jacques. *The Animal That Therefore I Am*. Ed. Marie-Louise Mallet. Trans. David Wills. New York: Fordham University Press, 2008.

———. *The Beast and the Sovereign, Volume II*. Trans. Geoffrey Bennington. Ed. Michel Lisse, Marie-Louise Mallet, and Ginette Michaud. Chicago: University of Chicago Press, 2011.

———. *De la grammatologie*. Paris: Les Éditions de Minuit, 1967.

———. *Dissemination*. Trans. Barbara Johnson. Chicago: University of Chicago Press, 1981.

———. "'Eating Well,' or, The Calculation of the Subject: An Interview with Jacques Derrida." In *Who Comes after the Subject?*, ed. Eduardo Cadava, Peter Connor, and Jean-Luc Nancy, 96–119. New York: Routledge, 1991.

———. "Le facteur de la vérité." In *The Post Card: From Socrates to Freud and Beyond*, trans. Alan Bass, 411–96. Chicago: University of Chicago Press, 1975.

---. "Force of Law: The 'Mystical Foundation of Authority.'" In *Deconstruction and the Possibility of Justice*, ed. Drucilla Cornell, Michel Rosenfeld, and David Gray Carlson, 3–67. New York: Routledge, 1992.

---. "From Restricted to General Economy: A Hegelianism without Reserve." In *Writing and Difference*, trans. Alan Bass, 317–50. London: Routledge, 2001.

---. Introduction to *The Future of Hegel*, by Catherine Malabou. Trans. Lisabeth During. London: Routledge, 2005.

---. *Life Death*. Trans. Pascale-Anne Brault and Michael Naas. Chicago: University of Chicago Press, 2020.

---. "My Chances / Mes chances: A Rendezvous with Some Epicurean Stereophonies." In *Psyche: Inventions of the Other*, vol. 1, ed, Peggy Kamuf and Elizabeth Rottenberg, trans. Irene Harvey and Avital Ronell. Stanford, CA: Stanford University Press, 2007.

---. *Negotiations: Interventions and Interviews, 1971–2001*. Stanford, CA: Stanford University Press, 2002.

---. "Nietzsche and the Machine (Interview with Richard Beardsworth)." In *Negotiations: Interventions and Interviews, 1971–2001*, ed. Elizabeth Rottenberg. Stanford, CA: Stanford University Press, 2002.

---. *Of Grammatology*. Trans. Gayatri Chakravorty Spivak. Baltimore, MD: Johns Hopkins University Press, 1976.

---. *Of Hospitality: Anne Dufourmantelle Invites Jacques Derrida to Respond*. Stanford, CA: Stanford University Press, 2000.

---. *Of Spirit: Heidegger and the Question*. Trans. Geoffrey Bennington and Rachel Bowlby. Chicago: University of Chicago Press, 1989.

---. *Philosophy in a Time of Terror: Dialogues with Jürgen Habermas and Jacques Derrida*. Ed. Giovanna Borradori. Chicago: University of Chicago Press, 2003.

---. "Plato's Pharmacy." In *Dissemination*, 61–172. London: Athlone, 1981.

---. *The Politics of Friendship*. Trans. George Collins. London: Verso, 2005.

---. *Positions*. Chicago: University of Chicago Press, 1981.

---. *The Post Card: From Socrates to Freud and Beyond*. Trans. Alan Bass. Chicago: University of Chicago Press, 2009.

---. *Resistances of Psychoanalysis*. Stanford, CA: Stanford University Press, 1998.

---. *Rogues: Two Essays on Reason*. Trans. Pascale-Anne Brault and Michael Naas. Stanford, CA: Stanford University Press, 2005.

---. "La structure, le signe et le jeu." In *L'écriture et la différence*. Paris: Éditions du Seuil, 1967.

---. "Structure, Sign, and Play in the Discourse of the Human Sciences."

In *Writing and Difference*, trans. Alan Bass. Chicago: University of Chicago Press, 1978.

———. "Telepathy." In *Psyche: Inventions of the Other*, vol. 1, ed. Peggy Kamuf and Elizabeth Rottenberg, trans. Nicholas Royle. Stanford, CA: Stanford University Press, 2007.

———. *La vie la mort*. Ed. Pascale-Anne Brault and Peggy Kamuf. Paris: Éditions du Seuil, 2019.

———. "Violence and Metaphysics." In *Writing and Difference*, trans. Alan Bass, 97–191. Chicago: University of Chicago Press, 1978.

Derrida, Jacques, and Elisabeth Roudinesco. "Violence against Animals." In *For What Tomorrow . . . : A Dialogue*, trans. Jeff Fort, 62–76. Stanford, CA: Stanford University Press, 2004.

Diderot, Denis. *Jacques le fataliste et son maître*. Ed. Barbara K.-Toumarkine. Paris: Flammarion, 2012.

The Discovery. Dir. Charlie McDowell. Endgame Entertainment, Netflix and ProtagonistPictures, 2017.

Dreyfus, Hubert. "Interpreting Heidegger on das Man." *Inquiry* 38 (1995): 423–30.

Dworkin, Ronald. *Law's Empire*. Cambridge, MA: Harvard University Press, 1986.

Dyer, Jay. "*Arrival* (2016)—The Film's Secret Meaning Explained." *21st Century Wire*, November 15, 2016. http://www.21stcenturywire.com/2016/11/15/arrival-2016-the-films-secret-meaning-explained/.

Edelglass, William, James Hatley, and Christian Diehm, eds. *Facing Nature: Levinas and Environmental Thought*. Pittsburgh, PA: Duquesne University Press, 2012.

Egan, Dave. "Das Man and Distantiality in *Being and Time*." *Inquiry* 55 (2012): 289–306.

Elias, Norbert. *The Society of Individuals*. Trans. Edmund Jephcott. Oxford: Basil Blackwell, 1991.

Esposito, Roberto. *Categorie dell'impolitico*. New ed. Bologna: Il Mulino, 1999.

———. *Communitas*. Trans. Timothy C. Campbell. Stanford, CA: Stanford University Press, 2010.

———. "Community, Immunity, Biopolitics." Trans. Michela Russo. *Política común* 3 (2012): n.p.

———. *Immunitas: The Protection and Negation of Life*. Trans. Zakiya Hanafi. Cambridge: Polity, 2011.

Forti, Simona. *New Demons: Rethinking Power and Evil Today*. Trans. Zakiya Hanafi. Stanford, CA: Stanford University Press, 2015.

Foucault, Michel. *Abnormal: Lectures at the Collège de France, 1974–1975*. Trans. Graham Burchell. New York: Picador, 2004.

———. "About the Concept of the 'Dangerous Individual' in Nineteenth-Century Legal Psychiatry." Trans. Alain Baudot and Jane Couchman. *International Journal of Law and Psychiatry* 1 (1978): 1–18.

———. *Discipline and Punish: The Birth of the Prison*. Trans. Alan Sheridan. London: Penguin, 1977.

———. *Dits et ecrits*. Vol. 4. Paris: Gallimard, 1994.

———. "Face aux gouvernements, les droits de l'homme." In *Dits et ecrits*, 4:707–8. Paris: Gallimard, 1994.

———. *Les mots and les choses*. Paris: Editions Gallimard, 1966.

———. *The Order of Things: An Archaeology of the Human Sciences*. New York: Pantheon, 1970.

———. *Politics, Philosophy, Culture: Interviews and Other Writings*. Trans. Alan Sheridan et al. New York: Routledge, 1988.

———. *Power: Essential Works of Michel Foucault, 1954–1984*. Vol. 3. Trans. Robert Hurley. New York: New Press, 2000.

———. "Preface to Transgression." In *Language, Counter-memory, Practice: Selected Essays and Interviews*, ed. Donald F. Bouchard, trans. Donald F. Bouchard and Sherry Simon, 29–52. Ithaca, NY: Cornell University Press, 1977.

———. *The Punitive Society: Lectures at the Collège de France, 1972–1973*. Trans. G. Burchell. London: Palgrave Macmillan, 2015.

———. *Remarks on Marx: Conversations with Duccio Trombadori*. Trans. R. James Goldstein and James Cascaito. New York: Semiotext(e), 1991.

———. "The Subject and Power." *Critical Inquiry* 8, no. 4 (1982): 777–95.

———. "What Is Critique?" In *Politics of Truth*, ed. Ed. Sylvère Lotringer, 23–82. New York: Semiotext(e), 1997.

———. "What Is Critique?" In *What Is Enlightenment? Eighteenth-Century Answers and Twentieth-Century Questions*, ed. Ed. James Schmidt, 382–98. Berkeley: University of California Press, 1996.

Fukuyama, Francis. *Our Posthuman Future: Consequences of the Biotechnological Revolution*. London: Profile, 2002.

Gamble, Christopher, Joshua S. Hanan, and Thomas Nail. "What Is New Materialism?" *Angelaki* 24, no. 6 (2019): 111–34.

Gasché, Rodolphe. *Georges Bataille: Phenomenology and Phantasmatology*. Trans. Roland Végső. Stanford, CA: Stanford University Press, 2012.

Gatens, Moira, and Genevieve Lloyd. *Collective Imaginings*. London: Routledge, 1999.

Ghosh, Amitav. *Blood of Fire*. London: John Murray, 2015.

———. *Gun Island*. London: John Murray, 2019.
———. *River of Smoke*. London: John Murray, 2011.
———. *Sea of Poppies*. London: John Murray, 2008.
Gilligan, Carol. *In a Different Voice: Psychological Theory and Women's Development*. Cambridge, MA: Harvard University Press, 2016.
Glynos, Jason. "Thinking the Ethics of the Political in the Context of a Postfoundational World: From an Ethics of Desire to an Ethics of the Drive." *Theory and Event* 4, no. 1 (2000): 1–16.
Gordon, Jane. *Creolizing Political Theory: Reading Rousseau through Fanon*. New York: Fordham University Press, 2014.
Gumbrecht, Hans Ulrich. *Prose of the World: Denis Diderot and the Periphery of Enlightenment*. Stanford, CA: Stanford University Press, 2021.
Habermas, Jürgen. *The Future of Human Nature*. Cambridge: Polity, 2003.
Hacking, Ian. *The Taming of Chance*. Cambridge: Cambridge University Press, 1990.
Hägglund, Martin. "The Trace of Time: A Critique of Vitalism." *Derrida Today* 9, no. 1 (2016): 36–46.
Hallward, Peter. "Ethics without Others: A Reply to Critchley on Badiou's Ethics." *Radical Philosophy* 102 (2000): 27–31.
———. *Out of This World: Deleuze and the Philosophy of Creation*. London: Verso, 2006.
The Handmaid's Tale. Dir. Bruce Miller. MGM Television, 2017–.
Haraway, Donna. *The Companion Species Manifesto: Dogs, People and Significant Otherness*. Chicago: Prickly Paradigm, 2003.
———. *Modest_Witness@Second_Millennium: FemaleMan©_Meets_Oncomouse™*. London: Routledge, 1997.
Hegel, Georg Wilhelm Friedrich. *Lectures on the Philosophy of World History*. Trans. H. B. Nisbet. Cambridge: Cambridge University Press, 1975.
———. *The Phenomenology of Spirit*. Trans. J. B. Baillie. New York: Digireads.com, 2009.
———. *The Phenomenology of Spirit*. Trans. Michael Inwood. Oxford: Oxford University Press, 2018.
———. *The Philosophy of Right*. Trans. T. M. Knox. Chicago: Encyclopaedia Britannica, 1952.
———. *The Science of Logic*. Trans. and ed. George di Giovanni. Cambridge: Cambridge University Press, 2010.
Heidegger, Martin. "The Age of the World Picture." In *The Question Concerning Technology and Other Essays*, trans. William Lovitt, 115–54. New York: Harper Torchbooks, 1977.

———. *Being and Time*. Trans. John McQuarrie and Edward Robinson. New York: Harper Perennial, 2008.

Herodotus. *The Persian Wars*. Trans. Alfred D. Godley. Cambridge, MA: Harvard University Press, 1990.

Hinnells, John R., ed. *The Routledge Companion to the Study of Religion*. London: Routledge, 2005.

Hobbes, Thomas. *Leviathan*. Ed. Richard Tuck. Cambridge: Cambridge University Press, 2016.

Hollywood, Amy. "Bataille and Mysticism: A 'Dazzling Dissolution.'" *Diacritics* 26, no. 2 (1996): 74–85.

Jackson, Dan. "The Guy behind Netflix's *The Discovery* Explains the Mind-Bender Ending." *Thrillist*, April 2, 2017. http://www.thrillist.com/entertainment/nation/netflix-discovery-ending-explained-theories.

———. "That Twist Ending of *Arrival* Makes You Rethink the Whole Movie." *Thrillist*, November 18, 2016. http://www.thrillist.com/entertainment/nation/arrival-movie-ending-big-time-twist.

Jacob, François. *The Logic of Life: A History of Heredity*. Princeton, NJ: Princeton University Press, 1973.

Jakobson, Roman. *On Language*. Ed. Linda R. Waugh and Monique Monville-Burston. Cambridge, MA: Harvard University Press, 1995.

Johnson, Christopher. *System and Writing in the Philosophy of Jacques Derrida*. Cambridge: Cambridge University Press, 1993.

Joseph, Miranda. *Against the Romance of Community*. Minneapolis: University of Minnesota Press, 2002.

Joyce, James. *Finnegan's Wake*. Oxford: Oxford University Press, 2012.

Kant, Immanuel. *Grounding for the Metaphysics of Morals with "On a Supposed Right to Lie because of Philanthropic Concerns."* Trans. James W. Ellington. Indianapolis, IN: Hackett, 1981.

———. *Groundwork of the Metaphysics of Morals*. Trans., ed. Mary Gregor. Cambridge: Cambridge University Press, 1997.

———. "Idea for a Universal History with a Cosmopolitan Purpose." In *Kant: Political Writings*, ed. Hans Reiss, 41–50. Cambridge: Cambridge University Press, 1991.

———. "Perpetual Peace: A Philosophical Sketch." In *Kant: Political Writings*, ed. Hans Reiss, 93–130. Cambridge: Cambridge University Press, 1991.

Kauffman, Stuart. *Humanity in a Creative Universe*. Oxford: Oxford University Press, 2015.

Keenan King, Dennis. *Hegel and Contemporary Continental Philosophy*. Albany: SUNY Press, 2004.

Keil, David. "The Ontological Prison: New Materialisms and Their Dead

Ends." *Contradictions: A Journal for Critical Thought* 1, no. 2 (2017): 41–59.

Kendall, Stuart. *Georges Bataille*. London: Reaktion, 2007.

Kirby, Vicki. "Grammatology: A Vital Science." *Derrida Today* 9, no. 1 (2016): 47–67.

Kleingeld, Pauline. "Contradiction and Kant's Formula of Universal Law." *Kant-Studien* 108, no. 1 (2017): 89–115.

Kolbert, Elizabeth. *The Sixth Extinction*. New York: Henry Holt, 2014.

Lacan, Jacques. "Seminar on 'The Purloined Letter.'" In *Écrits*, trans. Bruce Fink, 6–48. New York: Norton, 2006.

———. *The Seminar of Jacques Lacan Book III: The Psychoses, 1955–1956*. Ed. Jacques-Alain Miller. Trans. Russell Grigg. New York: Norton, 1997.

———. *The Seminar of Jacques Lacan Book VII: The Ethics of Psychoanalysis, 1959–1960*. Ed. Jacques-Alain Miller. Trans. Dennis Porter. London: Routledge, 2008.

———. *The Seminar of Jacques Lacan Book XI: The Four Fundamental Concepts of Psycho-Analysis*. Ed. Jacques-Alain Miller. Trans. Alan Sheridan. New York: Norton, 1981.

Lacan, Jacques, and Juliet Mitchell. *Feminine Sexuality: Jacques Lacan and the École Freudienne*. New York: Norton, 1985.

Latour, Bruno. "Agency at the Time of the Anthropocene." *New Literary History* 45 (2014): 1–18.

———. *Pandora's Hope: Essays on the Reality of Science Studies*. Cambridge, MA: Harvard University Press, 1999.

———. *The Politics of Nature*. Trans. Catherine Porter. Cambridge, MA: Harvard University Press, 2004.

———. *We Have Never Been Modern*. Trans. Catherine Porter. Cambridge, MA: Harvard University Press, 1993.

Levinas, Emmanuel. *Otherwise Than Being or Beyond Essence*. The Hague: Nijhoff, 1981.

———. "Le Scandale du mal." *Les Nouveaux Cahiers* 85 (1986): 15–17.

———. *Totality and Infinity*. Pittsburgh, PA: Duquesne University Press, 1969.

———. "Transcendence and Evil." In *Collected Philosophical Papers*, trans. A. Lingis, 175–89. Dordrecht: Martinus Nijhoff, 1986.

———. "Useless Suffering." In *Entre-Nous: Thinking-of-the-Other*, 78–87. London: Continuum, 2006.

Llewelyn, John. *The Middle Voice of Ecological Conscience*. London: Macmillan, 1991.

Lloyd, Genevieve. *Part of Nature: Self-Knowledge in Spinoza's Ethic*. Ithaca, NY: Cornell University Press, 1994.

———. *Spinoza and the Ethics*. London: Routledge, 1996.
Locke, John. *Two Treatises of Government*. Ed. Peter Laslett. Cambridge: Cambridge University Press, 2015.
Lodge, David. *Modes of Modern Writing*. London: Edward Arnold, 1977.
Luhmann, Niklas. *Social Systems*. Trans. John Bednarz Jr. and Dirk Baecker. Intro. Eva M. Knodt. Stanford, CA: Stanford University Press, 1995.
Lyotard, Jean-François, and Jean-Loup Thébaud. *Just Gaming*. Manchester: Manchester University Press, 1985.
Macherey, Pierre. *Hegel or Spinoza*. Minneapolis: University of Minnesota Press, 2011.
———. *Le sujet des normes*. Paris: Editions Amsterdam, 2014.
Macpherson, Crawford B. *The Political Theory of Possessive Individualism: Hobbes to Locke*. Oxford: Clarendon, 1962.
Marchi, Viola. "'The Alienation of the Common': A Look into the 'Authentic Origin' of Community." In *Critique of Authenticity*, ed. Thomas Claviez, Kornelia Imesch, and Britta Sweers, 73–100. Wilmington, DE: Vernon, 2019.
———. "Ethics, Interrupted: Community and Impersonality in Levinas." *SPELL* 32 (2015): 143–58.
Marcuse, Herbert. *One-Dimensional Man: Studies in the Ideology of Advanced Industrial Society*. Boston: Beacon, 1991.
Martin, Wallace. "Metonymy." In *Princeton Encyclopedia of Poetry and Poetics*, 4th ed., ed. Roland Greene, 876–78. Princeton, NJ: Princeton University Press, 2012.
Marx, Karl. *Capital*. Vol. 1. Trans. Ben Fowkes. New York: Vintage, 1977.
———. "The Communist Manifesto." In *The Marx-Engels Reader*, ed. Robert C. Tucker, 469–500. New York: Norton, 1978.
———. *A Contribution to the Critique of Political Economy*. Trans. S.W. Ryazanskaya. New York: International Publishers, 1972.
———. "Debates on the Law on Thefts of Wood." Proceedings of the Sixth Rhine Province Assembly, Third Article. *Rheinische Zeitung* 298, Supplement, October 25, 1842.
———. *Misère de la philosophie: réponse à la Philosophie de la misère de M. Proudhon*. Paris: A. Frank, 1847.
Marx, Karl, and Friedrich Engels. *The German Ideology*. New York: International Publishers, 1972.
Masolo, D. A. "Western and African Communitarianism: A Comparison." In *A Companion to African Philosophy*, ed. Kwasi Wiredu, 483–98. Oxford: Blackwell, 2004.
Maturana, Humberto R. "Science and Daily Life: The Ontology of Scientific Explanations." In *Selforganization: Portrait of a Scientific Revolution*, ed.

Wolfgang Krohn, Gunter Kuppers, and Helga Nowotny, 12–35. Dordrecht: Springer, 1990.

Maturana, Humberto R., and Francisco Varela. *The Tree of Knowledge: The Biological Roots of Human Understanding*. Boston: Shambhala, 1992.

McCance, Dawne. *The Reproduction of Life Death: Derrida's "La vie la mort."* New York: Fordham University Press, 2019.

Meillassoux, Quentin. *After Finitude: An Essay on the Necessity of Contingency*. Trans. Ray Brassier. London: Continuum, 2008.

———. *The Number and the Siren*. Trans. Robin Mackay. New York: Sequence, 2012.

Montesquieu, Charles de Secondat, baron de La Brède et de. *De l'esprit des lois*. Paris: Gallimard, 1995.

Moran, Dermot. "Nicholas Cusa and Modern Philosophy." In *The Cambridge Companion to Renaissance Philosophy*, ed. James Hankins, 173–92. Cambridge: Cambridge University Press, 2007.

More, Mabogo. "South Africa under and after Apartheid." In *A Companion to African Philosophy*, ed. Kwasi Wiredu, 149–60. Oxford: Blackwell, 2004.

Morton, Timothy. *The Ecological Thought*. Cambridge, MA: Harvard University Press, 2012.

———. *Ecology without Nature: Rethinking Environmental Aesthetics*. Cambridge, MA: Harvard University Press, 2007.

———. *Hyperobjects: Philosophy and Ecology after the End of the World*. Minneapolis: University of Minnesota Press, 2013.

Moss, Lenny. "Detachment Theory: Agency, Nature, and the Normative Nihilism of New Materialism." In *The New Politics of Materialism: History, Philosophy, Science*, ed. Sarah Ellenzweig and John H. Zammito, 227–49. London: Routledge, 2017.

Nancy, Jean-Luc. "The Confronted Community." In *The Obsessions of Georges Bataille: Community and Communication*, ed. Andrew J. Mitchell and Jason Kemp Winfree, trans. Jason Kemp Winfree, 19–30. Albany: SUNY Press, 2009.

———. *The Disavowed Community*. Trans. Philip Armstrong. New York: Fordham University Press, 2016.

———. "Exscription." Trans. Katherine Lydon. *Yale French Studies* 78 (1990): 47–65.

———. *The Inoperative Community*. Trans. Peter Connor et al. Minneapolis: University of Minnesota Press, 1991.

Neiman, Susan. *Evil in Modern Thought: An Alternative History of Philosophy*. Princeton, NJ: Princeton University Press, 2002.

Newman, Michael. "Sensibility, Trauma, and the Face: Levinas from Phenomenology to the Immemorial." In *The Face of the Other and the Trace of God*, ed. Jeffrey Bloechi, 90–128. New York: Fordham University Press, 2000.

Nguyen, Clinton. "China Might Use Data to Create a Score for Each Citizen Based on How Trustworthy They Are." *Business Insider*, October 26, 2016. http://www.businessinsider.com/china-social-credit-score-like-black-mirror-2016-10.

Ninotchka. Dir. Ernst Lubitsch. MGM, 1939.

Nisbet, Robert A. *The Sociological Tradition*. 1966; New York: Routledge, 2017.

Noble, Denis. "Conrad Waddington and the Origin of Epigenetics." *Journal of Experimental Biology* 218 (2015): 816–18.

Norris, Christopher. "Alain Badiou: Truth, Ethics, and the Formal Imperative." *Revista Portuguesa de Filosofia* 65 (2009): 1103–36.

Noys, Benjamin. *Georges Bataille: A Critical Introduction*. London: Pluto, 2000.

———. *The Persistence of the Negative*. Edinburgh: Edinburgh University Press, 2010.

Nussbaum, Martha. "Patriotism and Cosmopolitanism." In *For Love of Country*. Boston: Beacon, 1996.

Oliver, Kelly. "The Poetic Axis of Ethics." *Derrida Today* 7, no. 2 (2014): 121–36.

Osborne, Peter. *A Critical Sense: Interviews with Intellectuals*. London: Routledge, 2013.

Padui, Raoni. "Realism, Anti-Realism, and Materialism." *Angelaki: Journal of the Theoretical Humanities* 16, no. 2 (2011): 89–101.

Parikka, Jussi. *A Geology of Media*. Minneapolis: University of Minnesota Press, 2015.

Pietz, William. "Death of the Deodand: Accursed Objects and the Money Value of Human Life." *RES: Anthropology and Aesthetics* 31 (1997): 97–108.

Postman. Dir. Kevin Costner. Warner Bros, 1997.

Quashie, Kevin. *The Sovereignty of Quiet: Beyond Resistance in Black Culture*. New Brunswick, NJ: Rutgers University Press, 2012.

Rancière, Jacques. *Disagreement: Politics and Philosophy*. Minneapolis: University of Minnesota Press, 1999.

———. *On the Shores of Politics*. London: Verso, 2007.

Rasch, William, and Cary Wolfe, ed. *Observing Complexity: Systems Theory and Postmodernity*. Minneapolis: University of Minnesota Press, 2000.

Read, Jason. *The Politics of Transindividuality*. Leiden: Brill, 2016.

Red Angel. Dir. Yasuzô Masumura. Daiei Studios, 1966.

Rich, Adrienne. *Blood, Bread, and Poetry*. London: Virago, 1987.

Ricoeur, Paul. *Oneself as Another*. Trans. Kathleen Blamey. Chicago: University of Chicago Press, 1992.

Riera, Gabriel, ed. *Alain Badiou: Philosophy and Its Conditions*. Albany: SUNY Press, 2005.

Rorty, Richard. *Objectivity, Relativism, and Truth: Philosophical Papers*, Volume 1. Cambridge: Cambridge University Press, 1991.

Sankaran, Chita. "Diasporic Predicaments: An Interview with Amitav Ghosh." In *History, Narrative, and Testimony in Amitav Ghosh's Fiction*, ed. Chita Sankaran, 1–16. Albany: SUNY Press, 2012.

———. Introduction to *History, Narrative, and Testimony in Amitav Ghosh's Fiction*, ed. Chita Sankaran, xiii–xxvii. Albany: SUNY Press, 2012.

Schwab, Klaus. "The Fourth Industrial Revolution." *Foreign Affairs*, December 12, 2015.

Sloterdijk, Peter. "*Rules for the Human Zoo*: A Response to the Letter on Humanism." *Environment and Planning D: Society and Space* 27 (2009): 12–28.

Spiegel, Marjorie. *The Dreaded Comparison*. New York: Mirror, 1996.

Spiller, Hortense. "Mama's Baby, Papa's Maybe: An American Grammar Book." *Diacritics* 17, no. 2 (1987): 64–81.

Spinoza, Benedict de. *Ethics*. Trans. Edwin Curley. London: Penguin, 1996.

Spivak, Gayatri C. *A Critique of Postcolonial Reason: Toward a History of the Vanishing Present*. Cambridge, MA: Harvard University Press, 1999.

Starobinski, Jean. *Diderot, un diable de ramage*. Paris: Gallimard, 2012.

Statt, Nick. "Elon Musk Launches Neuralink, a Venture to Merge the Human Brain with AI." *The Verge*, March 27, 2017. http://www.theverge.com/2017/3/27/15077864/elon-musk-neuralink-brain-computer-interface-ai-cyborgs.

———. "How the Short Story That Inspired *Arrival* Helps Us Interpret the Film's Major Twist." *The Verge*, November 16, 2016. http://www.theverge.com/2016/11/16/13642396/arrival-ted-chiang-story-of-your-life-film-twist-ending.

Stevens, Wallace. *The Necessary Angel: Essays on Reality and the Imagination*. New York: Random House, 1942.

———. *Opus Posthumous*. Rev. ed. Ed. Milton J. Bates. New York: Vintage, 1990.

Stoekl, Allan. Introduction to *Visions of Excess: Selected Writings, 1927–1939*, by Georges Bataille, trans. Allan Stoekl, Carl R. Lovitt, and Donald M. Leslie Jr., ix–xxv. Minneapolis: University of Minnesota Press, 1985.

Szymborska, Wisława. "The Three Oddest Words." In *Poems New and Collected 1957–1997*, trans. Stanisław Barańczak and Clare Cavanagh, 261. New York: Harcourt, 1998.

Thacker, Eugene. *After Life*. Chicago: University of Chicago Press, 2010.

———. "Dark Media." In *Excommunication: Three Inquiries in Media and

Mediation, ed. Alexander Galloway, Eugene Thacker, and McKenzie Wark. Chicago: University of Chicago Press, 2014.

———. *Starry Speculative Corpse: Horror of Philosophy Vol. 2*. Alresford: Zero, 2015.

Todorov, Tzvetan. *Mikhail Bakhtin: The Dialogical Principle*. Minneapolis: University of Minnesota Press, 1984.

Tönnies, Ferdinand. *Community and Society*. Trans. Charles P. Loomis. Mineola, NY: Dover, 2002.

Turner, Denys. *The Darkness of God: Negativity in Christian Mysticism*. Cambridge: Cambridge University Press, 1995.

Tushnet, Mark. *The American Law of Slavery, 1810–1860*. Princeton, NJ: Princewton University Press, 1981.

Vernon, Jim, and Antonio Calcagno, eds. *Badiou and Hegel: Infinity, Dialectics, Subjectivity*. New York: Lexington, 2015.

Virno, Paolo. *Multitude: Between Innovation and Negation*. Trans. Isabella Bertoletti, James Cascaito, and Andrea Casson. Los Angeles: Semiotext(e), 2008.

Wagner, Andreas. "Jean-Luc Nancy—A Negative Politics?" *Philosophy and Social Criticism* 32, no. 1 (2006): 89–109.

Wallerstein, Immanuel. *The Modern World-System*. Vol. 4: *Centrist Liberalism Triumphant, 1789–1914*. Berkeley: University of California Press, 2011.

Weller, Shane. "Voidance: Linguistic Negativism in Blanchot's Fiction." *French Studies: A Quarterly Review* 69, no. 1 (January 2015): 30–45.

White, Hayden. *Metahistory: The Historical Imagination in Nineteenth-Century Europe*. Baltimore, MD: Johns Hopkins University Press, 1973.

The Who. "Pinball Wizard." Lyrics by Pete Townshend. London: Polydor, 1969.

Wiredu, Kwasi. "Mortality and Religion in Akan Thought." In *Philosophy and Cultures*, ed. Henry O. Oruka and D. A. Masolo, 6–13. Nairobi: Bookwise, 1983.

Wolfe, Cary. *Animal Rites: American Culture, the Discourse of Species, and Posthumanist Theory*. Chicago: University of Chicago Press, 2003.

———. *Before the Law: Humans and Other Animals in a Biopolitical Frame*. Chicago: University of Chicago Press, 2013.

———. *What Is Posthumanism?* Minneapolis: University of Minnesota Press, 2010.

Wynter, Sylvia. "No Humans Involved: An Open Letter to My Colleagues." *Forum N.H.I. Knowledge for the 21st Century* 1 (1994): 42–70.

———. "Towards the Sociogenic Principle: Fanon, the Puzzle of Conscious Experience, of 'Identity' and What It's Like to be 'Black.'" In *National*

Identities and Sociopolitical Changes in Latin America, ed. Mercedes F. Durán Cogan and Antonio Gómez-Moriana, 30–66. New York: Routledge, 2001.

———. "Unsettling the Coloniality of Being/Power/Truth/Freedom: Towards the Human, After Man, Its Overrepresentation—An Argument." *New Centennial Review* 3 (2003): 257–337.

Žižek, Slavoj. *Less Than Nothing: Hegel and the Shadow of Dialectical Materialism*. London: Verso, 2012.

Contributors

Alan Badiou is Professor Emeritus of Philosophy at the École Normal Supérieure in Paris and still holds seminars at the Collège International de Philosophie and at the European Graduate School. A philosopher, political activist, and playwright, he has published some of the most original, influential, and by now classic works of contemporary philosophy: *Theory of the Subject* (1982), *Manifesto for Philosophy* (1989), *Ethics: An Essay on the Understanding of Evil* (1993), *Deleuze: The Clamor of Being* (1997), and the three installments of his most ambitious work: *Being and Event* (1988), *Logics of the Worlds: Being and Event 2* (2006), and *The Immanence of Truths: Being and Event 3*, released in French in 2018.

Étienne Balibar is Professor Emeritus of Moral and Political Philosophy at the Université de Paris X Nanterre; Professor Emeritus of Humanities at the University of California, Irvine; and Anniversary Chair in Modern European Philosophy at Kingston University, London. His research in the fields of political, moral, and Marxist philosophy focuses on emancipation, citizenship, and on what he terms "equaliberty." The breadth of his thought can be gauged from his published works, from *Reading Capital*, released in 1965 and coauthored with his mentor Louis Althusser, to the more recent *We, the People of Europe? Reflections on Transnational Citizenship* (2003), *Equaliberty* (2014), *Violence and Civility: On the Limits of Political Philosophy* (2015), *Citizen Subject: Foundations for Philosophical Anthropology* (2017), and *Secularism and Cosmopolitanism* (2018).

Rosi Braidotti is Distinguished University Professor and Director of the Centre for the Humanities at Utrecht University. She is the founder of the interuniversity SOCRATES network NOISE and of the Thematic Network for Women's

Studies ATHENA, which she directed until 2005. Her research combines social and political theory, cultural politics, feminist theory, and ethnicity studies. She is the author of *Patterns of Dissonance: A Study on Women in Contemporary Philosophy* (1991), *Nomadic Subjects: Embodiment and Sexual Difference in Contemporary Feminist Theory* (1994), *Metamorphoses: Towards a Materialist Theory of Becoming* (2002), and *Transpositions: On Nomadic Ethics* (2006). Her latest publications, *The Posthuman* (2013) and *Posthuman Knowledge* (2019), call for a new type of critical knowledge, one able to address and challenge the intersections of power and violence, privilege and discrimination, arising out of human interactions.

Thomas Claviez is Professor for Literary Theory at the University of Bern, where he is responsible for the MA program in World Literature. He is the author of *Grenzfälle: Mythos- Ideologie- American Studies* (1998) and *Aesthetics and Ethics: Otherness and Moral Imagination from Aristotle to Levinas and from* Uncle Tom's Cabin *to* House Made of Dawn (2008) and the coauthor, with Dietmar Wetzel, of *Zur Aktualität von Jacques Rancière* (2016). He has published widely on issues of community, recognition, literary theory, and moral philosophy. He is the editor of *The Conditions of Hospitality: Ethics, Politics, and Aesthetics on the Threshold of the Possible* (2013) and of *The Common Growl: Towards a Poetics of Precarious Community* (2016) and the coeditor of *Aesthetic Transgressions: Modernity, Liberalism, and the Function of Literature* (2006) and of *Critique of Authenticity* (2019). He is currently working on a monograph with the title *A Metonymic Community? Towards a New Poetics of Contingency*.

Drucilla Cornell is Professor Emerita of Political Science, Comparative Literature, and Women's and Gender Studies at Rutgers University; Professor Extraordinaire at the University of Pretoria, South Africa; and a visiting professor at Birkbeck College, University of London. With a background in philosophy, law, and grassroots mobilization, she has played a central role in the organization of the memorable conferences on deconstruction and justice at the Benjamin N. Cardozo School of Law in 1989, 1990, and 1993. She is the author of *The Philosophy of the Limit* (1992), *Feminism and Pornography* (2000), and *Law and Revolution in South Africa: uBuntu, Dignity, and the Struggle for Constitutional Transformation* (2014). She has also coedited several books: *Feminism as Critique: On the Politics of Gender* (1987), with Seyla Benhabib; and *Hegel and Legal Theory* (1991) and *Deconstruction and the Possibility of Justice* (1992), with David Gray Carlson and Michel Rosenfeld. She is part of a philosophical exchange with Seyla Benhabib, Judith Butler, and Nancy Fraser entitled *Feminist Contentions* (1995). In addition to her academic work, she has written four produced plays.

Hans Ulrich Gumbrecht is the Albert Guérard Professor Emeritus in Literature in the Departments of Comparative Literature and French and Italian at Stanford University. As a public intellectual and highly prolific writer, he contributes to fields as diverse as the histories of national literatures in Romance languages, Western philosophical traditions, and forms of aesthetic experience in twenty-first-century everyday culture. He has published more than two thousand texts, translated into more than twenty languages. His latest books are *Atmosphere, Mood, Stimmung: On a Hidden Potential of Literature* (2012), *Explosionen der Aufklärung: Diderot, Goya, Lichtenberg, Mozart* (2013), *After 1945: Latency as Origin of the Present* (2013), and *Brüchige Gegenwart: Reflexionen und Reaktionen* (2019).

Viola Marchi is a postdoctoral researcher at the University of Bern. She studied English and Italian literatures at the University of Pisa and the University of Bern, receiving her PhD in English from the latter in 2019, with a dissertation titled "Fuori Luogo: Community and the Impropriety of the Common." In 2016, with support of the Swiss National Science Foundation, she was a visiting fellow at the Scuola Normale Superiore in Pisa. She has published the articles "Ethics, Interrupted: Community and Impersonality in Levinas" (2015) and "The Alienation of the Common: A Look into the 'Authentic' Origin of Community" (2019). She is currently working on her first monograph.

Michael Naas is Professor of Philosophy at DePaul University in Chicago. His research covers the fields of philosophy and comparative literature, with a particular focus on ancient Greek thought and contemporary French philosophy and with a strong interest in the thinkers Nietzsche, Heidegger, Derrida, Lyotard, and Levinas. He has edited and cotranslated into English a number of Jacques Derrida's texts: *The Work of Mourning* (2011), *Learning to Live Finally* (2007), *Rogues* (2005), and *Adieu: To Emmanuel Levinas* (1999). His most recent publications are *The End of the World and Other Teachable Moments: Jacques Derrida's Final Seminar* (2015), *Miracle and Machine: Jacques Derrida and the Two Sources of Religion, Science, and the Media* (2012), and *Plato and the Invention of Life* (2018).

Cary Wolfe is the Bruce and Elizabeth Dunlevie Professor of English at Rice University and the director of 3CT: Center for Critical and Cultural Theory. While he is most prominently known for his work in animal studies and posthumanism, his research and teaching covers fields such as systems theory, pragmatism, biopolitics, and American literature and culture. He is the founding editor of the University of Minnesota Press series Posthumanities, to which he contributed the monograph *What Is Posthumanism?* (2010). He is the author of

Animal Rites: American Culture, the Discourse of Species, and Posthumanist Theory (2003) and *Before the Law: Humans and Other Animals in a Biopolitical Frame* (2012). His latest projects are: the monograph *Ecological Poetics, or, Wallace Stevens' Birds* and a special issue of *Angelaki: Journal of the Theoretical Humanities* on "Ontogenesis beyond Complexity," on the work of the multidisciplinary Ontogenetics Process Group, of which he is a member.

Slavoj Žižek is Professor of Philosophy at the European Graduate School, senior researcher at the Institute for Sociology and Philosophy at the University of Ljubljana, Global Distinguished Professor of German at New York University, International Director of the Birkbeck Institute for the Humanities, and founder and president of the Society for Theoretical Psychoanalysis, Ljubljana. Since *The Sublime Object of Ideology* in 1989, his first book in English, Žižek has published over forty books, spanning from political theory to cultural studies and bringing together the influences of Hegelian idealism, Lacanian psychoanalysis, and Marxist thought. Among his most recent publications are *The Relevance of the Communist Manifesto* (2018), *Like a Thief in Broad Daylight: Power in the Era of Posthumanity* (2018), and *Sex and the Failed Absolute* (2019).

Index

acedia, 183
Actor-Network Theory (ANT), 21, 208, 217–19
aesthetics, 18, 41, 134–37, 164–66, 168, 170–72
affect, 16, 18, 145–48, 152–53, 155–56, 159, 171–72, 175, 177
affirmation, 96, 116, 122, 136, 145–48, 150–57, 162–69; and negation, 16, 97–98, 117, 153; nonpositive affirmation, 14, 96, 118–19; and position, 17. *See also* ethics of affirmation
Agamben, Giorgio, 1, 49, 105–7, 122n57, 183
agency, 19, 41, 63, 127, 151, 173, 190–91, 211–12, 224–28; and dialectics, 20; and moral subjecthood, 21–22, 206–9, 213–18, 222–23
alienation, 15, 113, 135, 141, 186, 191
alterity, 67, 74, 97, 108, 207. *See also* otherness/other
Althusser, Louis, 131, 142
animals, 28, 78, 85, 92n21, 201, 212, 214–15, 232–33, 235–36, 244–45
anthropocene, 22, 38, 155, 157, 159
aporia, 101, 115, 167
Arendt, Hannah, 128, 140, 171
Aristotle, 4–5, 7, 9, 11, 13, 25, 46–51, 56, 59, 64–65nn11,14, 70–72, 75, 94–95
Arrival, 20, 198, 201–2
autopoiesis, 146, 173–74, 233, 238–40, 243

Badiou, Alain, x, 1–16, 25–27, 194
Bailly, Jean-Christophe, 98

Bakhtin, Mikhail, 11
Balibar, Etienne, 1, 15–6, 27, 127, 140–41
Barad, Karen, 222
Barthes, Roland, 51
Bataille, Georges, 14–15, 96, 98, 100–114, 116–18, 120n30, 121nn31,39, 122n57, 123n105, 134, 136
Bateson, Gregory, 233, 237
Bauman, Zygmunt, 11, 47–48
becoming, xi, 10, 15, 27n33, 115, 132, 134, 137, 139, 151, 155–56, 158, 239, 242; becoming woman, 165–167; metaphysics of becoming, 146; as nondialectical, 16–17, 115–16, 148–49, 153
Benjamin, Walter, 136
Bennett, Jane, 208, 224
Bernstein, Richard J., 2–3
big Other, 19–20, 186, 189–93
biology, 22, 79, 230–31, 233, 235, 239–40
biosphere, 237, 239–42, 245
Black Mirror, 186
Black Panthers, 163
Blanchot, Maurice, 14–15, 95–96, 99, 101, 108–19, 135–36, 140, 143n21
Bloom, Harold, 229
Bourdieu, Pierre, 63
Bown, Alfie, 184–86, 189, 194
Braidotti, Rosi, 2, 16, 22, 159–61, 208
Brazil, 19, 186
Brown, Wendy, 170
Burckhardt, Jacob, 136, 143n24
Butler, Judith, 63, 138

Campe, Rüdiger, 63
capitalism, 16, 19, 40, 100, 128, 135, 142n12, 145–46, 148, 151, 154–55, 169, 171, 178, 183, 185
care: ethics of care, 178; 181n63; care of the self, 137, 139
cartographies, 150, 157–59
Cavarero, Adriana, 2
Celan, Paul, 22, 233
chance, x, 10, 12–13, 17, 45– 46, 50–51, 62, 69–70, 72, 77–78, 80, 82–83, 87, 90, 93n36, 96, 103, 184
Chiang, Ted, 200–201
code, 22–23, 75, 77, 82, 87–88, 92nn21,23, 148, 154, 156, 233–35, 237, 241
Colliot-Thélène, Catherine, 130
colonialism, 58
communitarianism, 100, 127
community, 14–15, 17–18, 27n29, 36, 47–48, 50–51, 54–55, 65n11, 98–101, 103, 105–15, 119, 147, 151–52, 171, 232, 246; apophatic community, 14, 27n29, 96; and contingency, 12, 58, 95–96; and cosmopolitanism, 11, 46–47, 58; and individuality, 15, 127–29, 132–36, 141n7, 175–76, 99; metonymic community, 12, 59–60
Constant, Benjamin, 7, 25n17
contingency, x–xii, 1–8, 13, 26n26, 46–47, 76–79, 84–85, 87–88, 90, 92n26, 242; and contiguity, 53, 59; as epistemological problem, 39–42, 48, 243, 246; and freedom, 10, 34–36, 38–39, 41–43, 64, 80–83, 92n26; and life, x, 10, 23, 34–35, 42–43, 51, 63, 70–72, 74–75, 77, 82–87, 91n12, 246; and necessity, x, 14, 37, 74, 92n26, 95; and otherness, 7, 12–13, 48, 50, 54–55; universe of, 11, 34–37, 41–43
contingent, x, 2–3, 8–10, 12, 14, 25n21, 26n23, 27n33, 43n1, 51, 55–58, 60, 62–64, 69, 73, 77, 80–82, 85–86, 92n32, 94–95, 107, 119, 233, 243
cosmopolitanism, 11, 46, 53, 59–60, 67n41, 158
Critchley, Simon, 26–27n27, 106–8, 116
Croesus, 70–71
Cusa, Nicholas, 114, 123n105

Darwin, Charles, 173, 240–42; neo-Darwinism, 235, 237
de la Boétie, Etienne, 133
de Sade, Marquis D.A.F., 194
de Tocqueville, Alex, 140n1

decision, 4–5, 8, 17, 28n40, 41, 49, 81, 87, 94–95, 163, 200–202, 210, 236; and the undecidable, 4–5, 18, 95, 112, 115, 169, 174
deconstruction, 4, 14, 22, 75, 96, 134, 163–65, 167, 169, 173, 223, 230, 232–34, 241
Defoe, Daniel, 232
Deleuze, Gilles, 1–2, 16–17, 27nn33,34, 29n47, 139, 143n17, 146, 148–49, 151, 155, 165–66, 172
DeLillo, Don, 69, 90
Democritus, 73
Derrida, Jacques, 1–8, 12–14, 17–18, 22–23, 24n12, 25n23, 27–28nn35,42,29n47, 60, 69, 72–76, 78–90, 91n17, 92nn23,26,32, 93n36, 95–96, 110–12, 114–15, 152, 162–69, 173–74, 177–78, 209, 224n2, 225n5, 230, 232–35, 241–42, 244–46
Descartes, René, xi, 39, 54, 146
Descombes, Vincent, 140n1
desire, 19–20, 36, 66n24, 102–4, 147–49, 152–55, 167, 182–86, 189–91, 193–94, 203n2, 232, 243
destiny, 12–13, 34, 38, 42, 54, 60, 100, 175
dialectics, 4–7, 14–18, 20, 22, 24n11, 26n25, 27n29, 98, 100, 104, 111–15, 118–19, 129, 131, 135, 142n10, 146, 148–49, 153, 169; and contingency, 2–3, 9, 96; of master and slave, 7, 15, 48, 136, 141n3; of the proper, 27n29, 96; of recognition, 7, 116–17, 146, 153; of self and other, 19, 24n11, 47, 113–14, 148, 183
Diderot, Denis, 11, 39, 41–43, 44n3
difference, 3, 6–7, 14, 24n11, 25n21, 60, 86–87, 93n36, 95, 107, 115, 118, 150, 156, 173, 207, 232; anthropological differences, 129, 135, 141n5; as nondialectical, 146; sexual difference, 164–66, 170, 177; and uBuntu, 18, 175–76
digitalization, 19–20, 189–93
dumb luck, 12–13, 69–78, 80, 83, 89–90
Dumont, Louis, 140n1
Dworkin, Ronald, 167
dystopia, 66n32, 184, 188

ecology, 22, 38, 221–22, 230, 232–33, 237
Elias, Norbert, 142n8
environment, 2, 21– 23, 37, 77, 208, 231, 235–37, 241–43, 245
equality, 60, 107, 128, 131–32, 136, 168, 170, 175
Esposito, Roberto, 52, 107, 119, 143n19

ethical feminism, 18, 164, 166, 171, 175, 177–78
ethics, ix–xi, 1, 3, 6–7, 9, 13, 15–20, 22, 24n12, 25n17, 27–28n35, 49, 59–60, 94–96, 101, 108, 116, 119, 127–28, 137–39, 177–78, 207, 209, 216–17, 222, 229, 233–34, 245–46, 249n54; environmental ethics, 2, 21–22, 208, 213, 225n5, 234; ethics of affirmation, 145–59; ethics of circular time, 19–20, 28n44, 195, 198, 200–203; ethics of the event, x–xii, 10, 16–17, 20, 25–26n23, 26–27n27, 152, 154, 194
event: and contingency, 14, 25n22, 26n27, 33, 42–43, 55, 59, 73, 77, 87, 94–96; and ethics. *See also* ethics of the event
evil, x, 2–3, 16, 64n11, 71, 148, 153, 182, 226n10, 227n18
evolution, 13, 23, 38, 40, 43, 52, 78–79, 85, 237, 240–42, 245

Fanon, Frantz, 173
Finitude, 22, 194, 233, 243
Forti, Simona, 2–3, 63–64, 65n11, 226n10, 227n18

Guattari, Felix, 16, 20, 29n47, 149, 151, 155, 165–66, 172, 193

Hobbes, Thomas, 12, 46, 51–52, 54, 63, 68n48, 109, 143n17, 185

imaginary domain, 165, 170–72, 177
imagination, 16, 18, 42, 67n41, 146, 152, 170–72, 224, 229
immanence, 99, 117, 146–47, 151
individual/individualism, x–xii, 3, 10–11, 15, 34–35, 38, 40–43, 49, 53–54, 62, 64, 65n24, 68n48, 76–77, 84, 98–100, 102, 110, 112, 127–40, 140n2, 141n3, 142n8, 144n26, 145, 167, 175, 232, 237; possessive individualism, 132, 140–41n3, 142n2; transindividual. *See also* transindividuality
interpellation, 131
Irigaray, Luce, 164
irreciprocity, 21, 116, 208–9, 214–17, 221

Jacob, François, 13, 72– 88, 91n17, 92nn21,26,28,32, 93n36, 234
Jakobson, Roman, 12, 56–57
Johnson, Christopher, 22, 234, 241
Joseph, Miranda, 95
jouissance, 19, 184

justice, x, 3–6, 8, 18, 26n23, 163, 165, 167–69, 178, 216–17, 224n2

Kant, Immanuel, ix, 7– 9, 12, 21, 25nn17,19, 52–53, 60, 62, 64, 65n24, 66n32, 67n48, 94, 129, 132, 170–71, 208, 180, 212–14, 216, 219–23, 226n12, 238–40, 244, 246
Kauffman, Stuart, 22–23, 235, 237–46
Keenan, Dennis King, 115
Kierkegaard, Søren, 28n40, 194
Kirby, Vicky, 230
Kojève, Alexandre, 110

Lacan, Jacques, 19–20, 164–66, 183–84, 186, 189–92, 194
Laruelle, François, 1
Latour, Bruno, 21, 208, 217–21, 223, 224n4, 227n24, 227–28n25, 243
Levinas, Emmanuel, 1, 7, 18, 20–21, 24n12, 25n22, 25–26n23, 49, 108, 116–17, 177, 209–11, 216–17, 221–23, 225nn5,7, 225–26n10
liberalism, 137–38, 141n8; neoliberalism, 99
liberty, 38, 41, 128, 131–32, 168
Locke, John, 46, 48, 129, 132, 140n3, 142n12
Lodge, David, 57, 67n36
Luhmann, Niklas, 173–74, 231, 233, 243
Lwoff, André, 234
Lyotard, Jean-François, 1, 209, 225n5

Macpherson, Crawford B., 140n3, 142n12
madness, 5, 8, 28n40, 136–37
Marcuse, Herbert, 171
market, 34, 61, 128, 130–31, 142n12, 168
Marx, Karl, 15–17, 41, 60–62, 128, 130–36, 139, 141n7, 142n10, 143nn19,24, 144n25, 155, 162–64, 169, 185, 189
Masolo, D. A., 175
Masson, André, 109, 111
materialism, 41, 102–3, 136, 147, 151, 228n17, 237, 244
Maturana, Humberto, 174, 230, 233, 243–45
Meillassoux, Quentin, x, 1, 9
metaphor, 3, 6, 9, 12, 14, 24n11, 25n18, 55–59, 64, 88, 166, 217
metonymy, 5–6, 9, 12, 25n18, 47, 56–59
modernity, 19, 80, 128, 137, 151, 183–84
Montesquieu, Charles, 138
More, Mabogo P., 176
Morrison, Toni, 166
Morton, Timothy, 208, 233
Musk, Elon, 189

Nancy, Jean-Luc, 14, 59, 67n39, 95–96, 98–101, 103–11, 113–16, 118–19, 123n103, 135
natureculture, 147
necessity, 11, 41, 135; and ethics, ix–x, 9–10, 94–95; and impossibility, 33–35. *See also* contingency and necessity
negotiation, 95, 162–63, 169, 172, 176
Neiman, Susan, 2–3
Newman, Michael, 209
Nietzsche, Friedrich, 15, 72, 101, 103, 128, 131, 133–34, 136–37, 143n24, 148, 169
Nisbet, Robert, 141n8
Noble, Denis, 22, 235–37
nomadic, 148, 185
nonhuman, 74, 86, 117, 147, 151, 153, 155, 157, 220–22, 224n4, 230, 233, 235
normality, 15, 89, 129, 132–33, 136–37

object, xi; 2, 10, 26n24, 39–41, 57, 88, 103–4, 118, 134, 182–83, 191, 193–95, 206, 230, 232, 243; and agency, 21, 208, 213–15, 221, 223–24; and juridical status, 217, 223; as a means to an end, 21, 206, 208, 210, 212–18, 220–23, 227n24. *See also* Actor-Network Theory (ANT)
ontology, 106, 108, 116, 128, 138, 146, 152–53, 156, 177, 228n27, 243
organism, 76, 78, 80, 83–86, 88, 230, 235, 237–40, 242, 245
otherness/other, 3, 17, 46, 49, 50, 54, 56, 64, 84, 97, 107–8, 116–17, 119, 140, 152–54, 158, 163, 166, 169, 170, 172–77, 182–83, 185–86, 200, 207–13, 216, 222, 245

Padui, Raoni, 244
panhuman, 157–58
paranoia, 191–92
parrhesia, 139
passivity, 20–21, 153, 208–10, 216, 218, 222–23, 226
physics, 237, 239–40
Pietz, William, 224n4
Plato, ix, 14, 73
Polanyi, Karl, 140n1
posthumanism, 20–21, 147, 152, 155, 157, 165, 172–73, 193, 207–8, 215, 217–18
Postman, 19, 185
precariousness, 63–64
program, 13, 22, 74–87, 93n36
proper, 14, 27n29, 105, 112, 118–19

property, 15, 62, 112, 119, 131–32, 135, 140n3, 218

Quashie, Kevin, 227n16

Rancière, Jacques, 1, 49, 134
realism, 244
reciprocity, 21, 107, 116, 206, 213–16, 221, 223. *See also* irreciprocity
recognition, 115, 127, 131, 133, 158; and contestation, 117. *See also* dialectics of recognition
Red Angel, 183
relationality, 16, 27, 107, 140, 152–53, 175
responsibility, 18, 21–22, 116–17, 131, 137, 175, 177, 194, 209, 211–12, 214–16, 222–23, 224n4, 225n7, 233
rhizome, 152, 165
Ricoeur, Paul, 209–10, 225n5
rights, 51, 53, 119, 127–33, 140n2, 144n31, 170, 177, 221
Roe v. Wade, 167–68
Rorty, Richard, 232, 243
Rousseau, Jean-Jacques, 46, 132

Sankaran, Chitra, 60
sexuate being, 171, 177
singularity, xi, 4–5, 10, 38, 67n39, 175–176
slave law, 213, 224n4
sociobiogenesis, 173
Spiller, Hortense, 227n16
Spinoza, Baruch, ix, 147–48, 155, 171–72, 218
Spivak, Gayatri Chakravorty, 158
Stevens, Wallace, 22, 229–30, 246
synecdoche, 3, 5–6, 58
systems theory, 22, 28n46, 232–33, 243

telos, 7, 13, 24n13, 25n19, 48, 50–51, 54–55, 60, 83
Thacker, Eugene, 97, 102, 105–7
The Discovery, 20, 10, 195–98
Tönnies, Ferdinand, 11, 46, 50
Transcendence, 12, 15, 26–27n27, 37, 97, 102, 108, 116, 139, 218; empirical-transcendental doublet, 128–29, 133, 141n4; transcendental signifier, 28n43, 164
transindividuality, 15, 19, 131–32, 136, 139–40, 144n32, 172, 175, 178
Trombadori, Duccio, 134, 136
Turner, Denys, 97–98
Tushnet, Mark, 227n15

uBuntu, 18–19, 175–78
universalism, 15, 47, 128, 131, 135
utilitarianism, 7, 18, 131, 139
utopia, 66n32, 135, 184–85

Varela, Francisco, 174, 230, 233, 244–45
violence, 51, 54, 119, 130, 138, 149, 153, 158, 226n12
Virno, Paolo, 117
von Uexküll, Jakob, 22, 232

Waddington, Conrad, 22, 235, 237, 242
Wagner, Andreas, 99

Wallerstein, Immanuel, 141n8
Weber, Max, 66n32, 128, 130–31
Weismann, August, 235
Weller, Shane, 118
White, Hayden, 59
Wilden, Anthony, 234
Wiredu, Kwasi, 176
Woolf, Virginia, 166, 170
Wynter, Sylvia, 164, 170, 172–74, 180

zoe, 147, 151, 155–56

just ideas

Roger Berkowitz, *The Gift of Science: Leibniz and the Modern Legal Tradition*

Jean-Luc Nancy, translated by Pascale-Anne Brault and Michael Naas, *The Truth of Democracy*

Drucilla Cornell and Kenneth Michael Panfilio, *Symbolic Forms for a New Humanity: Cultural and Racial Reconfigurations of Critical Theory*

Karl Shoemaker, *Sanctuary and Crime in the Middle Ages, 400–1500*

Michael J. Monahan, *The Creolizing Subject: Race, Reason, and the Politics of Purity*

Drucilla Cornell and Nyoko Muvangua (eds.), *uBuntu and the Law: African Ideals and Postapartheid Jurisprudence*

Drucilla Cornell, Stu Woolman, Sam Fuller, Jason Brickhill, Michael Bishop, and Diana Dunbar (eds.), *The Dignity Jurisprudence of the Constitutional Court of South Africa: Cases and Materials, Volumes I & II*

Nicholas Tampio, *Kantian Courage: Advancing the Enlightenment in Contemporary Political Theory*

Carrol Clarkson, *Drawing the Line: Toward an Aesthetics of Transitional Justice*

Jane Anna Gordon, *Creolizing Political Theory: Reading Rousseau through Fanon*

Jimmy Casas Klausen, *Fugitive Rousseau: Slavery, Primitivism, and Political Freedom*

Drucilla Cornell, *Law and Revolution in South Africa: uBuntu, Dignity, and the Struggle for Constitutional Transformation*

Abraham Acosta, *Thresholds of Illiteracy: Theory, Latin America, and the Crisis of Resistance*

Andrew Dilts, *Punishment and Inclusion: Race, Membership, and the Limits of American Liberalism*

Lewis R. Gordon, *What Fanon Said: A Philosophical Introduction to His Life and Thought.* Foreword by Sonia Dayan-Herzbrun, Afterword by Drucilla Cornell

Gaymon Bennett, *Technicians of Human Dignity: On the Politics of Intrinsic Worth*

Drucilla Cornell and Nick Friedman, *The Mandate of Dignity: Ronald Dworkin, Revolutionary Constitutionalism, and the Claims of Justice*

Richard A. Lynch, *Foucault's Critical Ethics*

Peter Banki, *The Forgiveness to Come: The Holocaust and the Hyper-Ethical*

Peter Goodrich and Michel Rosenfeld (eds.), *Administering Interpretation: Derrida, Agamben, and the Political Theology of Law*

Thomas Claviez and Viola Marchi (eds.), *Throwing the Moral Dice: Ethics and the Problem of Contingency*

www.ingramcontent.com/pod-product-compliance
Lightning Source LLC
Chambersburg PA
CBHW032030290426

44110CB00012B/736